THIS GAME OF FOOTBALL

THIS GAME OF
Football

LYNN O. WALDORF

McGRAW-HILL BOOK COMPANY, INC.

New York   London   Toronto

THIS GAME OF FOOTBALL

Library of Congress Catalog Card Number: 52-9457

SECOND PRINTING

PUBLISHED BY THE MCGRAW-HILL BOOK COMPANY, INC.

PRINTED IN THE UNITED STATES OF AMERICA

To my wife, Louise—
Who for twenty-seven years has provided
appreciation in victory,
support in defeat, and stability
in an unstable profession

ACKNOWLEDGMENTS

I should like to acknowledge the valuable contributions of the following, without whose help this book never could have been written:

Earl Rose and Cliff Bond of the Photography Department of A.S.U.C., for assistance in taking many of the pictures used herein

Mrs. Rena Hamilton, for help in preparing the manuscript

Our coaching staff at California—Wes Fry, "Eggs" Manske, Herm Meister, the late Bob Tessier, "Nibs" Price, Zeb Chaney, and Harold Grant—who have added so much to the ideas expressed in this book

And finally, the hundreds of players it has been my privilege to coach during the past twenty-seven years at California, Northwestern, Kansas State, Oklahoma A. & M., Kansas, and Oklahoma City University

Lynn O. Waldorf

CONTENTS

LIST OF ILLUSTRATIONS

CHAPTER 1 ON THE PERSONAL SIDE

IN 1939 when I was coaching at Northwestern University, we invited the University of Oklahoma to Dyche Stadium in Evanston, Illinois, to open our season. That was our first mistake. Oklahoma had a very fine football team and nearly closed our season that same afternoon. Just before we went on the field I gathered our team together and reminded them that we were playing a team from the South, where hospitality meant a great deal. I suggested to them that we demonstrate that the Northern brand of hospitality was equally good. I guess that's the first time I have ever had a team take me at my word, 100 per cent. We had hardly started the game when we fumbled on our own 5-yard line, certainly a very nice gesture of hospitality toward a visiting team. We thought the Sooners would recognize it as such and fumble back, but no such thing happened. Three plays later they had a touchdown; then they kicked a field goal, and at half time we were nine points behind.

As we discussed things between halves we thought that perhaps the long train ride might in some manner have jarred the delicately balanced sense of hospitality of the Southerners and that things would be different during the second half. Such was not the case. In the third quarter we fumbled on our 3-yard line and it took Oklahoma only two plays to score. However, in the fourth quarter Northwestern really began to roll. We put together a long march consisting of two consecutive first downs which had to be measured, and finally reached the hitherto untrodden territory of mid-field. It was at that precise moment that my sophomore fullback received the ball from center, faded back, and threw one of the most beauti-

1

ful passes that I have ever seen. It went 58 yards for a touchdown
—directly into the arms of the Oklahoma fullback. We were beaten
23–0 in our opening game!

Sometimes the mail which a college football coach receives on
Monday morning is very interesting. I shall never forget the Monday after the Oklahoma game. The postman dumped three sacks of
mail on my desk and I found therein some very choice bits of litera-
ture. The one that I'll always remember was a penny postal card.
It was addressed to me at Patten Gymnasium and bore the post-
mark of a town in Michigan where there is a convent. The message
read: "We don't have a football team, either." (Signed) "Sister
Mary."

Over the years I have learned never to be surprised at anything
that may happen in a football game; certainly American football is
a game that is totally unpredictable. There are so many intangibles
that no one can safely predict just how any given game or any given
season is going to turn out. That is one of the most interesting features of the game.

My first coaching job was at Oklahoma City University in 1925.
I had played at Syracuse University for three years under Chick
Meehan, a great coach and a fine gentleman. During that time we
had several games with the University of Nebraska, and I had been
greatly impressed with the size and the speed of the boys on the
Nebraska football squad. I had the naïve impression that all Middle
Western boys were of the same caliber. I was quite surprised, therefore, at my first practice at Oklahoma City University, to find
fourteen boys reporting, most of them a long way from the size and
quality of the Nebraska material. When we finally did get a ball
club together and lined up for our first game, I found that we had
a line which averaged 162 pounds from end to end and a backfield
which averaged 168. Six of the eleven starters had never played
football in high school. In one sense I might claim to have started
at the bottom so far as football coaching is concerned, but in a much
larger sense it was the best thing that ever happened to me. We had

a fine group of boys, and they taught me a lot more about football and a lot more about boys than I was able to teach them.

We won four games and lost six in that first season of 1925. I recall distinctly that in the fourth game of the season against Southwestern Teachers College of Weatherford, Oklahoma, played on home grounds, we broke the university record for gate receipts. We took in $86.50. Our games were played on a field immediately back of the one building which constituted the University, and before some wooden bleachers which seated 1200. There had been a dressing shack the previous year, but that had burned down during the summer. For the greater portion of the 1925 season our Oklahoma City University squad had dressed in a boiler room in the basement, with one shower in the corner. We had to climb a ladder and go through a basement window to get to the practice field.

I have a very real affection for that 1925 O.C.U. football squad and will always remember boys like Roy Allen, Bill and Ossie Doenges, Earl LaFon, Jim Perry, Joe Dumenil, the Schuneman brothers, Perk Whitman, Bob and Lee Dodson (two little 135-pound halfbacks), Taylor, Gutsche, and especially Bill Moore, our fullback, who won most of our games with place kicks. I owe them a tremendous debt of gratitude.

Those boys taught me valuable lessons—that young men like to play football; that they will go to any extreme of effort to participate in a rugged game; that they like to belong to an organization; and that, above all, the game is the thing that counts.

Early in that first season I decided to write a book on football, especially line play. A little later on that season I decided I had better postpone the writing of the book, for there were one or two points that I thought I ought to clear up. The next season I found a few more points that I wasn't sure of, and that has been true of each succeeding season ever since. Now I am not sure that there is anything on the subject of football of which I am definitely positive. Nevertheless, I think it might be worth while to set down some of the things that I have found significant and interesting about our greatest American game during the twenty-seven years that it has been my good fortune to coach.

On January 1, 1951, our California team lost to Michigan by a score of 14–6 in the Rose Bowl before a crowd of approximately one hundred thousand people. I don't know what the gate receipts amounted to, but I am sure that they exceeded the $86.50 from the O.C.U.–Southwestern game twenty-six years before. There was a lot of comment and second guessing in newspapers and on the part of men covering the game by radio and television, as contrasted to the two paragraphs which appeared in the local paper on the O.C.U. game. But in spite of the difference in crowd and interest, the same desire to play on the part of the boys and the same sense of belonging to an organization make those two football games very similar experiences.

Last fall some 50,000 boys of college age participated in football. Another 600,000 played as members of high-school squads. I don't know how many played as professionals or how many additional thousands of youngsters played on impromptu teams in sand lots; but certainly the game of football has a tremendous appeal for the boys who play it, and it has perhaps the greatest appeal of all American sports for the people who watch.

A football coach shares with a parent or a teacher the very keenest joy that there is in life—the joy of watching a youngster develop and find himself. Every coach has had the experience of watching a new boy join the squad for the first time. He is young, he is awkward, he is poorly coordinated, his suit doesn't hit him in the right places. As he joins the rest of the squad in practice it is soon apparent that he knows nothing about blocking, tackling, or perhaps even the rules of the game. But he has one great virtue—he stays with it. Gradually, perhaps later that same season or more likely in a subsequent season, you begin to see that boy in a new light. You realize that now he knows something about blocking, about tackling, that he has learned the rules. Perhaps there comes a day when he looks pretty good in a practice scrimmage in midweek against his teammates, and you wonder whether you dare take that green boy and put him into a tough, varsity contest. Finally, as a coach, you take your courage in your hands and put him in, and in ninety-five cases out of a hundred you are very happily surprised at the result.

Some people say that it is too bad that, when two teams meet on a field of play, one team has to win and the other team has to lose. I think that is the most American thing there is about the game of football. Some people say it is unfortunate that the youngster must be exposed to the pressures of an intensely competitive contact game. I feel that that is the finest thing that can happen to that boy, provided that the contest is fair. We shouldn't expect a fourteen-year-old kid to play with the eighteen-year-olds, nor the 130-pound guard to spend an afternoon trying to break through between a couple of 180-pounders. Provided that the contest is an equal one and the pressures are only those inherent in the game itself, football can contribute a great deal to a boy's growth and education.

The California squads and coaching staff during the past two years have derived a great deal of satisfaction and pleasure in watching a number of our boys develop. Roy Meuhlberger had never played in high school. He came out in the spring of 1948 and it was a pleasure to watch his development from an unheralded boy to a sturdy defensive left tackle. He started at that position in most of the games in 1949. Paul Andrew, another boy who did not play in high school, came out as a freshman at California in 1949 and attracted the attention of the freshman coaches, although his lack of experience didn't give him much opportunity to play. He came along in spring practice of 1950 and developed through the Ramblers, our junior varsity, during the fall of 1950 until he was starting right end during the latter part of the season. Another outstanding end at California who did not play high-school football was Dave Hood, who started most of our games in 1951 at right end on the offense. Dave developed into such a superior player that in 1951 he broke a university record by receiving 18 forward passes for 217 yards, including three touchdowns. Most boys who have football ability do play in high school, but it is a real thrill every once in a while to find a boy who, for one reason or another, has not had the opportunity to play in high school, and who develops so quickly in college that he takes his place as a starter on the varsity team. It is also a great satisfaction to watch youngsters who have not attained anywhere near their full development in high school become college players. Many develop late in high school and are overshadowed there by others who grew more rapidly. Yet, the late developers, if they will stick with it in college, often become fine football players. Such are the solid satisfactions of the football coach.

It is my conviction that nearly every boy playing football, on whatever level, enjoys the game. If a player does not derive some enjoyment from both the practices and the games, then certainly he is missing the most important part of football. Every player should be able to look back on incidents in his football career that made him a stronger, wiser, finer person. The humorous incidents, of which there should be many, are as valuable as any others.

In 1948 at California we had a tackle by the name of Jim Cullom, who was not only a fine lineman and an expert point-after-touchdown kicker, but also had the gift of wise-cracking at just the appropriate time. One Friday afternoon we were practicing in the stadium in sweat suits preparatory to the U.C.L.A. game. It was one of those days that a coach hates to see. Nothing went right. The linemen were jumping offside, the backs were fumbling, quarterbacks were spinning the wrong way, and the ends were letting passes roll off their fingertips. Nevertheless, we went ahead working on special plays we intended to use the next day. We came to a play that was one of quarterback Bobby Celeri's favorites, which we called the bootleg play, in which Celeri faked to the fullback going one way, the left half breaking the opposite way, and then tucked the ball on his hip and swung out around our left end. Cullom was left tackle on that particular play and his assignment was to momentarily block the defensive right guard and then swing sharply to his left to pick up Celeri.

But, as I said before, it was just one of those days. Cullom simply forgot and started to trot downfield. I called his attention to his error and the next team came on. The left tackle on that team was Herb Schmalenberger and he made the same mistake. I stopped the practice and said, "Herb, just because Cullom blew his assignment on the previous play is no reason for you to make the same mistake." Before anyone could say anything, Cullom piped up and said, "Pappy, if the kid has a case of hero worship, don't you interfere." We all had to laugh—in fact we enjoyed laughing—and somehow that wisecrack of Cullom's cleared the atmosphere and our practice moved a lot faster from then on.

At Northwestern in 1942 we had a captain by the name of Nick Burke, who had that same gift of repartee. Just before the opening of the season in 1941, when we were to play Kansas State in the first game, we had had a long chalk talk. I was discussing the rules and was particularly anxious to clear up a rule regarding a forward pass becoming incomplete in the opponent's end zone. The rule had been recently changed so that if a team had the ball on the other fellow's 8-yard line on fourth down, and a pass went incomplete in the end zone, the ball was brought out only to the eight instead of out to the twenty, as it would be if it were a touchback. I tried to make the case a little clearer with a hypothetical illustration. "Suppose that tomorrow we have the ball on Kansas State's 8-yard line. It is fourth down and goal to go. In the huddle Graham calls pass No. 64, we come out, line up, the ball is snapped back to Graham, he sees Motl, who is open in the end zone, and he throws him a pass. Motl drops it and it becomes incomplete in the end zone. What happens then?" At that moment Burke piped up, "Motl comes out of the ball game."

Football is first and foremost a game, and it must be kept just that. To those who play it, it provides an opportunity for all-round development, it provides great personal satisfactions, and it offers invaluable lessons in sportsmanship. The game that is lost is just as valuable an experience for the boy as the game won. Above all he has the sense of belonging to an organization; I don't believe that any fellow who has ever enjoyed playing the game of football forgets the team to which he belonged.

Sometimes spectators tend to expect too much from college football players. They forget that the twenty-two players on the field are merely young amateurs, and they demand perfection. Most fans identify themselves with one team or the other and root for their team, more or less violently. When mistakes are made (and they always will be), the spectator often becomes a grandstand quarterback and starts second guessing. "Why didn't State punt?" "If Brown had only been able to hold onto that long forward pass in the fourth quarter." "If our quarterback had only called for a pass, instead of a line buck." This is part of the fun and fascination of the game. But the spectator should remember that it *is* a game and should hesitate before demanding absolute perfection.

Football, perhaps more than any other sport, lends itself most readily to these postgame discussions of what might have happened. That is because it is a game where most anything can happen—and generally does.

CHAPTER 2 TWELVE MINUTES
OF FOOTBALL

"MODERN football is all right," said the Old Grad, "and I'll admit I like to watch it, but it's a sissy game compared with the way it was played in my day." He took a look at my gray hair and hastily amended, "*our* day." "With your platoon system and all those substitutions, there's no such thing as a sixty-minute player any more."

"There never was," I retorted. "The ball is only in play about twelve minutes out of sixty. The rest of the time, while the clock is running, the teams are huddling or otherwise preparing to put the ball in play."

My friend stomped off muttering about "six-minute offensive players," "six-minute defensive platoons," and "one-minute specialists."

It is four-thirty on a Saturday afternoon. The big stadium is slowly emptying after a hard-fought game which has left both players and spectators exhausted. It seems impossible that in the 2 hours and 20 minutes since the referee blew his whistle on the opening kickoff only 12 minutes of actual football have been played. Where did the time go?

Time was "in" and the clock running for a carefully measured 60 minutes, but only for 12 minutes was the ball actually in play— the interval covered by each "play" from the time the center snapped the ball to start the play until the officials declared the ball dead. The rest of the time while the clock was running, the teams were huddling and putting the ball in play.

9

But the clock wasn't always running. It was stopped between 70 and 100 times during the game for many different reasons. Not only is it stopped on a called time out, but also when the ball goes out of bounds, a pass is incomplete, a score or a touchback made, a penalty enforced, or the possession of the ball changes from one team to the other. The clock is stopped so often, in fact, that another 60 minutes elapses, a few seconds at a time. And then, of course, the intermission at half time covers about 20 minutes while the spectators are entertained by the bands, and the rooting sections perform.

Modern football is a game of great intensity which demands a strenuous effort from each participant. Frequent substitutions, which keep the players fresher, sustain the game's high pitch from start to finish. A great deal can happen in 12 minutes.

Based on statistics and the law of averages, during the course of the game *a college team will have about 65 chances to advance the ball* exclusive of punts or plays on which penalties occur. I have known teams to run less that 40 plays during a game as well as over 100 plays, but 60 to 65 is a consistent average.

Other things being equal, the team which controls the ball and has the greater opportunities to advance it by running or passing should win the ball game. This is not always true, however. I first started keeping statistics on the number of plays per game in 1935 at Northwestern. The largest number of plays we had that year was 88, and the smallest number 42, and yet we won the game in which we had only 42 plays by scoring an upset victory over Notre Dame 14–7, for the first Northwestern victory over Notre Dame since 1902. In the game in which we ran 88 plays we lost to Ohio State by a score of 28–7.

Whenever there is a great deal of passing, there will probably be more plays run than if the passing is limited. This is because the clock is stopped by an incompleted pass. In 1950, for example, Loyola University of Los Angeles had a very fine passing attack. Coach Jordan Oliver of Loyola told me that in one of their games they ran some 97 plays and in another one 103. Missouri in their game against Kansas in 1949 ran 105 plays. But the average team can count on between 60 and 65 plays per game.

Your team will come into possession of the ball for a series of plays 13 times during the game. This is one of the most consistent but least known football statistics. The series may be long or short, of course. Perhaps there will be a fumble on the first play or a drive of 15 or more consecutive plays may occur.

The longest sequence of plays that I can recall occurred in the 1946 Notre Dame–Northwestern game. Northwestern kicked off to Notre Dame to start the second half. A penalty took Notre Dame to their 1-yard line and for the next 12½ minutes, they kept possession of the ball without losing it or being forced to kick. In that sequence they ran 23 plays but did not score. The drive was stopped finally near the Northwestern goal line. Notre Dame won the game 27–0 and demonstrated a consistent and powerful attack which was hard to stop without some gain, although they did lack a real break-away runner.

In 1950 the smallest number of sequences for California and ten opponents was 10. The largest number was 15, and the average 12.7 sequences per game. A sequence will end with a score, a fumble, an intercepted pass, loss of the ball on downs, a punt, or time running out for the half.

The limited number of sequences in a game makes it important that the offensive team do everything in its power to keep the drive alive and avoid losing the ball. Mistakes such as poor ball handling, a missed assignment by a lineman, or a failure in pass protection, may cause the offensive team to lose ground and force a punt.

The number of sequences also enters into defensive playing. In 1950 in preparing for our game with the strong University of Washington team at Seattle, we knew that our defensive team had to be at its very best in order for us to win. Washington had a strong offensive team with fine backs like McElhenny, Kirkby, Seth, and Early, and a great passer in Don Heinrich. We stressed to our defensive team that Washington would probably have the ball for thirteen sequences. If our defensive unit was able to stop them from scoring in all but one sequence, we would probably win. If they scored in two or more sequences, our chances of victory were slim.

The game worked out along the lines anticipated. Washington did have the ball for thirteen sequences and they scored on one sequence; although they came close on at least two others, the California defense held and we finally won by a score of 14–7. I noticed that every time our defensive eleven came off the field during the second half they would tell each other, "six more times," "five more times," "two more times." In effect, the defensive team, instead of playing one game with the University of Washington, really had thirteen separate, individual games, one on each sequence.

In the Rose Bowl on January 1, 1951, Michigan and California each had ten sequences. The small number of sequences was due to the fact that there was not very much forward passing, and that each team on occasion controlled the ball for sequences which included a large number of plays.

Your team will punt five or six times. This will vary widely. Against a tough opponent, or under bad weather conditions, a team will naturally punt more than against a weaker opponent or under favorable weather conditions.

In 1950, Michigan and Ohio State played in a snowstorm. Under such extremely bad weather conditions, each team played very cautiously and punted frequently, Michigan twenty-four times and Ohio twenty-one. The combined total of forty-five punts in a single ball game established a new Big Ten record.

Twenty or thirty years ago a team would punt from ten to fourteen times per game. Under present-day conditions, with the development of the forward pass and a general increase in offensive power, the average will be from four to eight times per ball game.

During the 1951 season, the nine teams of the Pacific Coast Conference played a total of eighty-nine games. The following team averages per game give a reliable statistical picture of present-day football. Each team:

Scored 21.9 points per game
Made 15.5 first downs per game
Ran 70.7 plays, including passes, per game
Punted 5.8 times per game
Attempted 21.4 forward passes per game
Completed 9.6 forward passes per game
Had intercepted 1.8 forward passes per game
Fumbled 2.7 times per game

We regard the "intercepted passes" as an item of great importance. Our quarterbacks are told that if they have one pass in nine or ten intercepted, that is regarded as normal. Less than one in ten is all the better, of course; but if they have one pass in six or seven intercepted, we will probably lose the game on that factor alone.

Football is a comparatively young game. What is regarded as the first American contest was played on November 6, 1869, between Rutgers and Princeton, with Rutgers winning by a score of six goals to four. If you had been present on that occasion you would not have recognized the game. Each side had twenty-five players, the ball was round, and the emphasis was on kicking or batting the ball rather than on running with it. In fact, the only recognizable feature of that first game which has been retained was the placing of the goal posts 18 feet 6 inches apart and the crossbar 10 feet from the ground.

One account states that "the game was witnessed by a group of spectators numbering nearly twice the number of participants." Many of the spectators sat on a fence on one side of the field, a portion of which was demolished when several players ran into it in pursuit of the ball. It is also reliably reported that there was a dog on the field during a great part of the game.

The roots of our present-day statistics on football are to be found in the history of the game. It is a short history compared with some other games, but it affords an interesting study in the effort of the rules makers to balance the game between the offense and the defense. In the first few years it was largely a kicking game, somewhat similar to rugby. By 1880 the number of men on a side had been reduced to eleven and the offensive team was given possession of the ball for an offensive play. In those days no specific yardage had to be made in a certain number of downs. In 1881 the famous "block" game between Yale and Princeton was played in which each team had possession of the ball during an entire half. At that time if a team was pushed back behind their own goal line they merely brought the ball out to their 25-yard line and started all over again.

In 1882 there were some important changes in the rules. The safety—two points for the defensive team which forced the offensive team behind their own goal line—was adopted. A team had three downs in which to make 5 yards. Interference was allowed, that is, "blocking in advance of the ball." By 1888 the offensive line had become more concentrated and the idea of using a wing back or an end to flank the defensive tackle had come into vogue. Also, the now common procedure of sending a man through the line to lead the ball carrier was introduced.

During the nineties a type of "momentum mass" play developed. The offense was not required to have seven men on the line of scrimmage and could bring linemen to the backfield. These men could be in motion forward before the center snapped the ball. Such mass movements toward the line of scrimmage resulted in a great many injuries.

In 1906 the problem of football injuries had reached the point that President Theodore Roosevelt called a conference in the White House to consider ways and means of making the game safe. As a result the Rules Committee restricted the offense by requiring that six men be on the line of scrimmage at the start of a play. The offensive team had four chances in which to make 10 yards. The forward pass and the onside kick, with many restrictions, were introduced into the game. Despite these safety measures, it was during this period that many colleges gave up football as being too dangerous. California and Stanford gave up American football and returned to rugby; California continued rugby until the 1915 season and Stanford retained it several years longer. Columbia, Northwestern, and other schools also abandoned football for varying periods of time.

During this period the defense held the upper hand and often games were won by drop kicks. Many will remember Charlie Brickley's fine performance of five drop kicks against Yale in 1913.

By 1912 further changes were made to improve the offense. Previous restrictions were taken away from the forward pass, and an end zone of 10 yards back of each goal line was added to make scoring passes easier. Under the impetus of this legislation favoring the forward pass, the offense quickly returned to a proper balance with the defense, and our modern game of football came into being.

An interesting commentary on the early development of American football is contained in the following table of point evaluation for each method of scoring during the period 1884 to 1912:

Year	Touchdown	Goal after T.D.	Field goal	Safety
1884	2	4	5	1
1886	4	2	5	2
1897	5	1	5	2
1904	5	1	4	2
1909	5	1	3	2
1912	6	1	3	2

Football has always been a rugged game, but some of the schedules played by early-day football teams are awe-inspiring to the modern player. In 1899 the University of the South at Sewanee,

Tennessee, traveled 3000 miles by day coach and played six football games within a span of seven days. The squad consisted of a football team of eleven men plus one coach, one manager, and one substitute, and in those days a half was 40 minutes of play instead of 30.

Lafayette in 1886 played some twelve games between October 13 and November 24. With the resumption of American football at California in 1915, the California team played fourteen games between September 11 and November 25. And there was no platoon system in those days!

During the period since World War I, football has become steadily more interesting and more popular. The increased use of the forward pass has opened up the game and led to greater scoring year after year. The importance of the punt has diminished somewhat, although a team is badly hurt by any mistakes in the kicking department. Many games are won each year by a blocked kick, a punt return for a touchdown, or a successful try for point after touchdown.

The game has increased steadily in intensity and in spectator interest. Colleges and municipalities have built large stadia for the accommodation of spectators at football games. The following abbreviated table of the yearly attendance at the University of California football games is a definite indication of the growth and popularity of football. Practically all colleges and universities would show a similar steady growth in football interest.

Season	Total attendance (for entire season)
1895	14,500
1900	32,400
1905	43,000
1910	77,000
1915	88,800
1920	140,200

Season	Total attendance (for entire season)
1925	344,700
1930	382,978
1935	451,000
1940	395,000
1945	401,500
1950	497,200

The growth of interest in professional football and in high-school football parallels the development in college football. The first professional game was played in 1898 at Latrobe, Pennsylvania. The "pro" game developed rapidly in the Middle West, especially in Pennsylvania and Ohio. Massillon, Canton, Frankford, Portsmouth, Columbus, and a score of other cities supported teams in the development period of professional football. With the growing interest in the game and greater financial stability, professional football transferred to the larger cities. The game is now a permanent part of the American sports picture, and with the recent unification between the National Football League and the All-America Conference the professional game seems headed for a period of steady growth.

Professional football, with its many gifted passers and receivers, has developed the passing game to a very high degree of perfection. College teams have followed this trend, although I believe the college and high-school teams have retained a little better balance between the running and passing elements of the game.

SELECTION OF THE OFFENSIVE FORMATION

Football is a game played by eleven men on a side, on a field 300 feet long and 160 feet wide with a 30-foot end zone extending beyond each goal line. A person watching American football for the first time might wonder why, with all of the playing space available, it would not be possible to line up the eleven men on the offensive team in scores of different formations. Actually, 95 per cent of all football teams at the present time use some variation of the T formation or the single wing in attempting to advance the ball toward a score.

Before coaches and players are too quickly accused of lack of imagination, it should be explained that there are some sound reasons why offensive formations are limited in number. Within the scope of each of the major offensive systems is the possibility of a varied and powerful attack capable of putting the defensive team under considerable strain. The steady increase in scoring in the past few years bears witness to the strength and versatility of the offense.

A coaching staff will be influenced in their selection of the offensive formation to be taught at a given school by a number of factors, among which are:

1. *Rules.* Very early in American football the team on offense was given undisputed possession of the ball and the opportunity to start a play without interference. Neither team can cross the line of scrimmage (an imaginary line running through the point of the ball nearest each team and at right angles to the side lines) until the offensive center has passed the ball to one of his backfield men.

The team with the ball must have seven men on the line of

scrimmage. In the early days of football, before this rule was in effect, some very interesting formations were used, such as the "guards back" (Pennsylvania, 1895), and "tackles back" (Yale and Michigan, 1900). Such formations cannot be used today.

2. *Versatility*. Theoretically it is possible to spread the offensive team widely over the field from side line to side line and occasionally spread formations are used. Such formations are very limited, however, in the type of plays that can be run from them. The spread formation is good for passing but very weak on running, and the defense can drop back to cover the eligible receivers and ignore the running threat, making odds against a successful offense almost prohibitive.

A sound offensive formation must have its eleven players concentrated closely so that they can work together. Such a formation should be able to hit any spot in or around the defensive line with running plays, both those which hit quickly and plays of a delayed nature. There must be a constant threat of a forward pass with receivers in a position to break quickly downfield, and there should also be the threat of a kick. Any of the major offensive formations (see Diagrams 1–3 and Pictures 1–8) fulfill the above requirement and their continued use indicates their all-round effectiveness. Any of these formations can split an end or a flanker out 5 to 20 yards toward the side line, or put a man in motion wide to give the pass receivers greater range without sacrificing the threat of a sound running game.

3. *Personnel*. The offensive formation selected will depend somewhat on the men available. This is especially true with the key men. A standard T formation without a quarterback who is a good passer or backs with reasonable speed would not be very productive. A single wing spin attack with an awkward fullback is seriously handicapped. A double wing attack without a strong fullback, or a short punt formation without a tail back able to run, pass, and kick would similarly fail to realize the full potentiality of the formation.

When Clark Shaughnessy came to Stanford in 1940, he found some backfield men who were not adapted to the double wing, which Stanford had been using, but who were admirably suited to the T formation. Frank Albert was only a fair runner, but was a very fine passer and ball handler, and an ideal T-quarterback. Gallarneau and Kmetovic were not passers, but were fine runners and receivers, with a great deal of speed, and big Norm Standlee was an ideal T-fullback, strong enough to hit almost any place in the line and fast enough to go wide. These backs, who had had difficulty operating in the double wing, made the T formation go in fine style, won the Pacific Coast Championship, and defeated the University of Nebraska in the Rose Bowl.

The Michigan single wing attack depends a great deal on the ball-handling ability of the fullback. In 1940 Westfall at fullback was as versatile a ball handler and spinner as I have ever seen at the fullback spot in a single wing. His ball handling was a great help to fine backs like Tom Harmon. In 1950 Michigan had another fine fullback, Dufek. He was not the natural spinner that Westfall was, and so Michigan very wisely made use of the buck lateral series which Dufek ran as well as I have ever seen it run.

4. *Familiarity*. Other things being equal or nearly so, a coaching staff will choose a formation and teach a style of play they know and believe in. If a player has reasonable native ability he can step into a new formation and run it successfully even though such change may involve learning a new position, such as a shift from halfback to fullback or quarterback, or from fullback or end to guard. A squad with a high level of athletic ability, of course, should make any formation go.

Play diagrams mean very little in comparison with the mastery of the key details which make a play succeed. Two teams can run from the same identical formation and have the same assignments. One team will fail to make a given play go, while the other will make consistent yardage on the same play. The successful team

PICTURE 1. *Four offensive formations: (1) normal T; (2) split T; (3) single wing back, unbalanced line; (4) single wing back, Minnesota type (A.S.U.C., Berkeley).*

PICTURE 2. *Four more offensive formations: (1) single wing back, balanced line right; (2) double wing back; (3) deep punt—normal; (4) short punt—tail back 5 yards back of ball (A.S.U.C., Berkeley).*

PICTURE 3. *Two defenses against T with flanker: 6-man line* (top), *5-3-2-1* (bottom) (*A.S.U.C., Berkeley*).

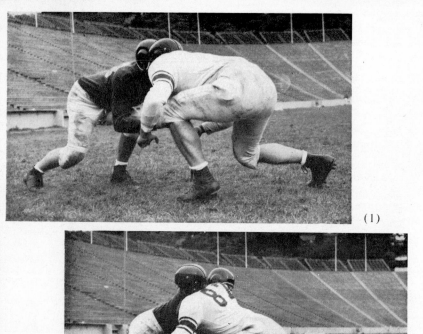

(1)

(2)

(3)

PICTURE 4. *The shoulder block: (1) the approach, offensive player (in white) in position to block with right shoulder; (2) contact, offensive player applying the "jolt"; (3) follow-through, offensive player brings legs up under him and turns opponent from path of ball (A.S.U.C., Berkeley).*

knows and can execute with precision the key items of footwork, ball handling, and timing. It is easy enough for a player to remember what to do on a play, but how to carry out his assignment and the ability to complete it successfully come only with constant practice and hard, intelligent work.

A well-designed play should improve with use. As the coaches and players become more familiar with the important details and eliminate any "bugs" in it, the play should be increasingly productive from game to game and from year to year until the defense has to overconcentrate against it, and thereby open up some other point of attack. A play will generally be designed to start like several other plays, and if one play is stopped, another running play or forward pass from the same action should have an added chance of success.

5. *Simplicity*. Most teams, college and high-school alike, try to learn too many plays. In the average game a team will have the opportunity of running sixty to sixty-five plays. Certainly plays that are going well should be repeated. I can see no reason to learn eighty or a hundred plays when there will be no opportunity to use a majority of them.

At California we use thirteen basic running plays and eight basic pass plays, and there are times when I think even that number is too many. Of course variations in backfield action may give the appearance of a greater number of running plays, and it is desirable to have the pass receivers use several different paths downfield on the same general pass action. Three or four special plays for specific situations should also be carried in the offense "book"; however, in one of our best games during the 1950 season we had sixty-one opportunities to advance the ball and used only ten different running plays and five pass plays.

An offense must be varied enough to hit every spot in or around the defensive line with plays that strike quickly and others that are delayed. A majority of the plays should look enough alike at the start of the play so that the defense cannot anticipate the point of attack. Pass patterns which send receivers to any spot in the defensive backfield which may develop a weakness are also essential. Whenever possible, the pass game should develop out of a running threat. This will not only help the running game by making the defensive linebackers and halfbacks hold back, but if they move up too quickly in anticipation of a run, receivers can get quickly into the open without complicated maneuvers.

PRINCIPAL OFFENSIVE FORMATIONS IN COMMON USE

On the following pages the reader will find diagrams of the principal offensive football formations. It is hoped that showing each formation in a photograph as well as in diagram may help anyone unfamiliar with a football diagram to visualize what it would look like in terms of a team lined up on the field of play.

	Picture	Diagram
Normal T formation	1	1
Normal T formation (with flanker)	2	1
Split T formation	3	1
Unbalanced split T	4	1
Unbalanced single wing right	5	1
Unbalanced single wing left	6	1
Unbalanced single wing Minn. type	7	1
Balanced single wing right	8	1
Double wing back		2
Short punt		2
Deep punt		2
Spread punt		2

Any of the above formations may split an end out 5 to 20 yards from his tackle. Or it may line up a flanker close or wide to the end, or put a backfield man in motion toward the side line.

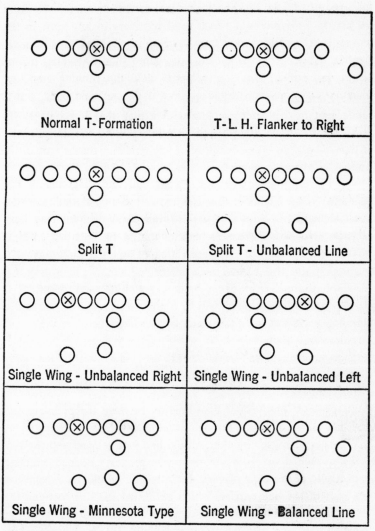

DIAGRAM 1

Common variations of T and single wing back formations

SELECTION OF PLAYS

After a coaching staff has determined the formation to be used, it is necessary to select the plays that will be used from the formations. The following factors should be considered:

1. *Variety.* The offensive team must be able to hit every possible spot in the defensive line with a play that hits quickly. In addition, it will be desirable to hit most spots on the defense with a delayed play to take advantage of any tendency on the part of the defensive player to move out of position. Also, the offense must be able to hit with a pass any spot which may be open. This would include the flat territory along the line of scrimmage on either side, the hooking spots down 8 to 10 yards in front of each offensive end, a short area over the center back of the linebackers and in front of the safety, and a deep central area behind the safety. An important spot is that behind each defensive halfback; then, too, it is desirable to hit in front of the halfbacks with delayed passes.

From most formations it will be found that a minimum of twelve running plays and six passes will be necessary to meet the above requirement. Many teams, of course, use more plays than this. If two or more offensive formations are used, it will not be necessary to have quite such a complete series of plays and passes for each formation.

2. *Timing.* The proper coordination between the blockers and the ball carrier is called timing. Bad timing might be indicated by a situation where the blocking in the line was delayed and the ball carrier reached the hole before it was properly opened, running into a pile of his own players. Equally bad would be a delay on the part of the ball carrier, which permitted the line to open the hole, and then have the defense close it before the ball carrier reached the point of attack. Generally speaking, a play should be designed so that the blockers contact the defensive men 2 or 3 yards in advance of the ball carrier, so that the defensive players do not have a chance to recover into the path of the play. On a

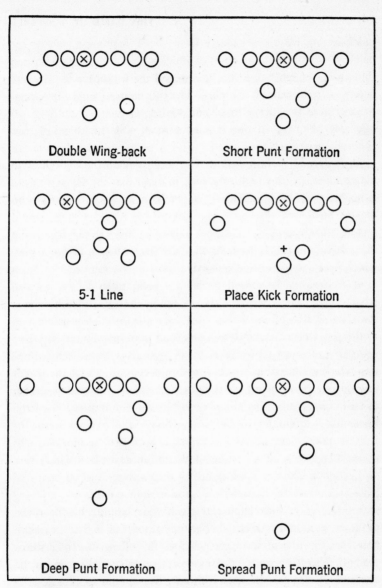

Double Wing-back

Short Punt Formation

5-1 Line

Place Kick Formation

Deep Punt Formation

Spread Punt Formation

DIAGRAM 2

Six more offensive formations

25

quick-hitting play, particularly from the T formation, where the
ball carrier will reach the point of attack with a minimum of elapsed
time, it is frequently possible for one offensive blocker to take one
defensive man out of the play: in other words, single blocking.
Where there is a delay involved, double teaming, or putting two
offensive blockers on one defensive man, and trap blocking are
generally necessary.

3. *Reasonable Assignment.* The assignment of each offensive
player must be drawn with the idea in mind that the offensive man
is no better than the defensive player he is assigned to block—no
bigger, no faster, no better coordinated. It would not be sound
football, for example, to expect a blocker who is playing inside
of a defensive player to take that defensive player in on a play
which goes outside of that defensive spot.

4. *Deception.* It is well to have several plays in the offense
which start exactly alike and end up by hitting different spots.
Reasonable deception of this kind does not tip off the defense as
to the point of attack and prevents their concentration at any one
spot. It is always well to have one or two plays from each formation which are based almost entirely on deception, where the threat
toward one point of attack is built up until the defense is drawn
to that point, permitting the play to hit at a different sector of the
line with a minimum of blocking. Many fake passes, Statue of
Liberty plays, and delayed reverses are of this nature. Straight
power plays without a vestige of deception and plays which rely
on deception alone cannot stand by themselves. A good series of
plays will combine reasonable deception with power.

5. *Flexibility.* The defense is given wide latitude by the rules,
as far as position is concerned. The only restriction is that they shall
not cross the line of scrimmage before the offensive center snaps
the ball. Therefore we see defenses with seven or eight men on the
line and we also see defenses with only five or four or occasionally
three men on the line. The defense will sometimes line up a yard
back of the ball. All of this complicates the picture for the offense.

The offense must have some reasonably simple system whereby assignments on any given play can be easily adjusted to meet whatever defense is set against the formation at the moment the ball is snapped. It is not at all uncommon to meet five or six different defensive alignments in the course of a single ball game. This is an added reason for keeping the offense simple and restricting the total number of different plays.

6. *Personnel*. Standard plays in any formation will have to be modified to fit the personnel of your team. If, for example, on the T formation the fullback is a good blocker but not a very fast runner, then it would be desirable to run wide with the halfbacks and use the fullback as a blocker. If, on the other hand, the fullback is an excellent open field runner, it would be well to utilize his ability going wide and depend on the halfbacks to help him with their blocking. Also, on the T formation, if one of the halfbacks or the fullback is a good passer, plays can be designed to take advantage of that ability.

At California in 1948 we were very fortunate in having a versatile fullback, Jack Jensen, who made All-American that year. Jensen had good straight-ahead power and enough speed to go off tackle or wide to either side. He was teamed with Jack Swaner at right halfback, another very fine back, with perhaps a little more straight-ahead power than Jensen. The third man in the backfield at left halfback was Billy Main, who was much smaller than either of the other two. Billy's particular strong point was in blocking, and it was always interesting to watch the little boy block for the two big fellows, but it worked out into a nice backfield combination. In addition, Jensen was a good passer and we developed plays that would permit him to forward-pass.

Plays will vary with any given team using the same system from year to year as the personnel varies. A play that worked very well last year may not work so well this year, because last year its success may have been due to the unusual ability of a player who has since graduated.

THE SIGNAL SYSTEM

As a part of the general offensive plan a simple and reliable signal system must be devised, so that the quarterback can inform his teammates in the easiest and surest way possible of the play which he has decided to run next. If a team uses the huddle, it is barely possible that the quarterback might gather the other ten players around him and describe the play that he plans to use. This plan, in most cases, however, would be highly unsatisfactory. The description would take too long, and it is sometimes very hard for a team to hear clearly during a game because of the noise, especially if there is a large crowd present.

Most teams find it easiest and safest simply to use one number which describes the entire play. Each player has learned his personal assignment on that particular play and the number conveys the picture of the entire offensive maneuver to him. It is desirable to have the play numbers follow some definite system of relationship which will indicate the point of attack, the ball carrier, and the general type of action that is to be used in setting up the play.

Until about thirty years ago it was customary for a team to line up in a set formation and for the quarterback to call a series of numbers, among which the play number and starting number were concealed according to a definite plan. In theory, this permitted the quarterback to look the defense over and find the weak spot. At that time the defense used only one or, at most, two alignments and did not change very much. Under present conditions, I doubt if such a plan would be desirable. Defenses use many alignments and shift around during the interval while signals are being called, so there is not much value in the quarterback having the opportunity of looking at the defense while he calls the signals.

During the past thirty years most teams have found it desirable to huddle around the quarterback while he gives the play. The team then lines up in the formation and the quarterback calls the starting cadence. Most teams have some way of adjusting or modifying the play in the event that it does not fit the defensive alignment.

Diagram 3 illustrates a typical huddle and a simple signal system. The huddle is formed around the center who stations himself about 7 yards back of the ball. The linemen face the rear and the backs face forward in a loose oval. The looser the huddle the better chance that everyone can hear the quarterback distinctly. We like to have the quarterback remain 4 or 5 yards outside of the huddle until

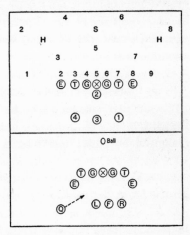

DIAGRAM 3
Huddle (below) and signal system

it is well formed. This gives him a chance to think for a moment about the play he is planning to call and it also gives the team captain a chance to make sure the huddle is well formed and quiet when the quarterback steps into it. After the quarterback is sure that everyone has heard and understands the play signal, he will hike them out of the huddle in unison to the offensive formation.

Diagram 3 also illustrates a simple signal system. In some cases the signal system numbers the holes between the defensive players. However, the one illustrated numbers the offensive players in the line of scrimmage, starting from left to right. Number 1, for example, is the area outside of the offensive left end, namely a wide play. Number 2 is the area over the left end, which would be an off-tackle play. Number 3 over the left tackle, 4 the left guard, 5 the center, and so forth, ending up with 9, which would indicate a play wide to the right.

The offensive backs are also numbered, with the right half No. 1, quarterback No. 2, the fullback No. 3, and left half No. 4. It is thus possible to put together a double-digit signal system which would indicate the ball carrier and the point of attack. As for example, Play 48 would be a play in which the left half carried the ball off tackle to the right. Play 35 would be a fullback buck over center, and Play 11 would be the left half wide to the left. In this way each play number means something to the entire team. Variations in basic plays can be given the number X or Y or a third digit could be added to the play number. In Diagrams 34 through 40 (below) the ball is passed directly to back No. 3 (see Diagram 34). Thus the play number would be 3-49. In Diagram 3 the numbers beyond the line of scrimmage indicate areas for pass receivers. For example, all passes might be designated as in the sixties, when thrown by the quarterback. A pass in which the left end crossed over behind the left defensive halfback in the 8-territory might be called 68. A flat pass to the left might be called 61. Any pass by the fullback might be in the seventies, so that the same two passes with the fullback throwing might be 78 and 71.

The signal system must be kept very simple so that it will not be a mental burden upon the players. The offensive team will need every bit of their energy to observe the maneuvers of the defense and to carry out the offensive assignments.

T-FORMATION PLAYS

All the plays that are diagramed on succeeding pages from the T formation have been used at the University of California in the past five years. Our T formation is a normal T, except that the tackles are generally split away from the guards from 8 to 24 inches. Our fullback lines up 4½ yards from the near point of the ball. The halfbacks line up with their heels in line with the fullback's toes, and line up far enough away from the fullback so that if the fullback and halfbacks raise their arms toward each other there is about a 3-inch interval between fingertips. We sometimes use a man in motion, but generally prefer to set the flanker directly from the huddle. The flanker lines up anywhere from 3 to 10 yards outside of the position normally occupied by the defensive end on his side.

The stances of the various players are illustrated in photographs in subsequent chapters on line and backfield fundamentals. The quarterback generally has one foot in advance of the other, and the position of the feet on each play will be indicated in the diagram by dots.

A complete series of basic plays, from both the normal T with three men back and the flanker, are diagramed on the following pages. Since the T is a completely balanced formation the same play can be run to either side. The first play diagramed, the hand-off to the right, will be shown against a normal five-, six-, and seven-man defensive line and its companion play, the hand-off to the left, will be shown in full detail against one defense. Other plays will be diagramed just to one side. The assignments to the opposite side can be worked out simply by transposing the entire play from right to left or vice versa.

Enough basic plays will be diagramed against three different defenses to illustrate the principles of adjustment to the varied defenses.

LEGEND FOR DIAGRAMS

○   Offensive Player

●   Ball Carrier

〜〜〜   Path of Ball Carrier

━━⊩→   Path of Back Faking to Receive Ball

━━→   Path of Offensive Interferers and Pass Receivers

-------   Path of Ball - Center's Pass Forward Pass - Lateral Pass

✕   Defensive Player

✕   Angle of Block on
○   Defensive Player

⊙   Position of Quarterback's Feet (R. Foot Forward)

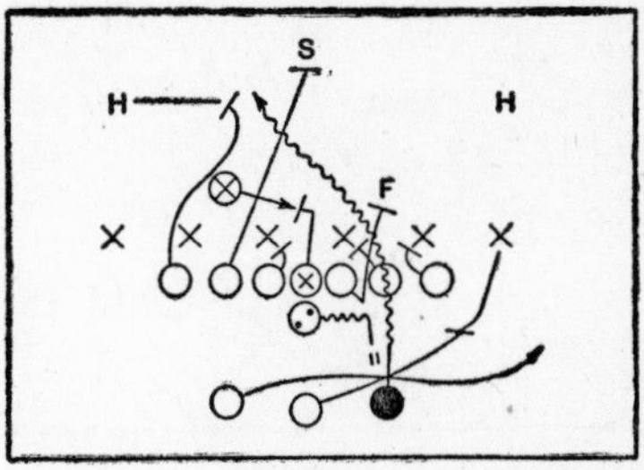

DIAGRAM 4
Play 17 vs. 6-man line

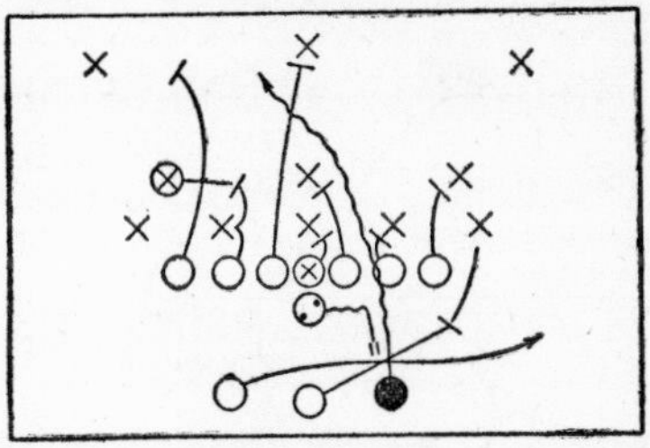

DIAGRAM 5
Play 17 vs. 5-man line

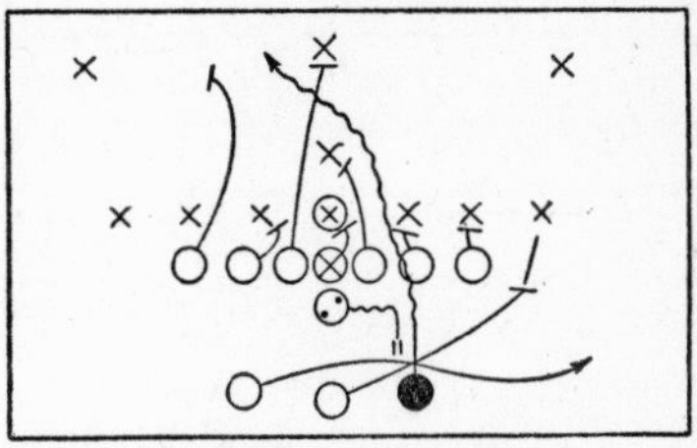

DIAGRAM 6
Play 17 vs. 7-man line

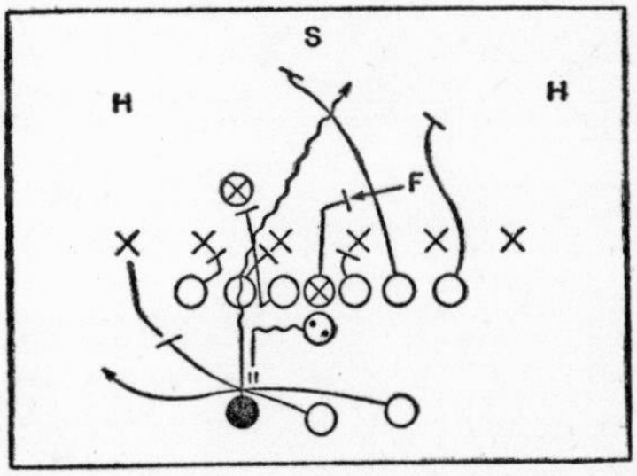

DIAGRAM 7
Play 43 vs. 6-man line

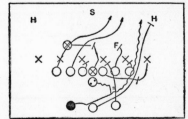

DIAGRAM 8
Play 48 vs. 6-man line

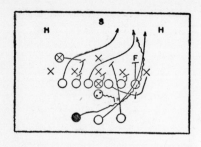

DIAGRAM 9
Play 48 vs. 5-man line

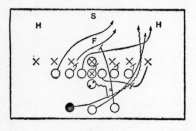

DIAGRAM 10
Play 48 vs. 7-man line

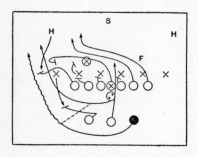

DIAGRAM 11
Play 11 vs. 6-man line

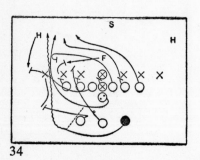

DIAGRAM 12
Play 11 vs. 7-man line

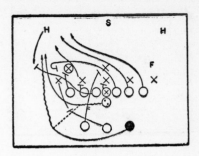

DIAGRAM 13
Play 11 vs. 5-man line

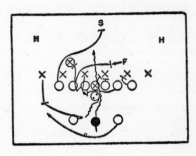

DIAGRAM 14
Play 34 (F.B. trap) vs. 6-man line

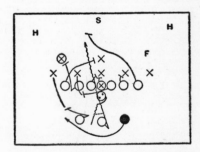

DIAGRAM 15
Play 34 vs. 5-man line

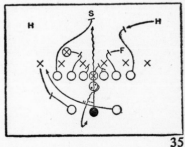

DIAGRAM 16
*Play 35 (F.B. power play) vs.
6-man line*

35

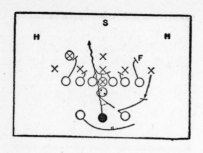

DIAGRAM 17
Play 35 vs. 5-man line

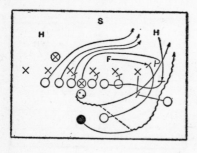

DIAGRAM 18
Play 39 (F.B. end run) vs. 6-man line

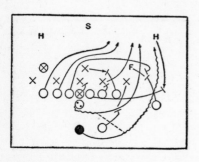

DIAGRAM 19
Play 39 vs. 5-man line

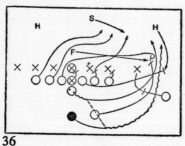

DIAGRAM 20
Play 39 vs. 7-man line

36

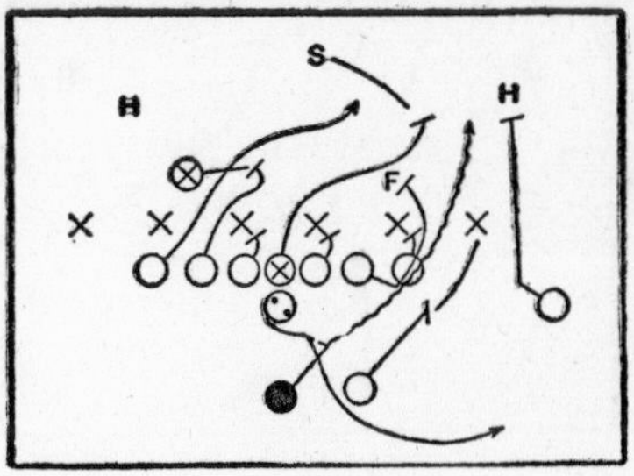

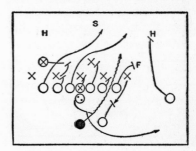

DIAGRAM 21
*Play 38 (F.B. off tackle) vs.
6-man line*

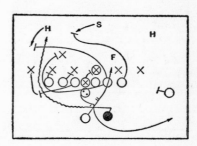

DIAGRAM 22
Play 38 vs. 5-man line

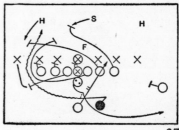

DIAGRAM 23
H.B. counter to left vs. 6-man line

DIAGRAM 24
H.B. counter to left vs. 7-man line

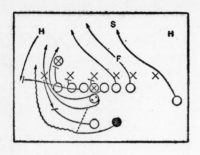

DIAGRAM 25
*Sweep to short side vs.
overshifted 6*

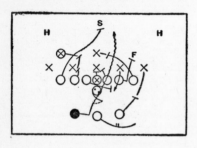

DIAGRAM 26
L.H. cutback (46) vs. 5-man line

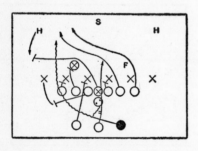

DIAGRAM 27
"Crossfire" (12) vs. 6-man line

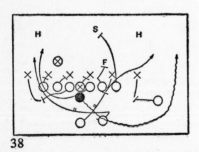

DIAGRAM 28
"Bootleg" play to right

38

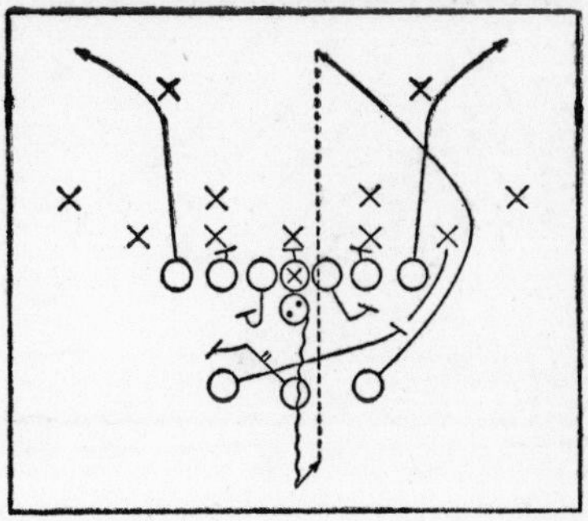

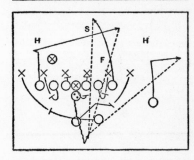

DIAGRAM 29
Pass 64 vs. 5-4-2 defense

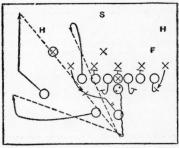

DIAGRAM 30
Pass 68 vs. 5-2-2-1 defense

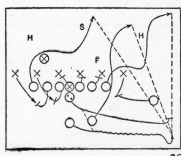

DIAGRAM 31
Pass 63

DIAGRAM 32
Running pass by F.B.

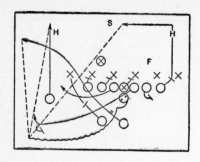

DIAGRAM 33
Q.B. roll-out pass (82) to left

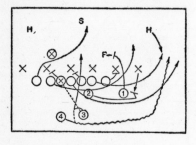

DIAGRAM 34
Play 3-49, single wing strong-side reverse

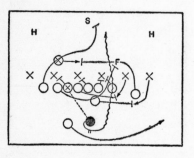

DIAGRAM 35
Play 3-37, F.B. spin inside tackle

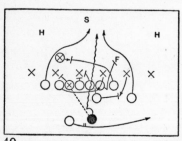

DIAGRAM 36
Play 3-36, F.B. half spin inside guard

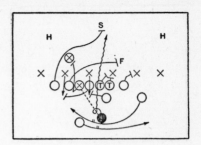

DIAGRAM 37
Play 3-34, fake reverse trap

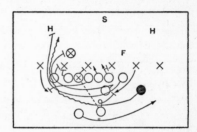

DIAGRAM 38
Play 3-12, short-side reverse

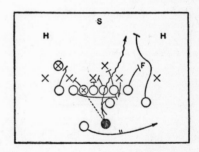

DIAGRAM 39
Play 3-27, buck lateral inside tackle

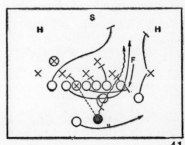

DIAGRAM 40
Play 3-28, buck lateral outside tackle

41

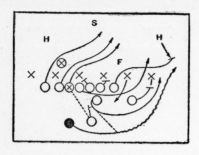

DIAGRAM 41
Lateral around end

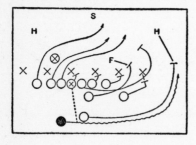

DIAGRAM 42
Single wing, balanced line, end run

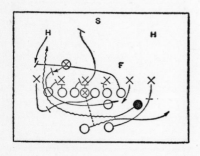

DIAGRAM 43
Half to half reverse

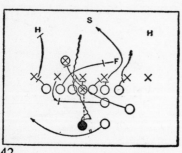

DIAGRAM 44
H.B. spin play to short side

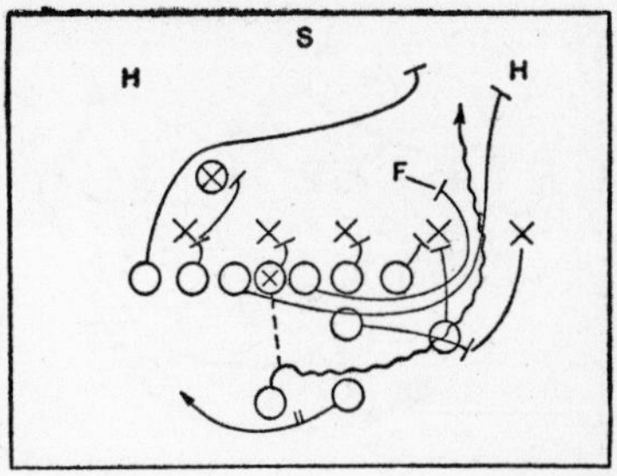

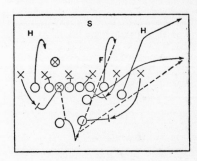

DIAGRAM 45
H.B. half spin off tackle

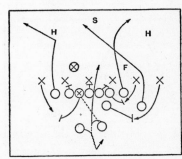

DIAGRAM 46
Single wing, 4-way pass

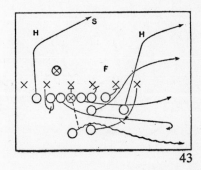

DIAGRAM 47
Single wing, pass from spin action

DIAGRAM 48
Single wing, running pass

DEFENSE is something of a stepchild in today's football. During the past twenty to thirty years the average score made in college games has been steadily creeping upward. A comparison of scores made today with those made twenty-five years ago reveals a surprising difference. I recall that the Syracuse team in 1923 on which I played, coached by Chick Meehan, held our first six opponents to a total of eleven first downs, and we were not scored upon until late in the season. The art of defense has made great progress since that day, but the offense has progressed even faster, and certainly our present game is a more interesting one for the spectator. A tight pitchers' duel is enjoyed by close students of baseball, but most people enjoy seeing a reasonable number of hits and an occasional home run. The same situation seems to hold true in football.

RECENT EMPHASIS ON OFFENSE

There are several reasons other than spectator interest which have contributed to the dominance of the offense in recent years. Among them, I would say, are:

1. *The Influence of Professional Football.* The pro game in the United States, with its many fine passers and excellent receivers and consequent emphasis on the forward passing game, has produced a high-scoring, crowd-pleasing type of football—perhaps too high scoring for proper balance. In many pro games nearly every sequence results in a score and that team will lose which fails on several occasions to go for a touchdown. I am by no means underestimating the great defensive ability of many of the pro players,

44

nor the ingenuity of professional coaches in designing defenses, but the wide-open pro game has had its influence upon the college game.

2. *Present Football Rules Slightly More Favorable to the Offense Than to the Defense.* This is not necessarily a bad thing. Through the years the rules have maintained a rather delicate balance between offense and defense and we seem to be going now through a period when the balance appears to be tipped in favor of the offense. Especially, the rules surrounding the forward pass have been liberalized in recent years. The passer may now make his pass from any point behind the line of scrimmage, instead of being forced to pass from a spot five yards or more back of that line. This, and other rules which tend to open up the game, have had the endorsement of spectators, players, and coaches alike.

3. *The Platoon System.* There are many desirable features of the so-called platoon system under which one team plays on offense and when the ball is lost a full team or nearly a full team is substituted to play the defense. We follow that plan at California and feel that generally speaking it has been beneficial. But the net result has undoubtedly been to make the offense stronger at the expense of the defense. The platoon system widens the base of competition and permits more players to participate in the game. Most coaches unconsciously select the strongest and fastest players to make up the offensive unit. These men specialize on offense and often receive no defensive practice at all. Men in the offensive platoon will have the opportunity to spend more time on offense to develop their timing of plays and to perfect their specialties. Many players learn defense more rapidly than offense and may play first on the defensive squad and then perhaps later on the offensive team. We try to keep our offensive and defensive units at California in good balance as to ability and opportunity for development. However, I cannot but feel that the net result throughout the country is a strengthening of the offense by the use of the platoon system.

IMPORTANCE OF DEFENSE

In spite of, or perhaps because of, the factors favoring the offense, defensive football is even more important today than it has ever been before. A team which neglects defense is building on sand. No matter how strong its offense may be, there will come a day when the offense is not functioning well and without the bulwark of the strong defense, that team is bound to go down in defeat, and perhaps a bad defeat. The offense may suffer from bad weather, their timing may be off that day, the opponents may present an unexpected and unbreakable defense—whichever one of many causes it may be, the offense may simply not function on any given Saturday. If the defense cannot step into the breach, then the team which has put all of its eggs into the offensive basket is in for a bad afternoon.

The importance of defense is something that most coaches have learned by bitter experience. I relearned it again the hard way in 1947, my first year at California. In teaching a new system of play we had been forced to spend a disproportionate amount of time on the offense. We were able to get by our first five games, and as we approached the sixth against one of Jeff Cravath's fine University of Southern California teams, we realized that we were not as strong defensively as we would like to be. In spite of every effort to bolster the defense, a good Trojan football team beat us by a score of 39–14. We redoubled our efforts on defense the following week and the results showed in our game with U.C.L.A. which we won by the close score of 6–0.

Confidence in the defense helps the morale of any football team. On several occasions I have seen a fine offense break its heart against a rock-ribbed defense. If a team feels that they can stop the other fellow, that feeling takes a great deal of the pressure off. A well-trained defensive platoon gives an element of stability to the entire squad and many times a healthy and good-natured rivalry develops between the two units.

Defense has developed a great deal in the past thirty years. It used to be that a team would present one or at most two defenses in the course of a ball game. A seven-man line was more or less standard with the six being used occasionally as a variation. At the present time one team in the course of a single afternoon may present a dozen different defenses. Furthermore they may "stunt" various players by having linebackers shoot unexpectedly through the line. They may play on the line of scrimmage or back off as much as a yard. The line may all slant or loop, as a unit, in a predetermined direction. An infinite variety of defensive line-ups is possible, and also a great variety in the maneuvers of the individual player.

THE DEFENSIVE PLAN

With a wide range of defensive formations and defensive maneuvers available, a defensive plan must be worked out for the team, just as a specific offensive pattern is developed. There are a number of factors which influence the choice of basic defensive plans. Among them are:

1. *Your Own Personnel.* This is by far the most important factor. If an opponent is to be stopped he will be stopped not by diagrams on a blackboard or by a slide rule, but by eleven human beings who may vary widely in size, height, speed and experience. Certain of the defensive players will be bigger, stronger, and faster than others. Just how to deploy the defense so as to take advantage of the strong points and hide whatever weak points there may be, is the first consideration. The opportunity to play players on defense, regardless of their position on offense, as is now permitted by the rules, has liberalized our thinking a great deal. Because a man plays tackle on offense is no reason that he would occupy the same position on defense. He might make a better guard or a linebacker. In the old days, however, the right tackle on offense generally played the same position on defense.

In 1949 the University of Washington used a defensive plan that bothered us a great deal. The line-up was that of a seven-man diamond (7–1–2–1) but six of the defensive players were listed as tackles, four as ends and one as a halfback. These six tackles on the defensive line were the biggest, toughest men on the squad and set up a formidable barrier. It is rather commonplace to find several centers in the game at the same time on defense, or an end playing defensive halfback.

A careful study of the squad personnel may reveal unexpected strength for key defensive positions. Two of the finest linebackers that California faced in 1950 played for Stanford. Bill McColl, a great offensive end, and Russ Pomeroy, an offensive tackle, fulfilled the function of linebackers in unequaled style.

In 1946 at Northwestern we had a talented defensive linebacker in "Buckets" Hirsch. He had always played in the backfield but was willing to change to guard, where his fine blocking on offense was of considerable help. "Buckets" was a great linebacker, but had never played in the line on defense; thus our defensive plans revolved around a five-man defensive setup where Hirsch's linebacking ability could be of best value to his teammates.

2. *Your Opponent.* Football is not played in a vacuum. The defensive plan, based on the most advantageous distribution of your own personnel, must be modified to meet each opponent. The first thing a scout is asked is, "What and who must we stop?" The answer to that question will form the basis of the defensive plan against that particular opponent.

The opponents' formation must be considered in planning the defense. A basic plan which might be very good against a T must be modified considerably against a single wing back. Any variations in the formation, such as flankers, men in motion, unusual spacing, must all be considered in planning the defense.

However, the personnel of the opponents will be even more important than the formation used. It is entirely possible that during the course of a season a team might meet six different T-formation opponents and use a different defense against each opponent even though each was using identically the same formation. One T-formation team, for example, might have a great passer, one end who is a fine receiver, and a fullback who is a power runner, and yet not be effective wide. Another T formation might have an average passer, but a great fullback with fine speed who could run wide but was not as effective in the middle of the line. Still another T-formation team might have ends who were very strong blockers but poor at receiving, and depend on the halfbacks to be the receivers. A careful evaluation of the opponent's personnel is the starting point for any defensive preparations. What are the things they can do well? What are the things they do poorly? What are their favorite plays and pass patterns?

A good example of the influence of opponent's personnel on the defensive plan occurred at Northwestern in 1941 when we were preparing for the Notre Dame game. Notre Dame was using basically the Notre Dame box, a type of single wing shifted right or left with a balanced line. When they shifted to the right the left half was Bertelli and the right half out at a semiwing position was Juzwik. Bertelli was one of the leading passers in the country but did not run very effectively. Juzwik did not pass but was an excellent runner and pass receiver. When they shifted to the left they put Bertelli in the wing spot and Juzwik back at the tail spot, where he was one of the most elusive runners and hardest drivers I have ever observed. At that time we were using a six-man defensive alignment as our basic formation. Quite naturally we undershifted the six when Notre Dame was in right formation because the running threat (Juzwik) was back to the left side, and over-shifted our six-man line when Notre Dame went into left formation because of this same strong threat of Juzwik running to the left. There were other factors, of course, which entered into the defensive plan, but the unusual abilities of Juzwik and Bertelli had to be very carefully considered. Incidentally, Notre Dame won the game by a score of 7–6, with a finely executed touchdown pass from Bertelli to the left end who made a great catch right at the Northwestern goal line.

3. *Basic Defensive Approach.* There are at least two general theories on the subject of defense. One theory goes something like this: a defensive plan should be simple so that every man understands exactly where he is to line up and exactly what his duties will be in defending his position. His defensive neighbor will know and can count on his action. Teach each man to play his position. Use one basic defensive plan with perhaps an occasional variation.

This plan has the merit of simplicity. There is no confusion as to where a man will line up or what his contribution will be to the defensive pattern. With defensive personnel made up of big, fast, active men, this plan has a lot to recommend it. Some of the toughest defensive teams I have ever seen were those at Minnesota the years 1935 through 1942. Their opponents knew generally where the Gophers were planning to line up and how they planned to charge, but their defensive execution was so effective and the line charge so hard that such knowledge availed the offense little.

A contrasting basic defensive theory might be described as the use of a large number of defensive formations and variations in the defensive action in an effort to confuse the assignments of the offensive team. If the defense constantly varies the position in which the players will line up, the offense has a tendency to become hesitant and confused, missed assignments result, and the defense frequently has a man free to penetrate into the offensive backfield. Under this plan a team might line up in the five-man line, a seven-man line, an overshifted six, a tight six, or a wide six on successive downs. The picture might be further complicated by having the players on the line of scrimmage one time and back a yard another time, by having the line charge straight ahead one time and slanting to the right or left another time, by using "stunts" in which a lineman might slant one direction and a linebacker shoot through the gap suddenly. In the hands of experienced personnel, this type of defense can be very effective; however, there is always the danger that some lineman will forget his assignment and line up out of position or charge in the wrong direction leaving a great hole through which the offense may happen to call a play at a most unfortunate time.

Many teams try to combine the strong points of both of the above theories. They teach position play; a lineman is instructed, by the use of various maneuvers, to maintain his own territory. However, several different defensive line-ups are used, so that the defensive players will not always be in the same spot; yet the defense is not complicated enough so that there is likely to be any uncertainty on the part of the defensive players. Using several different defenses also gives the defensive team an opportunity to vary the position of the linebackers so that the offense cannot peg them and know where they will be at all times. It is common sense also to vary the defense according to the ball's position on the field, for certain defenses are more favorable than others in sideline situations. The defense is also varied by the proximity to the goal line. If a team is on its own 5-yard line they are not in any position to give ground, and the linemen will play lower and tighter than in other situations. Similarly if the offense has only a short distance to go for a first down, the defense will tighten up. They will loosen up and play higher if the yardage to be gained is big.

PASS DEFENSE

Regardless of the exact defensive plan and formation decided upon, defense against passes will present a major problem. There is no perfect pass defense, but a sound one will carry out certain basic principles. The ingredients would assume about the following proportions:

1. *Sixty per cent*—rushing the passer and delaying receivers at or near the line of scrimmage.

2. *Twenty-five per cent*—the ability of the safety, halfbacks, and one or two linebackers to play the ball the instant it is in the air.

3. *Fifteen per cent*—the plan of cooperation used by the backs and linebackers or other assigned linemen in covering the pass pattern.

Rushing the Passer. Inexperienced linemen tend to feel that their duties on a pass play are relatively minor and that the backfield men should bear the brunt of pass defense. Rushing the passer is hard work, but once the defensive linemen have come to realize its importance and have enjoyed the opportunity of breaking through to throw the passer for a loss, they can appreciate the important part played by the pass rush in team pass defense. Any ordinary passer who is permitted 4 or 5 seconds from the time the center snaps the ball to look the field over and start his pass, will enjoy great success, and a good passer with that much time will riddle any possible defensive plan. But if the defensive linemen force the same passer to get rid of the ball in 2.3 or 2.4 seconds, the pass pattern has not had the opportunity to develop nearly as much depth and the defensive backs are in position to do a much better job. Linemen rushing the passer must expect to be blocked by the man assigned to them, and if they succeed in breaking through their man, there is generally an additional protector serving as a "clean-up" man to pick up anybody who breaks through. Inexperienced linemen have a tendency to give up too easily and to assume that the passer will get rid of the ball before they can reach him. A good lineman, however, will keep trying to break through the blockers and battle his way to the passer. This ability of the defensive linemen to "pick up" their rush as soon as they recognize that a pass play is under way and accelerate the drive toward the passer, is the foundation stone of all pass defense. The rusher must use his hands and forearm legitimately on the blockers, must learn to feint one way and side-step and, above all, must never stop coming until the ball has been thrown or he has tackled the passer. The pass rush, of course, should be varied enough so that the same men are not always rushing from the same spots. Sometimes if a linebacker rushes through while a teammate may protect his area, the linebacker may find himself unexpectedly in the passing zone with a clear shot at the passer.

Delaying Receivers. A defensive linebacker, tackle, or end is frequently in a position to jolt an eligible receiver with his shoulder and forearm and knock him off-balance or force him to detour, and thus delay him in getting downfield to take his place in the pass pattern. This opportunity is present most generally in the case of an eligible end or wing back occupying his normal spot in the offensive formation. If the end or the back widens out 10 yards, that same opportunity is not there, since the receiver has more room in which to dodge. However, by widening to that degree the receiver is not in a good blocking position for ordinary plays and this takes a little of the pressure off the defense against the running attack.

The defensive player who is attempting to hold up the eligible receiver must not hold him in an illegal manner. The rules of the game permit the defensive player to assume that the play is to be a running play until the pass is in the air, and he is entitled to protect himself against a potential offensive blocker by using his shoulders, forearms and hands to ward him off. He is not permitted to grab the receiver as he goes by, or to use any maneuver which would not be proper in warding off a potential blocker. The legitimate holding up of receivers, however, is a part of basic pass defense. If the receiver is delayed in his effort to get downfield, he cannot get as far into the secondary and the pass pattern will be much easier for the deep backs to cover.

Playing the Ball. All backfield men should be in a position to watch any man or area they are assigned to cover and at the same time see the passer. When the passer releases the ball every man must start instantly for the spot where it will come down, or put themselves in a position between that spot and their own goal line. Inexperienced backs do not appreciate the importance of breaking for the ball the instant it is thrown. A player can travel almost half as fast as the ball, but if he is slow in reacting, the area that he can cover effectively is greatly reduced. Instant ball reaction is essential on the part of a pass defender. The defensive man must also remember that he has just as much right to the football, once it is in the air, as any offensive receiver. The football traveling through the air belongs to no one, and is the property of that player, offensive or defensive, who can reach and catch it. Every effort should be made by the defense to intercept the pass. But reasonable judgment should be used so that the defender does not take himself out of the position from which he might make the tackle when it is clearly impossible for him to reach the ball. We like to stress the importance of interception and we feel that one intercepted pass is worth eight or nine knocked down. An interception enables the defensive team to turn instantly to offense and an alert rally of blockers may result in a runback of the interception for a touchdown. Many games are won every year by an intercepted pass and a return for a touchdown. Many more are won by two or three interceptions at critical moments, even if there is very little runback. Each interception deprives the offensive team of the yardage they might obtain by kicking the ball and breaks the continuity of attack.

The Plan of Cooperation of the Backs in Meeting Pass Patterns. It used to be customary to describe pass defense in terms of man for man, zone, or combination. In man-for-man defense each defensive player—halfback, safety, linebackers, or ends—is assigned to cover one eligible receiver in case a pass is thrown. In theory each defender covers his receiver all over the field. In actual fact, however, some system of switching responsibility on certain patterns, such as men crossing from one side to the other, is in general practice. Also, on a man-for-man defense, one player will generally be assigned to play the ball.

In zone defense, each defensive man who is not rushing the passer protects an area and covers any man who comes into that area to receive a pass. In actual practice, various ways of getting help from one zone to another which might be under attack by several different receivers, are necessary.

A combination pass defense would have certain men, in theory, covering a receiver man for man and others protecting zones. "Combination" is a rather loose term, and I suspect that practically all pass defenses in today's football must be so classified. A man-for-man defense would seem to be simple because it is definite as to the responsibility of each particular defender, and zone defense should result in less lost motion of the defensive players. Actually, a good pass defense will rely to a considerable degree upon familiarity with the basic pass patterns of the opponent and an evaluation of the opponent's personnel. Defensive backs who have been working together will frequently vary their tactics according to the type of pattern thrown against them and what seems to be working for the opponent on that particular occasion.

The defensive halfbacks and safety will generally watch the offensive ends, wing back, or flanker, for a clue as to the type of play to be expected. As soon as they sense a pass is developing, they should immediately warn their teammates. Pass defenders, particularly the deep men, should be continually talking to each other, and as the pattern develops and it is apparent that one area is under attack, a particular effort should be made to give warning of that fact. If an end or a back is crossing from one side of the field to the other, the man who observes the cross should call "Cross" or any designated key word to warn the men on the other side of the field that a receiver whom they may not be able to see is coming into their territory.

The greatest mistake that the halfbacks or safety can make on pass defense is to permit a receiver to get behind them and catch a pass. Such a pass will nearly always result in a touchdown, or at best a very long gain, even if the receiver is overtaken by a faster man. The halfbacks must at all times be conscious of this danger, and must at all costs protect the territory behind and outside of them. Quick reaction, the ability to estimate a potential receiver's speed, and the ability to run straight or diagonally backward, are important assets to the defensive halfback. The defensive safety is generally charged with protecting the territory deep over the middle. If the formation is unbalanced as with the single wing or T formation with a flanker or man in motion, the safety must give a little toward the strong side and be in a position to cover the inside man if two receivers come down deep. The safety has somewhat more latitude than the halfbacks, and in addition to the abilities required of the halfbacks, the safety should be a real ball hawk. The safety is in the best position of all to get the entire picture of the pass pattern as it develops. He can help warn the halfbacks on men crossing to their side, direct the pass defense, and lend his assistance to the deep spot under heaviest attack.

Pass defense is not the responsibility of any one man or any small group of the defensive team. It is in the truest sense a team responsibility and unless all eleven men are prepared to do their part, weaknesses will develop upon which the offense can capitalize with disastrous results.

DEFENSE AGAINST THE RUNNING GAME

Like offense, defense is a matter of team responsibility. Every man on the defensive team must defend his position and carry out his assignment in the team plan. This plan against the running attack may vary somewhat with different defensive alignments, and with the exact plan; for example, how the backfield may deploy to meet a wide play used by the offense. The various individual maneuvers and stunts of the linemen and linebackers (which will be discussed in greater detail in Chapter 12) may also modify the team plan. To illustrate a typical team defensive plan, refer to Diagram 49A. The offensive team is lined up in a normal T formation, and the defense is lined up in a normal six-man defensive line with the tackles playing slightly to the inside of the ends. The center and fullback act as linebackers stationed about a yard back from the tackles and slightly to their inside. The halfbacks are approximately 7 to 8 yards deep, and slightly outside of their own defensive ends. The safety is 10 to 12 yards deep and directly in front of the offensive center. The guards are lined up, head up with the offensive guards directly opposite them, and the ends are split away from the defensive tackles by approximately 3 yards.

In the diagram, the offensive team is starting a sweep to the right.

The basic plan of team cooperation for the defense—a normal one
—would be generally as follows:

The defensive ends will start across the line at the snap of the
ball aiming for a point slightly to the inside of the halfback on their
side. As soon as the end can diagnose the play he will go to it as

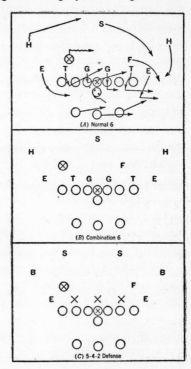

(A) Normal 6

(B) Combination 6

(C) 5-4-2 Defense

DIAGRAM 49
Defenses vs. normal T

rapidly as possible. In this case the left end, seeing that a sweep is
developing, will, once he is sure that the play is not coming inside
of him, widen with the play after he has penetrated a reasonable
distance. Using his hands to ward off blockers, he will try to force
the ball carrier wide and toward the side lines. If unable to make the
tackle, the end on the side under attack will attempt to strip the
interference to give his backfield a chance to make the tackle. The
end on the opposite side, in this case the right end, will follow

cautiously, chasing the play and making sure that nothing in the way of a delayed reverse is coming back in his direction.

The defensive left tackle will penetrate across the line; like all of the other linemen he will try to get a yard into offensive territory by a hard charge. As soon as he sees that the play is going wide, he will move out laterally, parallel to the line of scrimmage at such an angle that he can head the play off. He must be careful not to continue his penetration and merely chase the play. The tackle on the other side will penetrate a little deeper and then when he sees that the play is going away from him, he will drop back and follow it at a deeper angle, slightly toward his own goal line, so that he will be in position to tackle the ball carrier about 5 yards downfield in case the ball carrier cuts back.

The defensive guards will drive low and hard to protect their territory. As soon as they see where the play is going they will move laterally at such an angle as to be able to intercept the ball carrier several yards downfield and behind their own line of scrimmage.

All of the linemen must protect their own territory first and make sure that no delayed play is coming back over the ground they are defending. They must penetrate before they move to the ball.

The linebackers, in many respects, are the key to the defense. They must support the line vigorously against the running attack and yet must get back to assist the halfbacks and safety on pass plays. On the sweep to the right indicated in Diagram 49A, the fullback will move out laterally with the offensive back and attempt to meet the play with vigor on the line of scrimmage. The defensive center must play much more conservatively. As he sees the play apparently move away from him, his first step is backward, and he does not leave his territory until he is absolutely sure that no counter or delayed play or delayed pass is coming back in his direction. He then moves laterally to his left, taking an angle somewhat back, so that he will be in position along with the defensive right tackle to stop the ball carrier in case he cuts back.

The defensive left halfback, when he senses the play is coming in his direction, must move up to meet it, but he must be careful to meet it from the outside and drive it back in toward his teammates. He must not be caught inside and chase it from the inside. If that happens he is the only hope of the defense, for he can get little if any help from his teammates. If he will force the play to break inside of him, however, he will turn it back toward his teammates where he can receive plenty of help. The right halfback on the opposite side, when he sees the play going away from him, must become the most conservative man on the team. The first movement should be backward, and he should not leave his territory until he is sure that there is no delayed running play or any possible pass coming back to his side of the field. When he is sure of this fact, he will move conservatively over toward the spot originally occupied by the safety and, in fact, he becomes the new safety.

The defensive safety is a misnomer. The term "safety" implies a player that is playing very deep and is the last defensive hope on a long pass or in case a ball carrier has broken by every other defensive player. The safety man in today's football is anything but what his name implies. It would be more correct to call him a deep linebacker; for he is expected to take a very important and active part in the defense against the running attack. In Diagram 49A, therefore, the defensive safety, as soon as he has diagnosed the play, will move up vigorously to support the defensive fullback and left halfback. A good defensive safety is not merely a player who pulls down the ball carrier after a 30-yard gain, but he is a man who moves up sharply and makes tackles almost at the line of scrimmage.

One of the finest safety men I have seen in recent years was Johnny Lujack of Notre Dame. He was an excellent pass defender, but the thing which especially amazed me was his ability to diagnose plays rapidly and move up sharply to meet them. I have seen him make many tackles right on the line of scrimmage—coming up so fast and at such an angle that it was practically impossible for the offense to block him.

Diagrams 49B and 49C illustrate additional defensive alignments against the normal T. Diagram 49B is what may be called a combination six. On the defensive left side it is a wide six with the left tackle playing head on the end and the fullback protecting the gap to his inside. On the right side of the defense it is a tight six with a defensive right tackle playing on the outside shoulder of the offensive tackle and driving over the tackle. The defensive center, the linebacker on that side, is stationed behind the gap between the tackle and end and plays about head up with the offensive end. It would, of course, be possible to play a wide six on both sides of the defense, or equally possible to play a tight six on both sides.

Diagram 49C illustrates a 5-4-2 defense. On this defensive alignment, the three center linemen are lined up approximately head up with the offensive tackles and center, and they charge slightly to the inside, trying to seal the territory from tackle to tackle. The center and fullback play in the gap inside the defensive ends and about head on the offensive ends. Two backfield men are stationed approximately 4 yards outside of the defensive ends and 3 to 5 yards back of the line of scrimmage. Instead of one safety, there are two safeties, each about 12 yards back and approximately head up with the offensive ends. Since the defensive ends have help both to their inside and outside, they can afford to drive harder and at a little sharper angle, aiming perhaps for the offensive fullback.

There are an almost limitless number of defensive alignments possible against the T. I have tried to select just a few, but the defenses illustrated are those which I have seen used successfully against the T formation in the past two years. In Diagram 49C the 5-4-2 was a very tough defense as used by Washington against California in 1950 and 1951.

Diagram 50 illustrates three additional defensive formations against the T, and the adjustment made in each formation to meet a man in motion or a flanker. In each case illustrated, the T-formation offense has either put the left half in motion to the right, a very common procedure, or has stationed him about 5 to 15 yards outside of his own end as a flanker. Since this maneuver takes an offensive man from one side of the formation and places him wide on the other side, it is necessary for the defense to make some adjustment to meet it. The dotted lines on the defensive teams show

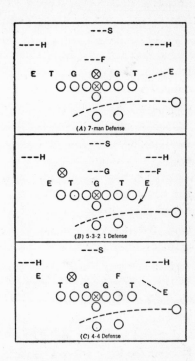

DIAGRAM 50
Defenses vs. T with flanker

the movement of the defensive players as the offensive left half starts in motion, in each case the starting point of the dots indicating the position they would occupy if the offense were to remain in the normal T with three men back. There are other ways of adjusting to the man in motion or flanker, but those shown are in common use. The offensive flanker is in position to break rapidly downfield to receive a pass and he is also in a good flanking position to block an end, a linebacker, or a halfback.

Diagram 50*A* illustrates a seven-man defensive alignment. As the offensive left half starts in motion or takes his position as a flanker as indicated, the defensive safety and halfback will have to move over a little in order to be in a position to cover the threat of a wide play or a forward pass. The right halfback will move over a short distance, too, although this is not always done, and the same is true of the defensive fullback. Since there is only one linebacker, the end on the side of the flanker or motion man will widen to meet the wide threat and drop back off the line a yard or so.

Diagram 50*B* illustrates a normal 5-3-2-1 defense. To meet the motion or flanker one method would be to have the end on the side of the flanker tighten down and protect against inside plays. To compensate for the inside responsibility of the end, the fullback would move to a position outside of the defensive end. The middle linebacker would move over a bit to compensate for the movement of the fullback, and the movement of the defensive halfbacks and safety would be similar to Diagram 50*A*.

Diagram 50*C* illustrates a 4-4-2-1 type of defense. Against the normal T the defense is lined up essentially in a wide six so far as the guards, tackles, and linebackers are concerned. The defensive ends are dropped back off the line about 2 yards and approximately at the same depth as the defensive center and fullback. This type of defense has been used by a number of teams with a great deal of success against the T formation. With the addition of various slants and stunts on the parts of the defensive linemen and linebackers the basic 4-4 can be varied considerably.

In 1949 and 1950 Red Saunders's team at U.C.L.A. used this general type of defense very effectively. They used a great many variations, especially in 1951, and we found it an exceedingly tough defense to work against. On the 4-4 defense a number of reactions to the flanker or man in motion are possible. One frequently used is illustrated. As the left half moves in motion or takes his position as a flanker, the defensive left end moves up from his position 2 yards back of the line of scrimmage. Here he takes his place on the line of scrimmage somewhat wider than he would normally occupy if there were no flanker.

There are a number of "stunts" which can be used by the defensive linemen and linebackers from almost any alignment and against practically any offensive formation. On all of the defenses illustrated so far the defensive linemen are taking a straightaway charge driving forward to protect their position, and the defensive linebackers are moving normally to meet the play as soon as they have diagnosed what is coming. By "stunts" we mean any variation in the normal procedure, as for example, a defensive linebacker shooting through the line at the snap of the ball with the adjacent linemen possibly slanting to protect his territory; or a movement of the entire line, such as slant charging or looping to the right or left as a unit with the linebackers moving in the opposite direction to compensate. On a slant charge the defensive linemen, instead of charging on the man directly opposite, will charge at an angle against the offensive player to the right or left of the man in front of him. A loop is generally a variation of the slant whereby the defensive linemen will side-step laterally and then drive into the man adjacent to the offensive player against whom he was originally lined up. Teams employing the slant or loop charge will frequently have the defensive linemen take their position from 1 foot to 1 yard back of the line of scrimmage in order to facilitate this maneuver. Even when a straightaway charge is planned, it makes an interesting variation to have the defensive line start from a position ½ to 1 yard back of the front point of the ball.

Diagram 51 illustrates a number of such "stunts" used against the T. Diagram 51A illustrates a six-man defensive alignment with a slant charge of the entire defensive line to their left. The two linebackers move to their right to help cover the territory weakened by the slant to the left. The same general type of maneuver could be used for a loop charge, as described above. Either the slant or the loop might work a bit better if the entire defensive line were back off the line of scrimmage ½ yard or so.

Diagram 51B illustrates a wide six with the tackles playing on the ends. In this stunt both defensive guards slant charge to their left, while the defensive center "shoots the gap" over the offensive tackle. The defensive tackles and ends play normally with a defensive fullback being alert for any play developing over the center as well as through his normal position. This stunt was used very effectively by Ohio State against California in the 1950 Rose Bowl game. Lininger, the Ohio State center, was particularly adept in its execution.

Diagram 51C illustrates a variety of possible stunts from the 5-3 defense. The guard over the center can slant either way—in the case illustrated, to the left—while the middle linebacker, at the snap of the ball, shoots to his right, attempting to drive through the line over the offensive left guard. Other variations of the linebacker stunts from 5-3 might have the corner linebackers, the fullback or center, "shooting the gap" over the offensive ends. It would probably not be desirable to have all three of the linebackers shoot at one time, but one of two linebackers shooting complicates the blocking problem of the offense.

Diagram 51D illustrates another stunt from the six-man line. In this case the defensive guards charge out and the defensive center shoots through between them. In the diagram illustrated the defensive tackles are holding up the offensive ends and then dropping back to cover the flat zone on their side against a possible forward pass.

Defensive stunts are always somewhat of a gamble, but a gamble often well worth taking. If the defense can get a player quickly into the offensive backfield and throw the ball carrier for a loss, that loss may be the means of interrupting the continuity of the attack and forcing the offense to kick. If a pass play develops and the stunter gets through cleanly into the area the offensive line is trying to protect, he may be able to throw the passer for a substantial loss before he can get the ball away. Even if the stunt succeeds only occasionally, the fact that it is being used by the defense will worry the offensive team and perhaps make them somewhat hesitant in their blocks. There are many other stunts and combinations of defensive charge that can be used beyond those illustrated here.

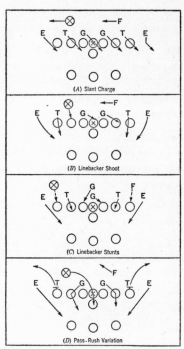

DIAGRAM 51
Line "stunts" vs. T

DEFENSE AGAINST THE SINGLE WING

Diagram 52 illustrates several different defenses against various types of the single wing formation. Since the single wing presents a backfield which is overbalanced in one direction and a line which is frequently overbalanced in the same direction, the defense must align their forces to meet the strongest threat. The basic principles described in Diagram 49A by which the defensive team deploys to meet the threat of an offensive play, would still hold true in principle. The defensive linemen facing the strong side of the formation are under especially strong attack. Since in most wing back formations the tackle is exposed to an immediate block by the end and wing back, the defensive strong side end finds two blockers in a position to move quickly against him. The men on the short side generally have a little more time in which to diagnose and meet plays. The single wing attack will not hit quite so fast as the T offense, but it will hit with more power, as double-teaming, or the use of two offensive players against one defensive man, is generally used at the point of attack.

Diagram 52*A* shows the offense lined up with the line unbalanced to the right and a normal single wing alignment in the backfield. The defense is in an overshifted six (by "overshifted" we mean that the defensive line has lined up laterally toward the strong side far enough to compensate or perhaps a little more than compensate for the concentration of strength on that side). The tackle on the strong side is lined up slightly to the inside of the wing back, while the short side tackle is playing the outside shoulder of the first man inside the offensive end. The guards divide the area between the tackles but are careful to play head on a man rather than in the gap between men. The defensive center is stationed slightly outside of the right defensive tackle, and the defensive fullback is in the gap between the defensive left guard and left tackle. Of course it is possible to stunt the linebackers from this formation.

Diagram 52*B* illustrates an undershifted six-man defense against a balanced single wing formation. In this defense, which could be used against the unbalanced line just as well, the defensive line has not shifted as far laterally toward the strong side. The defensive left tackle is lined up head on the offensive right end, and the defensive fullback has moved out into the gap between the left tackle and left end to strengthen that position. Defensive right tackle is playing head on the offensive left end, and the center can afford to move in a little closer toward the center of the line.

Diagram 52*C* illustrates a five-man defense against the Minnesota type of single wing formation in which the right half, instead of being stationed as a wing back, is lined up approximately even with the fullback. The 5-3 defense illustrated could be used against either of the above formations.

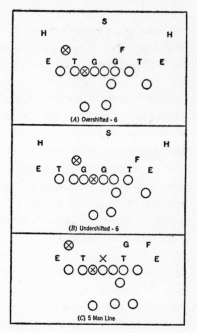

DIAGRAM 52
Defenses vs. single wing

DEFENSIVE SIGNALS AND GENERALSHIP

One player on the defensive team is assigned the duty of selecting the particular defensive alignment to be used on each play. This man is frequently, but not always, one of the linebackers. He must know thoroughly all of the defensive alignments that are planned for that particular game and he must vary them in such a way that the defensive players are not always lined up in the same spot. The defensive signal can be given by calling a number, but more frequently it is given by hand signals. In calling the defense to be used the defensive quarterback will stand with his back toward the offensive huddle. Because he must be careful not

to infringe on the neutral zone, his teammates will line up back of
the ball so that they can see the signal. An additional advantage of
hand signals is that they can be seen by the defensive halfbacks
and safety fairly easily, where the latter might not hear a spoken
signal. A little thought can readily devise a system of hand signals
which can be distinguished from each other to avoid any possibility
of confusion. If a stunt using the entire line is to be employed, it
also may be incorporated in the hand signal.

The defensive quarterback must be keenly aware of the situation
on the field, the down and distance to be gained, the time remaining
to play, the ball's proximity to side line and goal line, what plays
and passes have been gaining for the offense—all of these elements
must be taken into consideration in calling the defensive alignment.
On a first down, for example, it may be desirable to attempt a stunt
and try to throw the offensive ball carrier for a loss, so that the
offensive team is handicapped for that series of plays and must
gamble in their turn.

On a short yardage situation such as when there are 2 yards to
go on third down in the middle of the field, or fourth down and 1
or 2 yards to go inside the defensive 25- or 30-yard line, the defense
call should probably be one which emphasizes a tight line to prevent
the offense attaining the vital first down.

On a big yardage situation such as third down and 8 or 10 yards
to go, a looser formation may be called—one which provides for
better coverage on passes. If the offensive team has the ball around
their own 10-yard line where they may hesitate to gamble, a tight
defensive formation might be in order, so as to stop them and
force them to kick. On the defensive goal-line area every effort
must be made to fight for each inch of ground, and a tight defensive formation or a special goal-line formation would be logical
at this point. If the ball is in a side-line situation it might be well
to consider a formation which protects the wide side of the field;
however, this is not as essential as it used to be since the rules now
permit the offense to put the ball in play at least 17 yards from the

(1)

(2)

PICTURE 5. *The tackle: (1) the approach, low and in good balance; (2) contact; (3) the approach in action: California's Sam Williams* (right) *takes aim at Minnesota quarterback Giel, 1951* (A.S.U.C., Berkeley).

(1)

(3)

PICTURE 6. *The punt:* (1) *stance;* (2) *the foot meets ball about knee high;* (3) *follow-through (A.S.U.C., Berkeley).*

side line which allows plenty of maneuvering space in both directions. If there is only a short time remaining before the half, the defensive quarterback must take into consideration the possibility that the offense will try a long pass in an effort to score before the clock stops them.

Every member of the defensive team should be conscious of the defensive situation at the moment and should be constantly trying to read the mind of the offensive quarterback. In a short yardage situation the line should play lower and drive through to meet power plays. On a big yardage situation, they should play higher and be prepared to rush the pass but should also remain alert for a trap play. It is well to have one member of the defensive team assigned to remind his teammates of the down and distance and other pertinent data that might affect their play. If the opponent of that particular afternoon has shown a tendency to favor certain plays under certain conditions and on special areas of the field, the defense should remember that fact. If a particular defensive alignment seems to be bothering the offense more than others, then that defense should be used often.

There is just as much opportunity for alert, intelligent play on the part of the defense as there is on the part of the offense. A team with a strong defense has a bulwark which can on occasion carry them through to victory when the offense fails. The defensive team should have just as high morale as the offensive unit, and can take just as much pride in a job well done. The objectives and incentives of the defense are strong ones and among them are:

1. *To prevent the opponent from scoring.* Each series of downs, each possession of the ball on the part of the opponent, starts a new contest and there will be approximately thirteen such contests in the course of the game. The defense wins a minor victory on the contest if they prevent the opponents from scoring. The greatest defeat in any such contest that the defense could suffer would be to have the opponents score an easy touchdown by a long run or pass, due possibly to a missed tackle, a lineman playing out of

position, or a careless pass defender. Against a strong offense it might not be possible to win every single one of the thirteen minor contests, but that should be the primary objective of the defensive team.

2. *To hold each gain made against them to an absolute minimum.* It is hard for the offense to sustain a long drive of fifteen or more plays. Something may happen in the way of a fumble or a missed assignment, in a long drive made up of minimum gains, which will break the continuity of downs and aid the defense.

3. *To force the opponents to commit errors.* A sound defense which tackles hard may cause the offensive backs to fumble, giving the defense a chance to recover the ball. A hard rush by the defensive line may force the passer to throw before the pattern is fully developed and to throw wild. It is that kind of a rush which gives the defensive backs a chance to intercept a pass.

4. *To obtain possession of the ball as soon as possible and in as good a position as possible.* The attitude of a good defensive team is that circumstances have given the ball to the opponent and the rules permit them to have it, but that they, the defensive team, are going to get that ball back just as soon as possible. If the opponents can be held to short gains, forcing them to kick early, then our team has the ball in a good position to start a drive to score. If, on the other hand, the defensive team permits a long march which, even if it is not productive of a score, enables them to kick out of bounds inside our 10-yard line, then our offense is seriously handicapped.

5. *To score.* The defense must always be aggressive, and although their scoring opportunities are limited, such opportunities should always be kept in mind. Nothing gives a defensive team a greater lift than scoring on the opponents; such a score could come through blocking a kick and recovering it in the end zone, running a punt back for a touchdown, intercepting a pass and returning it for a touchdown, or catching a fumble in the air and running for a touchdown. If the defensive team realizes that it has

opportunities to score, and by alert blocking on an interception or a punt return make such a score possible, such an event gives them a tremendous lift. There have been games in which a defensive unit has actually outscored the offensive unit.

In 1951 Wisconsin defeated Pennsylvania 16–7 and all sixteen points were scored by the Badger defensive unit. In the first quarter, Deral Teteak, the Wisconsin safety man, recovered a bad pass from the Penn center in the end zone for a touchdown after several players had scrambled for the ball. Later in the first quarter, a Penn pass was tipped by Don Voss, Wisconsin's defensive left end, into the hands of Bob Leu, Wisconsin's 220-pound right tackle who ran 39 yards for the touchdown. In the third quarter with the ball on their own 16-yard line, Penn attempted a pass and the passer, Robinson, was rushed so hard that he was ultimately tackled behind his own goal line for a two-point safety by Pat O'Donahue, the Badgers' defensive left end.

In the course of a season there may be several games won directly through the efforts of the defensive team. Perhaps our most critical game in the season of 1950 was against the University of Washington at Seattle. We won the game by a score of 14–7. Our offensive team played very well, but I have always felt that it was the inspired play of our defensive unit which enabled us to win. They made each possession of the ball on the part of Washington a separate game, and some of them were very tough contests. In the fourth quarter, Washington, a very fine team, drove the length of the field despite every effort of our defensive unit. On fourth down, goal to go, inside our 2-yard line, Washington attempted to pass. Several of our men broke through and knocked the ball from the Washington passer's hands, recovered it in the air, and returned to our 14-yard line. Two plays later our offensive unit fumbled on our 15-yard line. This was a tough spot for the defensive team. Yet they went right to work, forced a Washington fumble, and on the second play recovered the ball once more.

I believe that the platoon system has brought about a new

appreciation by spectators of the part played by the defense in modern football. Our student rooting section at California seems to appreciate the efforts of the defense considerably more since the advent of the platoon system, and our defensive unit receives as much acclaim from the spectators for a good series of defensive plays as the offensive unit does for a fine offensive march. I cannot help feeling that such a situation is a healthy one for the game of football.

CHAPTER 5 THE KICKING GAME

THE number of punts per game has declined in the past twenty-five years. Yet the foot is still a most important part of today's football. A team which is weak in the kicking department is at a decided disadvantage. In discussing the kicking game we shall be concerned with team maneuvers in protecting and covering the punt from both the spread and regular punt formation, the quick kick, the kickoff, point after touchdown, and the goal from the field, as well as methods of attempting to block kicks of all varieties and return punts and kickoffs. (The discussion of the form of the kicking specialists will be taken up in Chapter 8, Ball Fundamentals.)

The ancestry and early history of American football mark it as a kicking game. Many things, such as the forward pass and blocking, have been added to our game to distinguish it from its first cousin, rugby, but the team which forgets that football is fundamentally a kicking game will find itself in trouble. Mistakes in the kicking department are penalized far more heavily than mistakes in other departments of the game. In a surprisingly large percentage of close games each season, a team lost because of a mistake in the kicking game, such as a blocked punt, a fumbled punt, failure to adequately cover a punt resulting in a run-back for a touchdown, or a failure to kick the point after touchdown. On the positive side, many games have been won because the winning team was definitely superior in the punting department and gained a lot of yardage thereby, or used a well-planned punt return to score, or to place the ball in position for the winning drive.

One time while coaching at Northwestern, I tried to analyze the reason why we had won or lost close games over a period of three or four years. In well over half of the games the defeat could be traced directly to a mistake in the kicking department. In recent years at California there have been several games where some phase of the kicking department decided the issue.

In the Rose Bowl game of January, 1950, Trautwein, the Ohio State left tackle, blocked a California punt in the third quarter deep in our territory, putting Ohio in a position to score several plays later. Toward the end of the game a low pass from center and a short California punt gave Ohio the ball again close to the goal line. With time running out they kicked a field goal on fourth down with less than 2 minutes remaining to win the ball game.

In the California–Southern California game of 1947 after a very close first half which ended with Southern California leading by a score of 20–14, the Trojans took the kickoff which started the second half and returned it for a touchdown and then went on to win the game, 39–14. It was poetic justice that in the 1949 game between the two teams, the situation was reversed. In the fourth quarter, after U.S.C. had kicked a field goal to go ahead by the score of 10–7, Frank Brunk of California took the ensuing kickoff in the end zone and ran it back 102 yards for a touchdown, with California eventually winning the game by a score of 16–10. There was good football in other departments of the game in both of these contests, but in each case it was a spectacular kick-off return which really turned the tide.

One of the most important and most spectacular games on the Coast during the 1951 season was the Stanford–U.S.C. game played in the Coliseum before 96,000 people. Stanford led at the half 7–0, and S.C. tied it up in the third quarter. Early in the fourth quarter, S.C. scored to lead 14–7. On the next kickoff Bob Mathias, Decathlon champion of the 1948 Olympics, took the ball on his own 4-yard line and ran it back 96 yards for a touchdown to keep

Stanford in the game. Stanford went on to win 27–20, but Mathias's kickoff return was an important factor in the Indians' victory.

The point after touchdown can also be extremely vital. Every Saturday key games are won by the slender margin of a single point. One of the most thrilling games I have ever suffered through was the Stanford-California contest in 1947. An underdog Stanford team played a magnificent game and it was only in the last 2½ minutes that California squeaked through by the narrow margin of 21–18. In the 1948 game between the same teams, the point after touchdown was equally important. California drove to score from the opening kickoff, and Jim Cullom kicked the extra point. After Stanford scored in the third quarter of that hard-fought contest, it was Cullom who broke through to deflect the try for point and save the slender margin of a 7–6 victory.

Even though superiority in the kicking department may not result in a score, it may have great influence in deciding the issue. Yardage gained in punting, for instance, either through longer punts or longer punt returns, can do a great deal to neutralize an opponent's superior running game or passing attack. The yardage gained in the punting game does not stand out in the statistics, but is just as important and frequently more so than running and passing yardage. If each team were to punt seven times and one team were to average, either through superior kicking or better runbacks, 8 yards more on each punt, that total of 56 yards might well have just as important bearing on the outcome of the game as a 56-yard run from scrimmage. The punt can be an offensive weapon as well as a defensive one and many teams use it as such. Generally such a team is possessed of a good punter and a strong defense, and they have been trained to cover their kicks well. With the advantage of a strong wind at its back even a team whose punting game is only average may use the kicking game to put themselves in a position to score, since the wind will carry its punts appreciably farther while retarding the punts of the opponents who are forced to kick into it. In most games the wind does not play such a vital part, but each year there are a few contests where the flip of a coin, which gives the winner the right to choose the goal he will defend, may well decide the issue.

PUNT PROTECTION

The first consideration of a kicking team is to get the punt away safely. A blocked kick may result in a touchdown for the opponent and at best it represents the loss of 35 or more valuable yards. A blocked kick, also, is a definite blow to the morale of the kicking team and a tonic for the other eleven. Even if a score does not result from the blocked kick, the team getting possession of the ball is frequently able to capitalize ultimately on their territorial and psychological advantage.

There are two general plans of punt protection and coverage in common use today. One is the normal, deep punt formation, with the punter back approximately 10 yards from the ball, and the line tight from tackle to tackle. The other is the spread punt formation, in which the punter is back 12 to 13 yards. The linemen are deployed wider with perhaps 1 yard between the center and guards, 1 to 2 yards between the guards and tackles, and the ends split the same distance or slightly wider from the tackles. Each plan makes use of two specialists: the center who must get the ball back accurately and swiftly to the punter, after which he picks up additional duties as a protector; and the punter who is charged with receiving the ball from center and kicking it downfield. The duties of the other nine men and of the center after he has passed the ball are first to protect the punter from the rush of the defensive players, so that the ball will get off safely, and then to break sharply downfield to cover the punt and tackle the ball carrier, holding him to a minimum return.

In the normal punt formation, illustrated in Diagram 53*A*, the vital area to be protected is indicated by the shaded triangle. The apex of the triangle is a spot approximately 2 yards in front of the punter's position and is the spot where the punter's foot will meet the ball. The triangle covers the entire area from which a defensive player could throw his arms or body at the football as it rises from the punter's foot. It is assumed that the center is going to make an accurate, quick pass, and that the ball will be leaving the punter's foot slightly less than 2 seconds after the center starts the pass back. The punt protection is predicated upon this timing, and if the center-punter combination can get the ball off in 1.8 seconds or less, so much the better. A blocked punt will generally result from the failure of one of the protectors to guard his territory, or from a punter who has become careless and allowed his rhythm to slow down or who attempts to make his kick outside the protected area. If the punter is planning to kick at an angle, he must be careful to line up to the opposite side so that the foot will meet the ball well within the protected area.

The first duty of the center is to make sure of his pass, after which he braces well. The guards and tackles have to make sure that nobody on the defensive team breaks through their territory since they are primarily responsible to the inside. They must take a short step with the inside foot and assume a well-braced position, not too low and in good balance, so that they can neither be driven back, pulled forward to make a break in the line, nor hurdled by an opponent. Generally one of the five center men is able to hit his opponent with a shoulder and continue on downfield. This is most often the left tackle, but occasionally it could be the center. The four linemen must maintain their position for approximately 1.5 seconds or until just before the ball is kicked and then break sharply downfield. With a right-footed kicker, the right end might line up wide enough to get a good angle of coverage. The left end should jolt the most dangerous opponent in his area, generally the defensive right end, with his shoulder and continue immediately downfield. The front back on the right is lined up approximately 1 yard behind his tackle. He must allow no one to break through between himself and the tackle, but force the defense around to his outside. When he is sure that no one is coming to his inside he may jolt any opposing player in the area to his outside. The fullback is lined up slightly inside of the front back, and 3 to 3½ yards deep. He must be careful not to line up so deep that there is any danger that the ball might hit him as the punter steps forward to kick. He too will protect his outside, and as soon as he is sure that no one is coming from the inside he will deliver his inside-out block against any opponent, generally the defensive left end, who may be in his area. The back on the left lines up in the seam between his guard and tackle and about 2 to 2½ yards back. If the left tackle is going downfield with the snap of the ball, the back on the left must be especially careful that no one comes inside of him. As soon as he ascertains this fact, he will also block from the inside out to force the defensive players on around.

THE SPREAD PUNT

The spread punt formation, as illustrated in Diagram 53B, has come into general use within the last three years, with a majority of college teams doing at least some kicking from this formation in the 1950 and 1951 seasons. Some teams have been using the spread punt longer than that, and Coach Amos Alonzo Stagg, illustrious veteran of more than fifty years' coaching at Chicago, College of the Pacific, and now Susquehanna University, has been using it with a great deal of success for many years. If a center is able to get the ball back 13 yards to the punter accurately and swiftly, the spread punt is just as safe as the traditional punt formation. Not all centers, however, are strong enough ball passers for the spread punt. The extra 3 yards frequently bother a center and he loses accuracy and speed with the longer distance. However, some other player on the squad, guard or tackle perhaps, may be found who can get the ball back there accurately and rapidly. Because of the extra distance involved, if the punter can get the ball off in 2 seconds from the moment the center starts his pass, the kick should be safe.

The line blocking for the spread punt is more aggressive, and most of the linemen can block and go downfield immediately. After the center has made his pass, if there is no defensive player within range for him to block, he will immediately start downfield. The guards will generally be more conservative. They should hold their position momentarily, then drive a hard block either to a man playing on them or to the outside, and immediately start downfield. The tackles drive a shoulder block into the most dangerous man in their territory and then release him instantly and go downfield. The ends should jolt any player in their territory as they start downfield. The two front backs play very close to the line and protect the area between the center and the guards. They must block aggressively any defensive player coming through that gap and must not release until the ball is kicked. The fullback is stationed 5 to 6 yards from the line of scrimmage, somewhat deeper than in the conventional punt formation. He must be alert to take the most dangerous man coming from any direction. The exact spread and the details of the blocking plan will vary with different teams. The entire kicking team must be alert to recognize any concentration of defensive players in any particular area for an organized blocking attempt. And it should be the duty of one player who is in a good position to see the entire area (generally either the punter or the fullback) to warn his teammates if the defense appears to be loading any particular area.

THE PUNT COVERAGE

From either formation it is very important that the men covering the punt break sharply downfield and run hard, all the way, at the earliest possible moment that they can safely leave their duties as protectors. Most bad punt coverage comes from the failure of the linemen to break sharply and sprint the first 10 yards. In the normal punt formation the ends should sprint downfield as fast as possible and ward off the blockers who will be assigned to them. They should keep the punt receiver inside of them, but should

not be merely spectators. They must force the play by driving in
from the outside to make the tackle. If they are forced to go inside
to get around a wide blocker on the way down, they should rectify
their position as soon as possible. The center, guards, and tackles,
as they break downfield, must be careful to fan out. If they fail to
do so, they will leave an alley inside their ends through which the
ball carrier might easily break. As soon as the backfield man on the
left and the front back on the right hear the sound of the punt, they
will break wide to support the end on their side. In fact, they act
as auxiliary ends and make certain that if the end is blocked in
they are in a position to make the tackle on the outside. The fullback and the punter will generally move along the flight of the ball
as soon as the kick is made, keeping in mind the desirability of
giving a little added protection to the wide side of the field.

Covering punts is hard work and a team may easily become
careless at it, but it is one of the most important parts of football;
a team must be urged constantly to break sharply downfield and
run hard. Covering punts is an excellent early season conditioning
exercise and it should be practiced periodically throughout the season. If the punter is planning to kick to the right or the left in
an effort to get the ball out of bounds or away from an unusually
good receiver, he should inform his teammates of that fact so that
they can be sure to cover the area of the kick. When kicking for
out of bounds, the protectors must hold a bit longer. The tackle
on the side toward which the punt will be directed should not leave
instantly, but should hold his ground, and the end on that side
should be careful to jolt any defensive player in his area before
he goes downfield. Even though the punter is aiming for the side
line, it is important that the rest of the team remember that he
might not succeed in kicking the ball out of bounds, and they must
not become careless in their coverage. I have sometimes seen a
team which is obviously attempting to kick out of bounds relax in
their coverage with disastrous results. A defensive back may catch
the ball near the side line and bring it straight back a considerable

distance, or he may swing toward the wide side of the field behind good blocking and go all the way.

Our California team in 1950 learned an important lesson in covering punts aimed out of bounds. Our game with the University of San Francisco was played on a very wet field in a pouring rain and the punt game naturally assumed great importance. In the second quarter Don Robison, our punter, got off a very nice kick aimed to go out of bounds to our right. The ball looked as if it would certainly cross the side line, but it came to rest on the soggy turf just inside the white side-line stripe. Our team had eased off in the punt coverage when Roy Barni, the S.F. safety man, suddenly picked up the ball and started down the side line. Two of our players had a shot at him but missed. He picked up a couple of blockers and was away for an 84-yard punt return for a touchdown. They kicked the point after touchdown and those seven points loomed very large, considering the condition of the field and the difficulty of obtaining traction for a sustained march. California was very fortunate when Ray Solari, a California guard, recovered a S.F. fumble in the air and ran 32 yards for a touchdown. It was not until late in the fourth quarter that we were fortunate enough to pull the game out of the fire by a narrow 13–7 margin.

In covering punts too much emphasis cannot be placed upon the instant change from protection to coverage. The team must be drilled to break sharply downfield at the proper moment, as there is no substitute for a fast start. They must also be constantly urged to fan out so that there is a good coverage and the players do not go downfield bunched together where one block by the receiving team might eliminate two or three tacklers. This would leave an alley between the linemen and the ends through which the punt returner might break. At California we like to have the men covering the punt take a quick look when they hear the sound of the foot meeting the ball, so they can get at least a rough estimate of the direction and distance of the kick. The linemen, when they reach the vicinity of the punt returner, should be in good balance and ready to make an aggressive attempt at tackling the ball carrier. The ends, and the backfield men who are backing up the ends, must be a little more conservative and must be able to drive the ball carrier into their own teammates.

Covering the Spread Punt. A team with a good ball passer at the center spot can use the spread punt formation with the confidence of adequate protection under almost all kicking conditions. We prefer to use the conventional punt formation when kicking out of bounds, but it is also possible to use the spread punt. We also like to use the conventional punt formation in most cases if we are forced to kick from close to our goal line, say, within the 5-yard line. A team kicking from its own 1-yard line might experience a little difficulty in using the spread punt, since there is a limit to the distance behind the ball that the punter can line up. The punter must be careful not to step beyond the end zone or even step on the end line in executing the punt or a safety will be scored against his team.

Coverage of kicks from a spread punt formation is generally better than from the conventional formation. The linemen are able to hit and go almost immediately so that they get downfield faster; furthermore, the linemen are already spread out so that the downfield coverage is more uniform and there is less danger of men being bunched together. Punt coverage from the spread formation was so uniformly good throughout the country during the season of 1950 that the Rules Committee restored the fair catch to the game, after an absence of one year, to protect the receiver. In executing a fair catch the punt receiver raises his hand clearly above his head as a signal of his intention to make a fair catch. After making this signal he cannot be tackled by the men covering the punt without a 15-yard penalty being assessed against the latter. In 1950 without the fair catch most safety men were faced with the hard choice of catching the punt which was well covered and risking a consequent fumble as a result of being tackled before having a firm grip on the ball, or playing it safe and allowing the ball to roll. The restoration of the fair catch gives the safety man an opportunity to catch the ball with less danger of fumbling or injury, and gives the tactical advantage of saving for his team the distance the ball might roll.

I believe that most teams enjoy using the spread punt as soon as they have had a chance to practice it enough to gain confidence in the protection afforded to the punter. Most linemen enjoy the opportunity of starting before the ball is kicked and this advantage provides an incentive to get downfield and get in on the tackle. I am only surprised that the spread punt did not come into general use long before the present time. The first spread punt that I can recall was encountered by my Oklahoma A.&M. team in 1930 when we went to Indiana to play Pat Page's team that year.

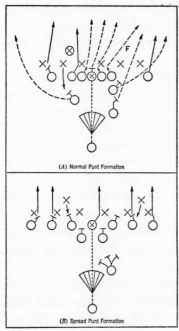

DIAGRAM 53
Punt protection and cover

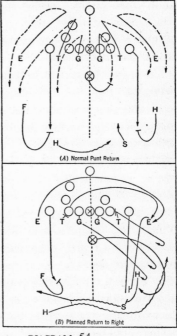

DIAGRAM 54
Punt returns

DEFENSE AGAINST THE PUNT

The objective of a kicking team is first to make sure that the kick gets away safely and next to hold the runback to a minimum yardage. Conversely, it is the primary objective of the receiving team to block the punt and obtain all the advantages of that action. It should be remembered that a strong rush on the part of the receiving team may not succeed in actually blocking the kick but it may force the punter to kick hurriedly, cut down the distance of the kick, or spoil the punter's accuracy. The second objective of the receiving team is to obtain a maximum yardage on the runback. If the kicking team is punting on any except fourth down, the defensive team must be alert for a running play or a forward pass. On fourth down, under normal conditions the defensive team can concentrate on either rushing the punter hard or bending every effort to obtain a good punt return. Even on fourth down, however, under certain conditions the defensive team must be alert for a run or a pass from punt formation. If the yardage to be gained is very short, the team with the ball may elect a running play from punt formation in an effort to make first down. With 1 minute or so to go until half time or 3 minutes or less to go until the end of the game, and the score against them, there is the strong possibility that the offensive team may elect to run or pass rather than kick, even if they line up in punt formation. When there is any possibility at all that some play other than a punt might be forthcoming from punt formation, the defense must be careful not to gamble on blocking the punt or commit itself to a planned punt return. Instead, it must keep players deployed in good position to stop a running play or a pass.

1. *Rushing the Kicker*. Because of the tremendous advantages to be gained in blocking a kick, it is frequently worth while to gamble a bit in order to put extra pressure on the punter. When the opponents are kicking on fourth down from within their 10-yard line every possible effort should be made to block the kick. If a kick

is blocked in this territory, the defensive team is almost sure to score. A blocked kick which goes out of bounds behind the goal line or is recovered by the kicking team in the end zone scores a safety worth two points to the defensive team. If the defensive team recovers the blocked kick behind the goal line, they have scored a touchdown. Even if a hard rush does not succeed in blocking the punt, the punter may be forced to kick hurriedly and a short kick will leave the defensive team in possession of the ball in good position to score.

One of the things which football scouts are always looking for when studying a future opponent is any opportunity to block a kick. If the center is a slow passer, if the punter is slow or takes too many steps or is careless in kicking outside of the protected area, if one of the blockers is careless or commits himself too quickly, then it is worth while to rush that opponent hard at any time and in any part of the field.

The hard rush may take the form of a planned play to take advantage of a blocker's weakness, or it may take the form of adding an extra man or two to the defensive line, with each lineman trying to fight his way through to the protected area to block the kick. In either plan it is very important that the players attempting to block the punt remember that they should not aim at the point where the punter is standing when the ball is snapped, but at a point 2 yards in front of that spot where the foot will meet the ball. The foot meets the ball about knee high and the ball takes several feet to rise above the fingertips of onrushing linemen. Many opportunities to block a punt are missed because the rusher goes too deep and passes the vulnerable point, or because he fails to accelerate his speed after breaking through. The punt rusher should be taught to protect himself by crossing his arms in front of his face as he hurls himself at the vulnerable point. In practice, sometimes the punt rusher can be taught the location of this point and confidence in his ability to reach it, by having the punter take his normal steps in the punt action and then instead of kicking the ball, just tossing it forward to avoid any possibility of injury.

Diagram 55A illustrates several plans for blocking the punt. All of them could not be used at any one time. On the short side where only one back is protecting, the right tackle may charge to the outside of that back to draw his block. The right end is lined up close to his tackle and back of the line just a bit, and drives inside the protecting back in case he takes the bait and tries to roll the tackle out. If this happens, the end should be able to reach the vital point in time to block the kick. If the protecting back remains in his position and blocks the end, the tackle should cut in sharply for the vital area.

On the right side of the punt formation, frequently the front back will have a tendency to be careless and commit himself wide too quickly. In that case, the defensive left guard will engage the offensive tackle, the defensive left tackle will draw the front back wide to make an alley through which the fullback can break quickly with the snap of the ball into the vital area. In case any of the offensive linemen have a tendency to play too low or to be overbalanced forward, one of the guards may be assigned to pull such a player forward while the other guard occupies the attention of the man adjacent, giving a linebacker an opportunity to break quickly through the split in the offensive line thus formed and get into the vital area. This stunt is illustrated in Diagram 55 A (below), with the defensive guard in the dotted-line position.

There are other methods which can be used in punt blocking plays. Some players are naturally quick and have a special aptitude for blocking punts. Such players should be given every encouragement to rush the punter hard and plays should be devised that will take advantage of their particular ability.

RETURNING THE PUNT

Against a fast punter with good protection, greater dividends will probably be realized in concentrating on the punt returns rather than attempting to block the kick. On fourth down in any

normal kicking situation it is well to have either a definite plan to
block the kick or one to return it for a maximum yardage. Otherwise the receiving team is liable to do neither one very effectively.
On any down but fourth, the defense must be prepared for anything, and if the ball is kicked, the rush will probably not be too
effective. If there is not a special planned return, the defense must
have a normal punt return play to save as much ground as possible.
Such a plan would have the halfbacks dropping back with the ends
on the punting team and blocking them deep. At least one linebacker should be in a position to block the first offensive lineman
down, and if two men are back to receive the punt, the man who
does not catch it can protect his teammate by blocking the nearest
and most dangerous man. A normal punt return is illustrated in
Diagram 54*A*. The linemen, after attempting to block the punt,

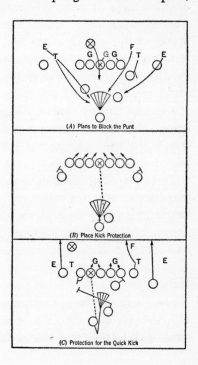

(A) Plans to Block the Punt

(B) Place Kick Protection

(C) Protection for the Quick Kick

DIAGRAM 55
Three kicking plays

must not regard their duties as finished, but must pick up immediately and come back to help the ball carrier.

The best punt returns generally come when the receiving team has a definite plan in which all eleven players participate. Such a plan is illustrated in Diagram 54B—a planned return to the right. The right end drops back with the offensive left end, forcing him if possible to the inside; the end and the defensive right halfback are assigned to block the left end. The defensive tackles jam hard against the offensive tackles and try to drive them in against their own guards; the defensive guards jam against the offensive guards. The entire action is planned to hold up the offensive line and prevent them from getting downfield very quickly. Just as the ball is kicked the defensive guards swing back fast at an angle of about 45 degrees. Both tackles swing around at the same time and come back to get as close to the guards as they can, forming a wall. The left end rushes the punt hard, and he, too, swings around to become a part of the wall. The defensive center allows the offensive left end to go downfield; then he cuts behind him and hustles downfield as deep as possible to pick up the punt receiver as a personal interferer. The defensive fullback who has dropped back into the left half spot, drops back still deeper and is in a position to protect against the most dangerous man, possibly the offensive right end. The fastest halfback and best punt receiver has joined the safety, giving the defense two men back to cover the punt. They should station themselves 15 to 20 yards apart and not too close to either side line. In case the safety receives the ball he will start to his left and hand it to the halfback, who then runs to his right seeking the protection of the wall formed by the linemen. In case the halfback receives the ball, he will run to his right and fake giving it to the safety who continues on to his left covering up as if he were carrying the ball. It is vitally important that the end on the side of the return should be well handled. If he insists on going wide, then he should be taken out. The linemen must hustle back to form the wall and must time their blocks so that they lead the ball carrier.

They must be careful not to form the wall any closer than 15 yards to a side line so that the ball carrier has enough room to maneuver. The ball carrier must make every effort to reach the protection of the wall and may even give a little ground backward in order to accomplish his objective.

A good punt return takes a lot of time and effort, but a return of a punt for a touchdown is one of the most thrilling and certainly one of the most satisfactory plays in the entire game of football. The most spectacular punt return of 1951 on the coast occurred in the U.S.C.–Washington game in Seattle. In the fourth quarter with the Trojans leading 13–7, Koch, the U.S.C. punter, kicked from mid-field. Hugh McElhenny, a great runner, was playing safety for Washington. He took the punt at the goal line in one corner of the field and ran the entire length of the field—100 yards— to tie the game up at 13–all.

THE QUICK KICK

The quick kick, as its name implies, is a surprise kick executed from the regular running formation. Safety men play very close in modern football, and a well-executed quick kick over the head of the safety man which takes a good roll, may well net considerably more yardage to the kicking team than a regular punt from the deep punt formation. In addition, the quick kick may have a psychological effect on the safety by causing him to worry about the possibility of its recurrence, and this fact may help keep him back a little deeper, giving running plays and passes a better chance to succeed. The quick kick should be executed on any down but fourth, any place from the kicking team's 10- or 15-yard line to its own 40- or 45-yard line. Beyond mid-field the conventional punt formation would probably result in a more accurate placement of the ball out of bounds. The quick kick should be executed with the wind and seldom against, and generally fairly early in the game to gain the desired effect on the defensive safety man. A well-executed quick kick can get the kicking team out of a hole deep in their own territory and if the roll is good, it may force the other team to put the ball in play deep in their territory, as generally there is very little chance for a return against a quick kick.

One of the most effective quick kicks I have seen in recent years occurred in the All-Star game of 1944 played at Dyche Stadium in Evanston. I had the privilege of acting as Head Coach of the All-Star team with the able assistance of Bo McMillan, Jeff Cravath, Henry Frnka and Wes Fry. We had a great many problems in preparing the All-Star team to meet the Chicago Bears, the professional champions of the previous fall. Practically all of the All-Star players were in the service, and many of our best players were unable to report until barely a week before the game.

In the first quarter the All-Stars had been driven back deep into their own territory when Glen Dobbs executed one of the finest quick kicks I have ever seen. It traveled 82 yards including the roll, and was downed very close to the Bears' goal line. Aided by this fine quick kick, the All-Stars went into a 14–0 lead. The Bears eventually won late in the game by a score of 24–21, but Dobbs's fine quick kick helped stave off defeat until the closing minutes.

The quick kick can be executed from almost any running formation. Diagram 55C illustrates the quick kick protection from an unbalanced single wing to the right. Earlier we have discussed the technique of the men executing the quick kick and we are now concerned with the protection. Nearly always at least two, and frequently three, men on the kicking team can leave with the snap of the ball so that if the kick is well executed and goes over the safety's head with a good roll, there is very little chance of any defensive player being in a position to pick up the ball and make any kind of a return. In Diagram 55C, the left end and the wing back go downfield immediately with the snap of the ball. The right end also starts with the snap of the ball, and jolts either the tackle or the linebacker, whoever appears to be the most dangerous man. The center and the three men to the right of center drive forward aggressively, shoulder to shoulder, just as if they were blocking for a running play. The blocking back drives hard just outside of his own right tackle and picks up the tackle or the linebacker or a wide guard, whoever may be in a position to come through outside of the tackle. The fullback takes a step forward and then blocks across in front of the kick to the short side. The left guard maintains body contact with his center, stepping first with the inside foot and then dropping his outside foot back. Similar protection can be worked out for almost any offensive formation. The essential feature of quick-kick protection is that the linemen must stay together and must make an aggressive charge forward, driving the defensive players back.

POINT AFTER TOUCHDOWN AND PLACE KICK

The action of the "team within a team"—the center, the holder, and the kicker—is discussed later, in the chapter on Ball Fundamentals. In executing the point after touchdown, the team lines up with the ends in tight and no gaps in the line. After the center passes the ball to the holder, he remains well braced; the guards drive forward one step with the inside foot and remain braced, and the tackles also step with the inside foot. The ends will step first with the inside foot, and then step back with the outside foot, keeping the inside hip in contact with the tackle. Every lineman is responsible solely to his inside and must not let anyone on the defensive team break through inside of him. The two backfield protectors line up about a yard back of the ends with their inside foot back of the end's outside foot. As the ball is snapped they step forward with the inside foot, completing a continuous team wall. The backs are responsible first to their inside, and then if they are sure that no one is coming inside, they may block from the inside out against any rusher who constitutes a threat.

Since time is out after a touchdown, substitutions can be made to make sure that the best center, holder and kicker are in the line-up for the try for point, and also that the strongest and biggest blockers are in to act as protectors regardless of the position normally played on offense. It is generally a good idea to substitute for any small backfield men. A well-executed place kick should take from 1.1 to 1.3 seconds from the time the center starts the ball back until it leaves the kicker's foot. The protection must be aggressive, and failures in protection are generally due to one of the blockers splitting off to the outside instead of protecting to the inside. The ends in particular must be constantly cautioned that their primary responsibility is to the inside.

THE KICKOFF

1. *Covering the Kickoff.* With our present liberal substitution rules an unlimited opportunity is provided to have the fastest and best open field tacklers on the squad in the game to cover the kickoff. Many teams will have what almost amounts to a "kickoff team." Nearly every squad will include several players who have speed and who delight in getting downfield on the kickoff to make the tackle. For the last two seasons we tried to make a contest on kickoffs to see who could get the tackle, and it was surprising what skill several of the players developed in getting downfield rapidly and in avoiding blockers.

In Diagram 56 the kicker is indicated by the letter "K" and the other players are simply numbered 1–10. Players 4, 5, 6 and 7 are the best open field tacklers on the squad, regardless of their regular position. They line up a straight line 5 yards back of the ball, in a sprinter's stance. As the kicker moves forward in a running start, these four players join him. Players 3 and 8 are stationed 1 yard ahead of the four best tacklers and they start forward when the kicker comes even with them. Players 2 and 9 are 1 yard ahead of 3 and 8 and when the kicker is even with them they start forward. The two outside men, 1 and 10, are 1 yard ahead of 2 and 9 and are not stationed too close to the side line. We like to have them 7 yards in from the side line where they have a better chance to be in the play than if they were stationed on the side line. All players move forward as the kicker comes even with them. Players 3 and

8 proceed downfield cautiously, each acting as a safety man on his side of the field. Just as in covering punts, all players must run hard and a fast start is very essential. If the kicking team can tackle the receiver on or behind his 25- or 30-yard line, then they have a distinct advantage at the start of the ball game. If one of the backs on the receiving team is a particularly dangerous open-field runner, the kicker should try to kick to the other side of the field.

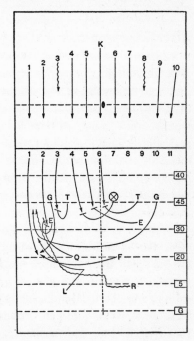

DIAGRAM 56–57
Covering kickoff; return left. Ball is kicked off from offensive 40-yard line over heads of 5 defensive linemen lined up on their 45-yard line. (Yard lines not drawn to scale.)

2. *Returning the Kickoff.* If the receiving team is able to return the kickoff to their own 35-yard line or beyond, then they receive an initial advantage. Even if the first series of plays is not productive of any great gains and they are forced to kick, the ensuing punt should put the opponent fairly deep in their own territory. The team receiving the kickoff will probably be the offensive team which would include the best blockers on the squad, as well as the best

ball carriers. The average T-formation quarterback or a pass-receiving specialist would be replaced by a strong blocker and a shifty open-field runner. In running the kickoff back several different plans are possible. The simplest would be to have all of the linemen drop back toward the vicinity of the man receiving the ball and then turn and block downfield against the nearest man on the kicking team. Most teams, however, use individual blocking assignments. Kickoff returns present fine opportunities for cross blocking against the players coming down to cover the kickoff. However, kickoff returns are hard to time because you never know just where the ball will be kicked and the men covering the kickoff will come down at varying speeds. Sometimes the kicking team will have an outstanding tackler or two who may be noticed by the scout, and it is well to be sure that one or sometimes two good blockers are assigned to take care of these men.

Diagram 57 illustrates a kickoff return to the left with individual blocking. The men on the kicking team are numbered 1 to 11 from left to right. The plan of this return is to block No. 2 in, giving the left end and quarterback the assignment of seeing that this is done. The left guard and the fullback block No. 1 out, shoulder to shoulder. The left tackle drops back and blocks No. 3 to his right. The center blocks No. 4 to his right, the right end blocks No. 5 to his right and the right tackle blocks the kicker No. 6 to his right. The right guard comes around to lead the play through the hole and also to act as cleanup man to take care of any player on the opposition who has broken through. The two best ball carriers, "L" and "R," are stationed on about the 5-yard line and 15 to 20 yards apart. Both of them start toward the center of the field as soon as the ball is received and then the one who did not receive the ball acts as a personal interferer for the ball carrier. It is also possible to use a crisscross on the kickoff.

There are a number of good ways to return a kickoff. This is a conventional method, but it has proved an effective one. It is easy to make the kickoff return too complicated and to spend too much time practicing kickoff returns relative to the number of kickoffs in any one game. A team, however, should have at least two kickoff returns and they should be kept reasonably simple. If the kicking team has a kicker who can get the ball high and deep toward the goal line, then the blockers must be cautioned to come back deeper in order to time the return. The five linemen, who by rule must remain in advance of their own 45-yard line until the ball is kicked, must be alert for a short kickoff that could be recovered by the kicking team. On the other hand they should keep away from most low kickoffs as such balls are very difficult to field and might result in a costly fumble. The man on the receiving team in best position to catch the ball should so inform his teammates. However, on a short kickoff, no player should move back from his position to field the ball, but should carry out his blocking assignment and let a player behind him, who will have the advantage of a running start, catch the ball. In spite of the difficulties of timing, a kickoff return for a touchdown is one of the great plays in our game, and when it happens, a team can feel well repaid for the time and effort put in practicing the play.

CHAPTER 6   TRAINING AND CONDITIONING

FOOTBALL is a rugged game which involves hard physical contact between players. In any contact game, and in many which are not, there is always the danger of injury, or rarely, of fatality. Because, rather than in spite of, the rugged nature of the game, football carries a tremendous appeal to boys and young men of all ages. It is the nature of boys to seek and enjoy a wide range of games and physical activities, and in any such pursuit there is always a danger of injury, especially to those who are poorly prepared. Any boy who attempts to play football owes it to himself to be in proper physical condition, and to wear adequate protective equipment. All of us who love the game and are involved directly with its supervision owe it to the players to see that proper safety techniques are taught, and that reasonable equality as to weight and age prevails, particularly in contests involving boys up to and including high-school age.

For the past twenty years Dr. Floyd Eastwood of Los Angeles State College has made an annual survey of fatalities and injuries for the American Football Coaches Association. His report of January, 1952, states that during this period, in which a careful record has been kept on a nationwide basis, there has been a fatality rate of 1.54 per 100,000 participants in high school, and a rate of 2.36 per 100,000 participants in college football. The annual automobile and pedestrian fatality rate per 100,000 exposures is 36.3 for the same age group. This would indicate that it is approximately 15 times safer to play football than it is to ride in an automobile or be a pedestrian.

SAFETY MEASURES FOR BOYS OF HIGH-SCHOOL AGE AND YOUNGER

Football can and should be a reasonably safe game if it is played under the proper conditions. It is played, however, under widely varying conditions, all the way from impromptu sand-lot games between very young boys to well-organized college games played under the supervision of large coaching staffs and with the best protective equipment that money can buy. It would seem that the following might be principles which would tend toward greater safety in football under most conditions.

1. *Physical Examination.* Every boy planning to play football should receive a thorough physical examination from the family or school doctor. Very occasionally an unsuspected heart ailment or other condition may be discovered which would make it undesirable for the boy to participate in a strenuous sport such as football.

2. *Equality of Competition.* A boy should play with and against other boys of approximately his own age and weight. It is when he attempts to play with older boys or heavier boys that the danger of injury increases. Most high schools have long recognized the importance of physical equality. Such schools will provide a varsity team for the older and more experienced players, a junior varsity or B-team for the less experienced players, and a frosh-soph or lightweight team for the younger and lighter players. Competition with other high schools within the same age and weight limitations is provided, and under those conditions football can be an exciting and beneficial sport for all concerned.

3. *The Practice Field.* The practice field as well as the playing field should be free of all obstructions. A post or bench too near the side line might lead to a serious injury. The surface of the field should be even and free from unexpected holes which might cause

an ankle or knee injury. It should also be free of stones, glass, or other objects which might cause cuts, abrasions and infection. The lack of adequate practice fields is most serious in many cities, not only for football but for all games.

4. *Proper Supervision.* The presence on the field of an experienced coach, physical education teacher, or at least an older person with athletic experience and mature judgment during practices and contests is most important. An experienced supervisor will recognize injuries and see that they are properly treated; he will prevent a boy from playing past the exhaustion point or when he is injured, and above all he will insure equality of competition. Any normal boy hates to have his teammates think he is lacking in courage, and if left to his own judgment he will often attempt to play when he is injured or tired, or he will join in a game with bigger or older fellows who outmatch him. The game of football provides plenty of opportunity for a boy to demonstrate courage, but such demonstration should not occur under conditions that are detrimental to the player. It is here that older judgment can step into the situation and see that competition is maintained on a basis of equality.

5. *Equipment.* Very young boys playing impromptu games with four or five on a side probably need a minimum of equipment, but as soon as they grow a little older and can run faster and hit harder, protective equipment must be used to cut down the danger of injury. High-school-age boys, playing in team units with full blocking and tackling, should be provided with equipment designed to protect vulnerable parts of the body.

Head Guard: Head injuries are not as common as injuries to other parts of the body, but when they do occur they are the most severe. Among football players of all age groups, nearly 70 per cent of the fatalities are caused by blows to the head.

An adequate head guard must fit well; it must be neither too loose nor too tight. The crown, back, and ear pieces should be made of molded fiber or leather strong enough to afford real protection. It is most important that there should be an adequate webbing or head suspension so that the top of the head does not come in direct contact with the helmet. Some helmets use a thick layer of sponge rubber or felt between the head and the fiber crown of the helmet; others use both a suspension and an absorptive material between the suspension and the crown. An adequate chin strap is necessary to keep the helmet on the head.

Very young boys may not need quite the head protection that high-school and college players must have. Good helmets are now available in a wide variety of sizes and types. The sporting goods manufacturers have made great strides in developing all types of equipment, even for young boys. The perfect football helmet, however, has not yet been devised, although steady progress is being made in that direction.

Shoulder Pads: Most good tackles or blocks involve the use of the shoulder and this vital part of the body must be protected. Good shoulder pads of fiber or leather, lined with felt or sponge rubber and of cantilever or flat construction, are available in all sizes. Here again, a good fit is most essential, for a pad that is too big or one that is too small will not give adequate protection.

Hip Pads: A painful, and sometimes serious, injury can be sustained in the hip and kidney area unless these extremely vulnerable parts of the body are adequately covered. Some football pants have hip and kidney pads attached to them. Other hip and kidney pads are separate from the pants and can be buckled around the body under the jersey or sweat shirt. Either arrangement is good. Most hip and kidney pads are of rubber, kapok, or felt, with molded pieces of fiber or leather to give added protection to the hip, kidney, and tail bone (coccyx) area. Good hip and kidney pads are available in a wide range of types and sizes.

Football is a much faster game than it was twenty-five or thirty years ago, and fortunately the development of protective equipment has kept pace with the development of the game. I recall, for instance, that thirty years ago we made our own hip pads. Each player cut a piece of felt to what he considered the proper size for himself, and laced it inside each side of his pants to protect the hip and kidney area.

Pants, Thigh Guards, and Knee Pads: Football pants are made of many different materials. A set of varsity game pants made of satin or nylon, with a lastex back or knit inserts, in a variety of colors, dresses up a team and can be quite expensive. Adequate protection, however, can be obtained at reasonable cost and good practice pants are a sound investment. Football pants for any age group are available in all price ranges.

A good fit is essential if a pair of football pants are to accomplish the purpose for which they are designed. They should fit snugly and yet not interfere with the freedom of movement in running. If too big, particularly through the legs, they will not hold the thigh pads in the proper position. Most football pants are cut a little higher in the back because so much of the game is played from a crouching position. Pants should be made of a good sturdy material; those made of canvas or similar durable material will last a long time.

To prevent injury to the large muscles of the thigh, an area particularly vulnerable to a painful muscle bruise or "Charley horse," a thigh pad should be worn. This pad must be large enough to protect the entire front of the leg, and give some protection to the side. Most thigh pads fit into pockets in the pants and are effective only if the pants fit snugly enough so that the thigh pads cannot be moved out of position under a blow, exposing the leg muscles to injury. Many teams tape the thigh guard directly to the leg with adhesive tape for scrimmages and games in order to avoid this danger. A number of good thigh guards have been developed, generally made of molded fiber and lined with felt or rubber. Care should always be taken to see that thigh guards are well dried out after playing, as moisture makes the fiber soft and ineffective. Thigh guards made soft by constant use should be replaced.

Most football pants make some provision for protection of the knee against a direct blow, in the form of a pad attached to the pants

PICTURE 7. *The pass and the place kick: (1) passer's stance, ball cocked; (2) ball released high, point up; (3) right foot follows through after ball is released; (4 and 5) place kicker and holder watch the ball, before and after (A.S.U.C., Berkeley).*

(1)

(2)

(3)

PICTURE 8. *The center: (1) stance for pass to T-quarterback; (2) pass to quarterback; (3) stance for pass to punter (A.S.U.C., Berkeley).*

or fitting into a pocket and made of felt, kapok, or rubber. A knee pad is an important piece of equipment, not only to protect the wearer, but also to protect other players. Statistics show that a high percentage of the accidents occur when the knee comes in contact with another player, particularly in the head region. For the same reason thigh guards are required by rule to have the hard surface of the fiber padded on the outside so that other players will be protected.

Shoes: A well-fitting pair of shoes is a most important article of equipment. Football shoes are cut high enough so that a good fit should not only support the foot but the ankle as well. The shoes should not be so tight that the feet are cramped, nor so loose that blisters will occur. Clean socks, heavy enough to protect the foot, help the shoe perform its proper function.

For very young boys competing in impromptu games, the shoe is not as important a piece of equipment as some others, but for the high-school and college player the shoe becomes the most important single article of equipment; many teams provide their players with a pair of shoes to use in practice and another pair somewhat lighter in weight to use in games. Good football shoes have cleats of either a conical or rectangular variety on the sole, which enable a player to pick up speed rapidly and to cut sharply and still keep his footing. Our present-day cleats are very efficient—perhaps too efficient—since they enable the player to change his direction so suddenly that he may suffer a knee injury. Practice cleats should be shorter and blunter than game cleats so that they will give in case of a sudden cut or hard contact, and not put all of the strain on the knee.

Good protective equipment is an absolute necessity in any game or scrimmage between boys who run hard enough to produce severe contact. No equipment is effective, of course, unless it is being worn. In the past, some players occasionally thought it was smart or daring to play without a head guard, hip pads, or some other piece of equipment. Such action is foolhardy, and the rules provide that every player in an organized game must wear a head guard. It is up to whoever is supervising the practice or the game to see that full equipment is worn. Practice equipment is generally heavier, and with an even greater emphasis on protection than game equipment. Players sometimes become careless and frequently will select equipment because it is light and "feels good" instead of considering it from a protective standpoint. A thorough check should always be made, not only to see that all equipment is being worn but to ascertain that all pieces fit properly.

6. *Safety Techniques.* In teaching the fundamentals of the game, such as blocking and tackling, players should be taught to protect themselves. A ball carrier being tackled, for example, should be taught to tuck his chin down against his chest when he sees that contact is inevitable, so that there is no danger that his head will be thrown back violently against the ground. He should also bring his arms in, not only to protect the ball, but also to avoid landing on the point of the elbow. Once down, he should bring his feet up to avoid having them stepped on.

Good techniques are nearly always safe techniques. A blocker should be taught to keep his arms close to his body, not only to widen his shoulder for a more effective block and to avoid any temptation to hold illegally, but also to avoid landing on the elbow point or having an arm spread out where it can be stepped on in case he goes to the ground. A defensive man coming in to block a kick will not only cover a wider area and have a better chance of blocking the kick if he raises his arms and crosses them in front of his face, but he will also protect himself from injury. The runner who drives through the line low is not only a more effective ball carrier, but is in a much better position to protect all parts of his body upon contact than is the boy who is running too high. The same thing is true of the blocker or the tackler who approaches the moment of contact in a low, well-balanced position, with his knees bent and his feet well spread.

MEDICAL SUPERVISION

A thorough physical examination should be given all prospective players on a high-school or college level. Each year at California the examination for candidates for the freshman football team reveals several men, who, in the opinion of the doctors, should not attempt to play football. Sometimes it is a heart condition. Sometimes it is an old high-school knee or shoulder injury. A thorough medical screening will catch these conditions that perhaps even the player himself does not suspect.

During all games a doctor should be present and his judgment as to whether an injured player should continue in the game must always be final. During practices, especially those in which there is to be a scrimmage or other physical contact, it is desirable to have a doctor present if possible. Decisions of a medical nature should never be left to the coach or to the player himself.

Practically all colleges and most high schools employ trainers who will make immeasurable contributions to the welfare of the squad. A good trainer not only prevents injury by taping ankles and devising proper pads, but also treats minor injuries and generally supervises the physical fitness of the team. He also adds a great deal to the morale of the boys; a good trainer earns the respect and affection of every member of the squad and works closely with the team doctor, each in his own field. Such a trainer is absolutely indispensable and luckily that fact has become appreciated in the sports world. Fine men are now attracted to this field. I feel that we are exceptionally fortunate here at California in having such men as Jack Williamson, Bob Peterson, and Dick Abreu on our training staff. They are certainly among the most skillful trainers in the country and I shall always be grateful for their efforts.

Good equipment and proper medical supervision can go a long way to prevent injuries. In addition, the general practice of wrapping or taping of ankles before contact work has done a great deal to cut down ankle injuries. The knee, however, continues to be particularly susceptible to injury. All possible effort should be made to strengthen the knee in pre-season preparation by means of walking, running, or even special exercises. Shoes and cleats seem to put the knee joint under unusual strain. An injured knee should receive the immediate attention of the doctor, who should not only determine whether the boy can continue to play in a game, but also when he should be allowed to return to practice and to physical contact, in order that there is no recurrence of the injury. A head injury, as before indicated, might be serious. Any boy who receives a blow on the head in the course of a game or a practice should receive immediate attention of a doctor and should not be moved except under the doctor's direction.

CONDITIONING

Any young man who plans to play football should make every effort to see that he is in the best possible physical condition. A month before the ball season starts he should take definite steps to improve his all-round physical condition, particularly his legs, in preparation for a strenuous season. It is generally a good idea to send a letter to all candidates for the football squad about a month before the fall practice season opens to remind them that they should report in excellent physical condition. It is important that the large muscles of the body, particularly the leg muscles, be well conditioned. The legs are most important in football, not only for the ball carrier who must depend on his legs to drive and cut, but also for the blocker and the tackler. Football is a game of fast starts and quick sudden movements, rather than sustained and constant effort. People do not walk as much as they did years ago. A definite, planned effort is necessary to insure proper leg conditioning. Walking is fine; running is even better. Any game that a boy enjoys playing during the summer period which develops the leg muscles, such as golf, tennis, or handball, is good preparation for football. Best of all is a definite program of running. Long-distance running is not necessary, although that will help to some extent, but a daily series of short runs, coupled with one of middle distance, is preferred. It is, of course, essential that a boy be warmed up before he attempts any hard running, summer or fall.

We like to suggest to our football candidates at California that they appear for the opening practice well rested, with their legs in good shape, and from 3 to 5 pounds overweight. The first two weeks of practice will be very strenuous and if a boy comes back with his legs in good shape, but not trimmed down too fine in weight, he is in the most advantageous position for this hard work. Once practice has started there will be a lot of running, both sprints and longer runs, as well as in the execution of the kicking game and the fundamental movements which must be perfected. Early-season drills are planned specifically to speed up the conditioning process. Good football condition must be attained in the first three weeks. After that, the effort will be to maintain condition while working on team development, timing, and the finer points of the game. Conditioning is the joint responsibility of the player and the coach. A well-conditioned team will play better football, will have greater stamina (particularly in that tough fourth quarter), and will be far less susceptible to injury.

TRAINING

Conditioning means more than the preseason effort of the player to prepare himself. It calls for a continuing effort, once the season has started, by rigorous physical activity, to reach and maintain a proper state of physical efficiency by means of a definite physical exercise and development program. Whatever a player does off the field is just as important as what he does on the field, as far as his conditioning is concerned. Teams will vary widely in their training rules but certainly the following must be considered as essential.

1. *Sleep.* Adequate and regular sleep is a must. Depending on age and individual variation, a young man should have a minimum of 8 hours sleep per night, and most players find 8½ or 9 hours

sleep desirable. Regular sleep habits are important. A regular time for going to bed, particularly on week nights, and the same amount of sleep each night, is most beneficial. Six hours' sleep one night, and ten the next are mathematically an average of eight, but from a practical training standpoint it is most difficult to make up sleep which has been lost. I have always regarded the proper amount of sleep as the most important single factor in good training.

2. *Food.* Coaches and trainers agree that a normal, well-balanced diet is very important in attaining proper physical condition. Heavy pastries, fried foods, and any particular food which does not seem to "agree" with the individual should be avoided. Some colleges and universities maintain a training table, generally limited to the evening meal. For this meal the diet can be controlled. But for other meals, college and high-school players should be careful to get a sensible, well-balanced diet with a proper balance of fruits, vegetables, meat, and other proteins.

3. *Things to Be Avoided.* The use of tobacco in any form is most undesirable and detrimental to attaining the highest degree of physical efficiency. The same will hold true of the use of alcohol in any form. Training rules should be couched in a positive rather than in a negative form, and most football players have a pretty good idea of the things that are good for them and the things that are detrimental to their health.

Any player who is conscientious about putting himself in proper physical condition before the season, who will work hard on the practice field and train consistently throughout the playing months, will find that he can learn the game more easily, that he has greater stamina, that he is most effective in his play, and that he is freer of injury than would otherwise be the case. A training schedule calls only for some minor sacrifices; if a boy is not willing to make these, he probably is not cut out for the game of football anyway.

Day of the Game. If the game is to be played on Saturday, a good night's sleep on Friday is essential. If the game is to be played some distance away from home, frequently it is a good idea to travel on Thursday night. Or if travel is to be by air, on Friday. Most boys sleep pretty well anywhere, but some have difficulty in sleeping on a train at night. A quiet place to sleep, whether at home or away from home, is highly desirable. Many colleges, if there is a possibility of considerable noise on the night before, as on a homecoming occasion, find it desirable to take the players off campus after the Friday workout to a quiet place where conditions are more conducive to a good rest.

A squad should not eat heavily too soon before engaging in the intense physical activity of a football game. There are several ways of handling the pre-game meal or meals. One way would be to have a fairly hearty breakfast about 8 o'clock on the morning of the game, followed by a very light meal 3 hours before the game. Such a meal might consist of poached eggs, tea, and toast; or sliced oranges with powdered sugar, tea, and toast. In recent years we have found that our players prefer to sleep a little later on the morning of the game and to eat one fairly substantial meal about 4 hours before game time. If the game is to be at 2 o'clock we have breakfast at 10:00 A.M.: a large glass of orange juice, a small steak, baked potato, toast, tea (or coffee for those who prefer, but no milk), and a small cup of custard. After the pre-game meal the trainers take advantage of the interval immediately after the meal to do the routine taping of ankles and so forth. We like to have our squad lie down and rest or at least keep off their feet before the game. They should arrive at the stadium about 1½ hours before game time, and the procedure from then on is indicated in the chapter on the Organization of Practice. It is important that the work shall have been planned during the week so that there is a slight tapering-off period on Thursday and a very light practice on Friday. The team should appear at the stadium rested, relaxed, and looking forward eagerly to the contest.

It is important that every player be thoroughly warmed up before entering the game. Statistics have shown that there is a higher percentage of injuries when a player fails to warm up properly. A 15-minute warm-up period just before the beginning of the game is highly desirable, and when the teams return for the second half, there should also be a short impromptu warm-up period. Any player entering the game for the first time after sitting on the bench for a considerable interval should also be carefully warmed-up. This is particularly important on cold days. Before each practice that is to include any contact work, players should be equally careful to warm up, either individually or as a squad, by means of calisthenics, or some form of running. We have found systematic loosening and stretching exercises, which bring into play all of the large muscles of the body, to be most helpful. Before each practice our squad gathers briefly to hear any announcements and the practice plan for the day before taking one lap around the field at a moderate pace. There follows 5 minutes of brisk mass exercise before breaking into groups to begin organized practice.

CHAPTER 7 THE BIG THREE—THE
FOUNDATIONS OF A
FOOTBALL TEAM

THE football team which you see perform in a college stadium on Saturday afternoon is the end result of a great deal of effort, hard work, and much thought on the part of players, coaches, and all those connected with the football organization. The team probably had its inception the previous spring in an off-season practice period. At that time the coaches met the new players from the freshman team of the previous season, and the whole squad became acquainted with the system of plays to be used in the fall. A lot of hard work was put in on the individual skills of the game. The squad started with the stances of the linemen and the backs, learned to block and to tackle and to handle the ball on the simplest plays, and were trained in the special skills of punting, forward passing, and pass receiving. Some experiments were conducted in new plays and new methods of defense and possibly a new formation or two was tried out.

All of this preliminary work was necessary because the fall season is a race against time, and there are not enough hours available once the fall practice season is under way to properly evaluate the players and find out the position in which they will contribute the most to the team. Above all, there is not time to begin the development of individual skills which must become habitual if the team is to enjoy success.

Once the fall season starts, a very strenuous period of practice

109

on individual skills must be combined with the learning of plays, the practice of various defenses, the development of the kicking game, passing game, and all of the other elements of team play.

Spring practice has an important place in college football. At California each year between 150 and 250 men come out for the team for the next fall. Many of these players have had no previous college experience and frequently many of them have had no high-school experience. I have always admired the desire of the least-experienced to participate in football. Long hours are spent in individual development and the learning of basic plays. At least three spring practice games, complete with officials and the taking of movies, are held to give each man an opportunity to test his new-found skills and to point out his deficiencies. In the Pacific Coast Conference before 1952 we were permitted thirty practice sessions in the spring. This is about the right amount; for spring practice, while very essential for good football, can be overdone. Thirty days is sufficient to get acquainted with the squad and yet not so long that the period will become boring without the excitement of games with other teams. In 1952 spring practice was limited to twenty sessions.

The team which takes the field in the fall for its opening game on Saturday afternoon does represent a lot of effort and hard work on the part of all concerned. I have sometimes felt that the team in the fall as it is presented for public inspection at a game is like the superstructure of a fine bridge across a body of water. Those who observe the graceful lines of the bridge often fail to realize how much work, effort and planning went into the foundations which hold the bridge up to public view. Just so, it is hard to realize that the team visible on a Saturday afternoon in the fall has its foundations in so many hours of unseen and publicly unappreciated toil.

No football team can be successful unless the individual members who make it up are proficient in the basic skills. Every sport has fundamentals. In basketball, a player has to be able to shoot, dribble, pivot, and pass. In baseball, a player must throw, hit, field, and run the bases. The football player must learn to block, tackle, and handle the ball in the very beginning; and certain members of the team must be able to forward pass, receive passes, punt, kickoff and place-kick. We are concerned in this chapter with what we believe to be the "Big Three" of football—blocking, tackling, and "getting off with the ball."

The ability to teach individual skills is the true test of a coach. Mastery of blocking, tackling, and "getting off" call for hard work and sound teaching. Sometimes the process becomes monotonous to player and coach alike, especially if the player is frequently discouraged at his apparent lack of progress. It is the job of the coach to make instruction as varied, interesting, and competitive as possible.

I like to tell our squad, particularly in the spring, that there are no short cuts to development in the individual skills of football. We feel that the only way to learn to block is to block a thousand times. Fortunately it is possible with the requisite effort to learn most of the fundamentals of the game. We have had players never required to block in high school who developed into good blockers.

THE SHOULDER BLOCK

Blocking is the solid rock upon which all offense is built. Protective blocking is necessary for a successful kicking or passing game, but blocking is, above all, the cornerstone of the running game and a team without a reasonably good running game faces a bleak season indeed.

Some coaches have said that a running play is a series of individual battles between offensive and defensive players. On any given play there will be nine and sometimes ten players blocking to remove defensive players from the projected path of the ball carrier. Possibly one or two players on the offense will be either delivering the ball, as in the case of the T-formation quarterback, or faking to draw defensive men out of position, and possibly two defensive players will not be in a position to get into the play. If the offense can win five of the individual contests between blockers and defensive men, particularly if those contests are won at the immediate point of attack, then the play is bound to gain ground. The more individual contests that are won, particularly those downfield, the more likely a long gain will result.

In the past we have taught a great many different blocks and have had fancy names for them. At the present time we concentrate almost entirely on teaching the shoulder block. Occasionally an offensive player will use the side of his body to keep a player out of the path of the ball on the line of scrimmage, either directly or as a follow-up of the shoulder block. Occasionally a flanker or a man blocking in the open field on a punt or kickoff return will throw his body into the side of an opponent. But by and large, offensive blocking means the use of the shoulder block.

The shoulder block is pre-eminently a power block. It is used when we want the ground on which the defensive player is lined up. He must be forcibly and legally removed from the path of the ball or restrained from entering that path. A player may execute a shoulder block against a man directly opposite him across the line of scrimmage, he may block a linebacker, he may pull out and shoulder block an end, or he may travel across the field to get ahead of his ball carrier, blocking against a defensive halfback or safety. Whether the block is delivered near the line of scrimmage or after traveling 20 yards downfield, the basic principles are the same.

The form of the shoulder block can best be illustrated by the three steps in Picture 4. We feel that there are three important parts of the shoulder block.

1. *The Approach.* Whether the shoulder block is applied immediately across the scrimmage line or at the end of a run of several yards, just previous to actual bodily contact, the blocker should be in a well-balanced position. His knees should be well bent and his feet well spread, his head up and eyes directly on

the target. "You can't hit what you can't see," and many inexperienced players have a bad habit of ducking the head and closing the eyes just previous to impact. This is a normal reaction and a great deal of effort and work must be put into keeping the head up and the eyes open.

2. *The Jolt.* At the instant of impact the blocker should obtain added impetus to his forward movement by a well-timed straightening of his knees. The head, which has been aimed at the mid-section of the defensive player, should slide to one side so that the full impact of the entire width of the shoulder may be delivered just as is the punch of a well-trained boxer. We are not concerned with which foot happens to be forward at the moment of impact. We like to have our linemen step with the back foot first in close line play regardless of the shoulder which is to deliver the block. A blocker who is delivering a block against an end after traveling 4 or 5 yards would find it most difficult to arrange his feet so as to have any certain foot forward. As the shoulder hits the defensive player, the arm on that side should move up with the hand legally against the body in order to widen the shoulder and, together with the head on the other side of the shoulder, form a "V" to prevent the defensive man from slipping off. A well-timed jolt will aid in moving the defensive man back.

3. *The Follow-through.* The instant the jolt is delivered the feet must be further widened and short, digging steps used to prevent the defensive man from sliding off by keeping continuous pressure against him. As soon as good, firm contact has been established, a blocker must make every effort to drive the defensive man not only back, but also farther away from the path of the ball carrier. Too many blockers merely hit and go to the ground. The ability to sustain the block for several steps is most important.

METHODS OF TEACHING THE SHOULDER BLOCK

We like to start teaching the shoulder block by having the man who is learning it execute the shoulder block against a moderately heavy dummy. We prefer a dummy weighing 26 to 30 pounds, with handles on the sides that can be gripped by a teammate to give a firm blocking surface without danger of injury to either man. On the command "set," the blocker takes his position and the man holding the dummy raises it from the ground and moves it to a position about 8 inches in front of the shoulder of the blocker. On "hike" the blocker straightens his knees, driving into the dummy as hard as possible, head up, without moving his feet. In this manner he gets the feel of the jolt and learns that a considerable impact may be delivered extending in a straight line from his toes up to the shoulder which delivers the blow.

As soon as the blocker understands the principles of the jolt, we move the dummy back 1 yard so that the blocker must take a step before he delivers the impact. The next step is for the blocker, after driving hard into the dummy, to attempt to drive it not only back, but to the side away from the play. The final step places the blocker approximately 5 yards away from the dummy. We have him approach at about three-quarters speed, eyeing his target, and then deliver the full impact as hard as he can with the jolt and follow-through, again driving the dummy away from the path of the ball carrier. The man holding the dummy can be of great assistance in thrusting the dummy toward the blocker at the moment of impact and giving him good resistance. It is, of course, desirable to have six or eight men execute this drill at one time under the supervision of a coach. They may all block simultaneously, or one right after another rapidly, so that the coach may see the block of each man.

After a blocker has gained confidence working against a dummy held by a teammate, we then execute the block without the dummy, using a defensive man trying to break through the block of the offensive man. It takes many hours of hard work for a boy to learn the correct form for the shoulder block, but a good blocker is a priceless asset to the attack. Sometimes a blocker may seem to lose his timing, and in those cases we will bring him back to the dummy again so that he may rapidly relearn blocking principles.

All players on the team must learn the shoulder block. There is no place in today's football for a man who cannot do his share of blocking. I think one of the finest all-round T-formation back-fields I have seen was our California backfield of Monachino, Olszewski, and Schabarum in 1950. Each of the three back men on the T was both a good runner and a good blocker.

The ends also must be able to execute the shoulder block and their form is similar to that described above. The end blocking a tackle out on a quick opening must learn to drive his head to the inside of the tackle and raise quickly to prevent the tackle from reaching over to grab the ball carrier. Sometimes an end playing against a fast-charging tackle will turn his head to the inside across the path of the tackle when he is attempting to block the tackle in. These blocks of the ends are illustrated in Picture 4. Various additional blocking drills will be described in the chapters on Line Play and Offensive Backfield Play.

TACKLING

Just as blocking is the cornerstone of the offense, so is tackling the basis of all defensive play. The old football adage that "eleven good tacklers are hard to beat, and you can't beat them badly" is as true today as it ever was. Many touchdowns are scored each year because a defensive player in position to tackle missed, or merely arm-tackled, and a strong runner drove through him for a touchdown. Many of the old-timers in football tell us that our men today do not tackle as well as players did thirty or forty years ago. They may well be right, for there are many things to be taught in present-day football—forward passing, pass defense, and other special phases of the game—that have assumed an importance they did not have in the early days. However, good tackling always pays off, and always will, and a team that strays too far away from the basic principle of good tackling is sure to find itself in con-siderable difficulty some Saturday afternoon.

Teaching Tackling. A good tackle is essentially a shoulder block delivered with vigor and with use of the arms to hold the body of the runner against the tackler's shoulder. I am not sure that tackling can be taught to the same degree that blocking can. Certainly tackling is at least 90 per cent desire on the part of the tackler, and only 10 per cent technique.

We teach tackling along the same principles as blocking.

The Approach: The tackler must be in good balance, feet well spread, knees bent, arms extended, and eyes upon the belt buckle of the runner. If the tackler attempts to watch the runner's eyes he may find himself badly misled, and the same is true of the runner's feet. A good runner may use the cross-over dodge and swing the feet widely to one side, but he is hard put to fake with his belt buckle.

The Impact: The tackler drives his shoulder into the thigh or waist of the runner, in the same manner in which he would deliver a good shoulder block, trying to get the full width of the shoulder in contact with the runner. If he turns his head aside too early and has only the arm in front of the runner, a good runner will drive through that flimsy barrier without difficulty. The knees are straightened at the moment of impact just as in the case of a good block.

The Follow-through: The tackler, once he has made contact, drives on through the runner carrying him back with short, digging steps and clubbing his arms around the runner's knees to bring him to earth.

We attempt to teach tackling by demonstrating the form at about half speed and letting the players tackle each other. The man being tackled must learn to relax at the moment of impact and tuck his chin in against his chest so that his head will not hit the ground too hard. After a tackler has learned something of the form of tackling by working against a teammate, we put him on the tackling dummy. Tackling against a dummy suspended from a frame will give a player confidence and teach him to meet the runner at full speed. We then do a limited amount of live tackling with one player representing the runner and the other the tackler. It is generally best to restrict the area in which this drill is carried out, in order to avoid a full-speed impact and the danger of injury. One drill we like is to have the runner approach a stationary dummy and cut one side or the other, while the tackler keeps in balance, alert for the cut, and executes the tackle. Another drill is a sequence tackling drill—a line of men representing runners face another line representing tacklers, with about 5 yards separating the runner and tackler and 5 yards separating each pair. The first runner approaches the tackler, who then executes the tackle. As soon as the tackle is completed, the next runner starts, and so on down the line. In this manner the coach can get a very quick look at every player. It is inadvisable to do too much live tackling, however.

Sometimes we have a runner run the "gauntlet." Several tacklers are spaced 10 yards apart with a line 5 yards on each side representing the side lines. In this restricted area the runner attempts to get by one tackler after another. This exercise is good training in balance, timing, and general open field tackling, but results in rather severe contact and we do not use it often. As a matter of fact, I am still looking for the ideal tackling drill which will teach without injuring. Many coaches maintain that the best way to teach tackling is to teach blocking, and there is a good deal of truth in this observation.

GETTING OFF WITH THE BALL

The longer I coach football the more I am convinced that the basic, true fundamental of the game, at least of offense, is the ability of the entire offensive team to "get off," or start in unison, legally, and with the ball. All plays are designed on the assumption that all of the players on the offensive team start together. If one or two players lag back and are slow getting off, it may spoil the timing of the entire play. We spend a great deal of time in drilling our team to get off with the ball, and I feel that it has paid us dividends. This is a department of the game in which players tend to become careless and I am convinced that at least two out of three football teams are late in their start. The rules of the game permit the offensive team to use a starting number which lets them know when the ball will be passed. Thus they can move with the ball and not behind the ball. Nearly every night of the fall season we insist that each team execute three perfect starts at the end of practice before going to the shower. A perfect start means that all eleven players are getting off together, legally, with the ball, without any lineman infringing on the neutral zone before the ball is passed, and without any backfield man starting before the ball is passed. A perfect start also implies that no player will lag behind the ball a count or two.

In drilling a team in starting we like to have one coach in the position of a head linesman just in front of the offensive line to make sure that no linesman lines up offside, jumps offside, or infringes on the neutral zone in any way until the ball is passed. Another coach lines up just behind the offensive line to make sure that there is no false step backward or any kind of a preliminary movement. Another coach stations himself so that he can watch the offensive backs and the ball at the same time, to make sure that there is no movement on the part of any back until the moment the ball is passed. Sometimes we will start on a silent count, with the quarterback giving the first number and the other men counting to themselves and going on the proper cadence. Sometimes the quarterback will call "set" and then after a varied interval "hike" to start the team. The "hike" may come early or late and everyone must be alert for it. Sometimes we will start on our regular cadence which we will vary in the course of the drill just as we do in a game.

The physical act of starting together not only helps the timing of plays but gives the players on the team a sense of unity. A team that "gets off" well not only looks but feels like a real football team. Getting off with the ball is the basic fundamental of offensive football and continuous vigilance must be exercised to see that the team does not get careless in that department.

Blocking, tackling, and getting off are not sensational aspects of football, but they are the foundation for a good team. It is easy to talk about the "Big Three" in principle, but it takes steady and continuous effort to obtain precise execution in those departments.

CHAPTER 8 BALL FUNDAMENTALS

EACH member of the team is expected to be proficient in the fundamentals of his position, as well as the basic "Big Three." Certain players will specialize in the ball fundamentals, and their contribution to the team may be a considerable one. The players entrusted with punting, forward passing, place kicking, kicking off, or holding the ball for the place kicker, may, by superior individual skill, give the team a considerable advantage in the course of a ball game. The men selected to execute these fundamentals must spend additional time in practice in perfecting their individual skills. It should be obvious that these skills are of no value unless the entire team carries out its assignments and protects the punter, the passer, or the place kicker. But since these ball fundamentals are individual skills, I think it worth while to consider them in a separate chapter.

THE PUNT

As we have seen in the chapter on Statistics, football teams do not punt as often as they once did years ago, but every team must have at least one player capable of kicking the ball downfield a reasonable distance, and able to kick fast enough so that he can be sure of getting the kick away. A slow, erratic, or inaccurate punter will place his team under a considerable handicap against a strong opponent; while a superior punter, who kicks high and far, or who is an expert at placing his kicks out of bounds, may present his team with one or more scoring opportunities in the course of a game and by his superior ability keep the opponent under constant

120

pressure. In any given year there are only a few great punters, men of unusual ability. Any boy with average coordination and a desire to learn, can by hard work become a reasonably accurate punter.

There has been a decline in the art of punting in recent years, probably due to the slightly less important part played by the kicking game in today's football. It is also undoubtedly due to the change in the size and proportions of the football itself. Our present-day football is appreciably narrower through the belly and more pointed at the ends. The gradual change of the shape of the ball helps a forward passer, particularly one with a small hand, but it handicaps the punter by requiring greater accuracy in the manner in which the foot meets the ball.

The Punter's Form

Stance: We like to have our punter, kicking from the normal punt formation, stand 10 yards behind his center. If kicking from the spread punt formation, he must stand 12 to 13 yards back. In either event, he should stand relaxed, with the right foot slightly forward if he is a right-footed kicker, watching the center, with hands extended forward to meet the ball. The center plays an important part in the execution of the punt. If his pass is slow or inaccurate, he will force the punter to hurry or to kick off balance. If the center's pass comes back hard, fast, and accurately, it will give the punter confidence and enable him to get the ball away in plenty of time.

The Steps: We like to have the punter take a short step forward with the right foot just before the ball reaches him, then a normal step with the left foot, and kick. Deviations from this standard method will be described under the Rocker Step method and also under the Quick Kick.

The Catch and Drop: The punter watches the ball into his hands, and the hands should give slightly with the ball. On a wet day, the punter must be more careful, and the ball will be brought nearly in to his body. Under normal conditions, this is a needless waste of time. The ball is adjusted quickly by the punter so that the laces are on top or to the right; the right hand is well spread and extended along the right side of the ball; the left hand gives support while adjusting the ball and starting the drop. As the ball is extended forward over the kicking leg, it is held with the front point slightly in and slightly down. The left hand leaves the ball, and the punter attempts to lay the ball on the foot with his right hand. A spiral kick is obtained by having a certain point, slightly to the outside of the instep of the foot, meeting a definite spot on the belly of the ball. The more accurately the punter can drop the ball, and the longer the right hand remains in contact, the more accurately the foot will hit the ball and the better control the punter will have of the ensuing kick. The kicking leg is swung forward under the impetus of the step, with the knee slightly bent and the toe extended and turned down and in. As the foot meets the ball, the knee is straightened with a snap, and it is this snap at the moment of impact, combined with a full follow-through, which gives distance to a punt.

The Follow-through: The foot is met by the ball at approximately knee height, and the kicking leg swings forward in its arc until the foot is higher than the punter's head. A man with a long leg and loose muscles generally makes a better punter than the short-legged man.

We like to have the center deliver the ball to the punter at a spot just inside of the right knee or slightly above. We feel that if the punter receives the ball in a fairly low position it helps his balance, shortens the distance of the drop, and enables him to get a better snap. This description of the punter's form is illustrated in the three steps of Picture 6.

1. *Variations in Punting Form.* Some punters prefer a "rocker step" instead of the traditional "step-and-a-half" method described above. Many such rocker-step kickers have been very successful and there are several varieties of this technique. In one type the left foot is forward and as the punter receives the ball he steps back

with the left foot, transferring his weight to the right foot. He adjusts the ball, steps forward quickly with the left foot, and kicks in the conventional manner. Another method is to have the right leg forward, to take a short step back with the right foot, a full step back with the left foot, then a full step forward, and kick. I have also known punters who have rocked back with the left foot, then a short step forward with the right foot, a full step with the left foot, and kick.

Sometimes a punter will hold the ball with the right hand underneath, with the laces on top, and the middle finger of the right hand extended along the underseam of the ball. The ball is then thrust forward, the left hand leaves it, and the ball is dropped on the foot by withdrawing the support of the right hand.

In instructing an inexperienced punter, it is probably most desirable to teach the conventional form detailed above. However, an experienced punter, who is getting good results and is getting the ball away in good time with reasonable distance and accuracy, will probably have better success in continuing his accustomed form rather than attempting to change it.

2. *Speed*. The punter must always remember that there is a definite limit to the time interval during which his teammates can protect him by blocking out the defensive team. If the entire punting process, from the moment the center starts his pass back until the ball leaves the punter's foot, occupies 2 seconds or less, the punt should get away without being blocked. We like to have our punters try to get the ball away in 1.8 or 1.9 seconds, in the case of the conventional punt formation, or 2 seconds flat in the case of the spread punt.

3. *Accuracy*. The longest punt is not always the best punt under the circumstances. If a punter kicks 65 yards down the field with a low trajectory which enables the safety man to field the ball and the defensive team to put into execution a plan of return, the result may be a 40-yard return and certainly that could not be called a successful punt. A 35-yard punt that went out of bounds

with no possibility of a return, or a high punt which did not travel as far but could be well covered by the punter's teammates would be more successful.

If a team is punting on the opponent's 45-yard line and the punter gets off a booming 70-yard punt which goes out of the end zone, the ball is put in play on the opponent's 20-yard line—a net gain of 25 yards. But if the punter is able to kick out of bounds on the opponent's 10-yard line, the net gain is 35 yards and the opposing team must put the ball in play precariously close to its own end zone.

In order to place his kicks the punter must face squarely in the direction toward which he plans to kick. The toe of the left foot (on a right-footed kicker) must accurately face that direction. The punter must always kick in the direction toward which he faces. We like to tell our punters that they should regard themselves as a gunboat with one fixed gun on the bow. The only way to aim the gun is to aim the entire boat. In placing his kicks the punter must be careful always to kick behind the core of his protection. That is, if he is kicking toward the left he should line up slightly to the right so that when he faces left, receives the ball and takes his step in that direction, his kick will be made at the spot of greatest safety. If he is kicking to the right, he should line up slightly to the left for the same reason. The entire team, including the center, must be aware of the punter's intentions as to direction. The punter may unobtrusively line up to the right or left of his center still facing forward and then turn his body in the intended direction of his kick at the last moment so as not to tip off the defensive players as to the direction of the kick.

In kicking out of bounds it will help to have an object toward which the kick can be aimed. In training the punters to kick out of bounds, we like to place a flag on the goal line, one on the 5-yard line, and one on the 10-yard line, with the punter using the 5-yard flag as his aiming point. In a game the punter will not have the advantage of such artificial aid; therefore, in the huddle, he should select some object on the side line to serve as an aiming point. It will help him if, previous to the game, or during the warm-up period, the kicker moves around the field and selects some object, such as a ramp entrance, a stairway, a flagpole, or other object that will not be obscured by the crowd, as a possible aiming point from that section of the field.

4. *Teaching the Punter.* All punters, whether experienced or beginners, have a very natural tendency to enjoy seeing how far they can kick. This very natural tendency must be curbed if the punter is to show improvement. He should be given training in balance, in holding and dropping the ball, in accuracy, and in speed in getting the ball away. A book could be written just on the subject of punting, and several have been. It is our purpose here to suggest exercises and drills which may be helpful to the punter.

Balance: Most punters have a tendency to pull the ball to the right or the left. This can be demonstrated by having the punter close his eyes firmly after aiming toward an object 25 or 30 yards away. If, with his eyes closed, he goes through his kicking form ten or twelve times in succession and then opens his eyes, he will be frequently surprised how far off course he is. Various exercises may be used to help the punter correct balance, such as having the punter swing the kicking leg forward trying to touch his instep to the palm of the hand of the instructor held at varying heights.

Dropping the Ball: We like to start our punters out by pairing them off about 10 yards apart and kick back and forth to each other. This is good training in watching the foot hit the ball and in laying the ball on the instep. The distance apart of the two players may be gradually increased. The same drill can be used in teaching accuracy by requiring the punter to get the ball to his teammate in such a manner that the latter does not have to move, or by having the kicker see if he can hit the hand of the receiver, extended either to the right or to the left.

Accuracy: An extension of the above drill is used in connection with the side-line flag. The kicker starts about 15 to 20 yards from the 5-yard flag, faces the flag, takes careful aim, and drops the ball—carefully watching it—onto his foot. After the kick he takes two steps in the direction of the flag. The distance is gradually increased, and this routine should be tried both to the right and to the left side lines.

Speed: At least once a week the punter and his center should work against a stop watch, as otherwise the punter may become careless and slow in getting his kicks off, a mistake which could be fatal in a tough ball game. Constant vigilance is necessary to see that no extra motions have crept into the punter's form. By stepping forward to meet the ball and adjusting it quickly, the punter should be able to get the kick off in around 1.8 seconds without feeling crowded or hurried.

Once a punter has his leg in shape and has shown good consistency, he should not kick too much during the week. Two or three sessions should be ample and never after Thursday if the game is to be played on Saturday. Whenever a punter starts to have trouble with his form, and especially with dropping the ball, we like to have him go back to early season procedure and kick to a teammate at a distance of 10 to 20 yards until his form returns.

It is well to remember, however, that punters will vary somewhat in individual form. They do not all come out of the same mold. In my second year of coaching, at Oklahoma City University, I watched a young freshman end by the name of Bob Eaton practice punting. He did everything all wrong according to the form with which I was familiar. He held the ball with his right hand underneath (which in later years has become an accepted form) and he used a rocker step which was totally different from the action I had been teaching other punters. However, I noticed that he was getting nice high spirals of 50 and 55 yards downfield, and I decided to leave him alone. I did make a suggestion or two to him about placing his kicks, and Bob became very much interested in the subject of accuracy. Eaton's punting became an important part of our game and in 1927 against the Haskell Indians, which we won by a score of 7–0, Eaton kicked out of bounds inside the Haskell 15-yard line about six times.

I can recall many other fine punters whose form deviated somewhat from the standard procedure, and I think most experienced punting coaches will agree that there are times when it is a good idea to leave well enough alone.

THE QUICK KICK

The quick kick, as its name implies, is a surprise weapon—a kick unexpectedly delivered from a normal running formation, in which the kicker is 5 to 7 yards back of the ball. This kick can be executed easily, of course, from the short punt formation in which the tail back is back 6 or 7 yards. It can also be executed without very much difficulty by the fullback or tail back in the single wing formation. It is a little more difficult from the T formation, but can be executed by having the center pass the ball through the legs of the quarterback directly to the fullback who executes the kick.

Most defenses place the safety man up where he is in a position to help on forward-pass defense, and indeed in most cases he is a sort of glorified linebacker. A well-executed quick kick can sometimes upset a safety man and worry him, as well as result in a long gain.

There are several types of footwork which may be employed in the quick kick. Possibly the simplest is to have the center pass the ball toward the inside of the right knee, for a right-footed kicker. As the ball comes back toward the kicker, he steps back and in with the left foot, then steps forward with the left foot and kicks. Some kickers prefer to step back with the left foot, then a short step with the right foot, a step with the left and kick. Others like to step back with the right foot, then another step back with the left foot, a step forward with the left foot, then kick. Regardless of the footwork used, the kicker must be able to get the kick away in about 1.2 seconds.

A well-executed quick kick does not depend on a high spiral for its effectiveness. In fact, too great height is a handicap. An end-over-end quick kick which travels 30 to 35 yards with a good roll is much more effective than a high kick. The quick kick is best used by a team within its own territory, though not too close to the goal line, with the wind at its back, and on first, second or third down, when a kick is not expected. I have seen on a number of occasions a well-executed quick kick change the whole course of the ball game. In blocking for the quick kick, the line should move forward aggressively and keep a solid front.

THE PLACE KICK

A team may score by a kick, either by kicking the ball through the uprights and above the crossbar on the try for point after a touchdown, or making a goal from the field by a similar kick from scrimmage. At one time the drop kick had a considerable vogue as a method of scoring, but at the present time, teams almost universally use the place kick. Here one player receives the ball from center, places it on the ground or on a tee for a teammate who in turn executes the kick. In professional football with the goal posts on the goal line and many experienced, long-distance kickers playing, the field goal is frequently used as a scoring medium. In the college game with the goal posts on the end line 10 yards behind the goal line, the field goal is not seen nearly as often as it used to be. However, the try for point is extremely important, and more college games are won and lost by the margin of the point after touchdown than is the case in the professional game.

In the California-Washington game in 1951, the Huskies scored early in the fourth quarter and converted to lead 28–27. Late in the quarter, on fourth down, Les Richter kicked a field goal from the Washington 14-yard line to put California ahead 30–27. It was the first field goal made by a California football team in eleven years. A last-minute touchdown made the score California: 37, Washington: 28, but Richter's field goal was the deciding factor in the game. During the same season, Richter kicked 40 out of 44 points after touchdown to set a new Conference and University of California record in that department.

A successful place kick requires, of course, good protection by nine members of the team, but especially important is the "team within a team," consisting of the center, the holder and the kicker. Each of these men must do his part and they should practice together continually. The center must get the ball back to the holder accurately and quickly. The holder must place the ball in exactly the right position before the kicker can do his part.

1. *The Holder.* Assuming a right-footed kicker, the holder will place his left knee about opposite the spot where he will put the ball. The right leg is extended toward the line of scrimmage and the holder's hands are extended as far toward the center (to reach the ball at the earliest possible moment) as is consistent with a generally relaxed position. The rules now permit the use of a 1-inch tee for the place kicker. There are a number of good tees available, but a very simple one can be made by taking two ½-inch pieces of sponge rubber, about 6 inches in diameter, and taping them together. The two lines of tape can mark the exact spot where the ball is to be placed at their intersection, and can also be used by the kicker to help line up the target. As the ball comes back to the holder, he watches it into his hands and places it quickly on the spot planned. The ball will be held firmly but lightly at the top by the fingers of the right hand, and the left hand helps to guide the ball to the proper place and then is quickly withdrawn. If convenient the laces of the ball should be toward the front, but this is not necessary and no extra time should be taken to adjust the ball, as speed in getting the kick off is what counts. Some kickers like the ball leaned back slightly, others in an upright position. The

holder must be consistent about getting the ball to the proper spot and in holding it steadily until it is kicked out from underneath his fingers.

2. *The Kicker*. The kicker stations himself with his kicking foot on an extension of the line from the middle of the crossbar through the spot where the ball is to be placed. His exact distance back from the ball will vary somewhat with men of different builds. The kicker will generally take a short step with the kicking foot, a hop step with the nonkicking or aiming foot, and the kicking foot will swing through the ball. In a right-footed kicker, at the moment of impact, the left foot will be firmly planted with the toe slightly behind the ball and about 4 to 6 inches to the left of the ball and pointed straight toward the target. The toe of the kicking foot should hit the ball about 4 or 5 inches from the ground or the lower point of the ball. It is most important that the kicking foot swing through the ball on a straight arc just as if the foot were to follow the ball on through the goal post. The most important single thing, however, is that the kicker must keep his eyes on the ball, his head down, and resist a natural tendency to look up. I have known kickers who, in order to help accomplish this aim, watch the ball steadily as they kick; then pick up a piece of grass before they permit their eyes to raise and follow the flight of the ball.

The kicker should be provided with a shoe for the kicking foot which has a hard square box toe and a fairly stiff sole. A kicking toe of this nature can be specially built on the shoe or a rubber kicking toe can be slipped over an ordinary shoe.

The center, holder, and kicker should practice together at every opportunity until they truly become a unit. If the kicker is sure of a fast pass from center and accurate placement by the holder, he can start forward as the ball starts back and before it is actually placed by the holder.

THE DROP KICK

Since the drop kick is executed by one man without benefit of a holder, thus releasing an extra man for protection, one might wonder why drop kicking is not used more. Through the years the place kick has been found to be more accurate and our modern, sharp-pointed football is much more difficult to drop-kick than the old football. As a result, one seldom sees a drop kicker any more. Very few boys take it up in high school and I can only recall one drop-kicker in college who operated with any degree of consistency on points after touchdown. In twenty-six years of coaching college football, I have had only three boys who have even attempted the drop kick, and they were not used regularly because we found that the place kickers were more accurate.

At Northwestern in 1935 we had a very shifty left halfback named Ollie Adelman. Ollie practiced the drop kick at every opportunity and kept asking me to let him try a drop kick in a game. Half jokingly I told Ollie that if he ever scored three touchdowns in a game he would have his long-sought opportunity. I forgot about our conversation, but Ollie didn't.

Late that season Ollie had a great day against Wisconsin and did score three touchdowns. I started to send a place kicker into the game, but Ollie waved him away and called for a drop-kick formation for the point after touchdown. Adelman took his position, the ball came back from the center, he kicked—and missed the conversion as the ball went wide of the uprights.

In executing the drop kick the kicker bends forward, drops the ball carefully on the nose and kicks it just as it rises from the ground.

THE KICKOFF

The kickoff is a glorified place kick with the opportunity for a longer run to gain momentum and no pressure as to time, since the defensive players cannot advance beyond the restraining line until the ball is actually kicked. There are a number of satisfactory kickoff tees on the market which hold the ball in an upright position and yet permit some degree of tilting as desired by the kicker. The technique of kicking off is exactly like that of the place kick, except that the kicker will have to work out his run so that he will be certain that the left foot (if he is a right-footed kicker) hits the same spot every time. A high kick which goes into the end zone is the most desirable type. Not all teams have kickoff men who can deliver this highly desired kick. Our present-day rules have an automatic time-out after each kickoff and it seems reasonable that the team might develop a kickoff specialist. Lacking a reliable kickoff man, it is sometimes more desirable to lay the ball on its side and attempt a kick which sails erratically and bounces unpredictably, even though it doesn't travel as far. Such a kick makes it very difficult to time a kickoff return, and is frequently used when the opponents are known to have a good plan for returning the kickoff.

THE FORWARD PASS

A courageous forward passer can put a defensive team under great pressure. Not only will his accurate passing pay off in yardage gained and scores made, but the threat of a pass at any time may force the defensive halfbacks and linebackers back, delaying their support of the line on running plays and presenting the offensive team with much better blocking angles. A difference of even a yard back on the part of a linebacker or a halfback may make it infinitely easier to block him. Moreover, if the offensive line concentrates on rushing the passer, they open themselves up to trap plays and quick skirts around the ends. A good passer, therefore, not only sets up the pass game, but makes his team's running attack much easier to execute.

In 1950, for instance, California played against Don Heinrich of Washington, Gary Kerkorian of Stanford, and Chuck Ortmann of Michigan, and I can testify that their accuracy complicated our defensive problems considerably.

Some say that good passers are born and not made, and there is a large measure of truth in that statement. Most boys can learn to throw fairly well, but knowing the exact moment at which to turn the ball loose is something that is extremely difficult, if not impossible, to teach. A fine passer generally has big hands with strong fingers, so that he has good ball control and can grip a wet ball almost as well as a dry one. He is generally fairly tall so that he can get a good view of the field over the heads of onrushing linemen. He has good eyes, something in the nature of a wide-angled lens, so that he can see a large portion of the field and pick his receivers. He has quickness, so that he can avoid a blind rusher, and he has the courage to wait until his receiver is open, even though he knows that in the next split second he will be tackled hard. He has the judgment to realize when there is no chance of completing the pass and he doesn't throw the ball blindly to get rid of it, but recovers as much ground as he can and takes his loss.

Otto Graham of Northwestern was a fine example of a great college passer. He had big hands, good ball control, and truly remarkable eyes. Otto seemed to be able to observe all sections of the field at once, pick his man coolly, and time his passes accurately.

Passers will vary somewhat in the exact form used, but most of the good ones will follow this general form.

1. *Grip.* The passer must have sure control of the ball. Most passers like the feel of the laces against the fingertips, and believe that with the fingers in that position, better control is obtained. The hand is well spread over the ball, fingers on the laces, and somewhat to the rear of the ball. The fingers grip the ball firmly and there is daylight between the palm of the hand and the surface of the football.

2. *The Throw.* The ball is raised with both hands to a position somewhat back of, and slightly to one side of the head, with the left arm dropping down as the right arm finishes bringing the ball all the way back. The ball is delivered with an overhand motion, with the arm swinging through on a straight arc reminiscent of the base-

ball catcher's "snap" throw to the second baseman. The wrist is cocked and is snapped forward at the moment of release. The wrist action is a very important part of the throw, as it pulls the rear point of the ball slightly down, raising the front point and making the ball a little easier to handle for the receiver. The snap also imparts speed and helps in controlling the direction of the throw.

3. *Follow-through.* A right-handed passer will step forward with the left foot as he throws and most of his weight will be on that left foot as the ball is released. The force of the throw should bring the right side of his body around smoothly as a continuation of the throwing process. Of course, the passer will seldom have the time, since he is being rushed by the defense, to make a perfect picture-book throw. He will frequently have to throw off-balance.

A medium length pass will be thrown largely with the wrist, forearm, and fingers. The long pass will be arched higher so that the receiver can run under it, and the passer will get a considerable body action into the throw, somewhat like a javelin thrower.

These points in the passer's form are physical, and pertain to throwing only. A real passer is far more than a thrower. He seems to have an inborn sense of timing, which enables him to anticipate the break of his receiver and throw the ball to him just as the receiver is getting open and before he can be covered by the defense. Most mechanical passers wait until the receiver is clearly open, and then try to hit him. By the time the ball reaches the vicinity of the receiver, the defense has had time to rally and knock down or intercept the pass. I have never seen a passer who could anticipate the break of his receiver better than Sam Baugh. I was greatly impressed with his gift in that direction one summer when he had just graduated from T.C.U. and was a member of the All-Star squad putting on a demonstration for our Northwestern coaching school. His record with the Washington Redskins has stamped him as one of the great passers of all time.

A good passer knows how to use his protection. He stays in the "cup" formed for him by his teammates, and is much easier to block for than the passer who goes back too deep or wanders all over the field. If the passer has running ability and natural quickness, he can often make a great deal of yardage when he finds his receivers covered and spots an opening among the onrushing linemen. Bob Celeri made good use of his ability along those lines at California in 1948 and 1949. He could take advantage of any opening to run when he went back to pass which made him a doubly difficult man to stop. It is hard to rush a passer and stop a runner at the same time.

4. *Teaching Methods.* While it is true that the great passer comes along only at long intervals, still it is possible to help a passer develop. The T-formation quarterback has some advantages in that he has the opportunity to make a good fake to one or more of his backfield teammates and thus add a quality of deception to the pass attack. However, he suffers from one great disadvantage. He must generally turn his back to the field of play and go back to reach a position 5 or 6 yards back of the line from which he can be adequately protected. The passer, from the short punt formation, double wing or single wing, has the advantage of receiving the ball directly from center and keeping the entire field of play in his view. It is therefore very important that the T-formation quarterback be able to get back quickly to a spot about 6 yards behind the line and then step up into the protection of his "cup." The opportunity to throw a "choice" pass—one in which the passer will select one of several possible receivers—is limited in the T formation but the added opportunities for deception sometimes make up for that lack. Regardless of the formation, the passer must be drilled in getting as rapidly as possible to the point from which he is going to pass and taking at least a quick look over the field of play to make sure that his receiver is open or has a chance of getting open.

An inexperienced passer will find it desirable to spend some time each day throwing to a teammate, facing him 10 or 15 yards away. In this way he can work on his form, get the feel of the ball, and become thoroughly warmed up for the later drills. During this process it is sometimes a good idea for the passer to stand on his "wrong leg." That is, if he is a right-handed passer he should stand on his right foot and throw the ball by using his wrist, forearm, fingers, and to a certain extent his arm, without any body movement in the throw at all. This action will help develop the forearm and wrist snap and may be of assistance to the passer when he has to throw off-balance under pressure in the ball game. A passer needs to throw constantly and he should concentrate on the teammates he will be called upon to pass to in a ball game. In this way he will become familiar with the comparative speeds of his receivers and the manner in which they break to get away from a defender. It is by this constant practice that a good passing combination is built up. A passer should do considerable throwing to a receiver whom a defensive man is attempting to cover. He should get experience in leading his receiver away from trouble, placing the ball so that the defender cannot reach it, and, if the receiver is very closely covered, throwing the ball so that neither man can catch it. The passer also should throw a great deal in team drill under the pressure of a rushing line. Knowing when to throw and when not to throw and when the receiver is about to break so that the ball can reach him before the defense gets there, are things that only a great deal of experience will give to a passer. Some passers never do seem to develop the proper judgment on these items. A careless or an inaccurate passer can greatly handicap a team by allowing the pass to be intercepted and run back for a touchdown or to a spot which puts the opponent in an advantageous offensive position.

5. *Pass Receiving.* Good receivers who can catch the marginal passes make an ordinary passer look good, and a great passer unbeatable. A fine receiver has reasonable height, speed, a good change of pace, and the agility that enables him to catch passes that are not perfectly thrown.

Once the ball nears him, the receiver must concentrate his attention on it. He watches the ball right into his hands. Many passes are missed because the receiver worries about the proximity of a defensive man and tries to take a quick look. A fine receiver has agile hands, he knows when to stretch toward the ball and when to give with it. Generally speaking, if he is running away from the passer he will catch the ball over his shoulder, hands together, little fingers almost touching, and elbows in. If the ball is a bit out of line he will adjust his run by turning with its flight. If the pass is on the side he doesn't expect, he will pivot in stride. If the pass receiver is cutting across or hooking so that he is facing the passer, he will extend his arms toward the ball with thumbs together. Above all, a good receiver is determined. He will make a desperate effort to get the ball, even though he is well covered, and if successful he will tuck it away and protect it, even though he is hit the instant he catches it. If the pass is short he will come back toward it and make an effort to catch it, or at least be in a position to tackle the interceptor.

The first problem of the pass receiver is to break sharply from his position, unless it is to be a delayed pass. This is not always easy to do. Frequently a tackle or linebacker will attempt to prevent the receiver from getting downfield, which the defensive man is legally entitled to do, so long as he does not hold the receiver. A well-trained defense will make every effort to have men in position to impede the progress of the receiver. The pass receiver may line up a little bit wider to give himself more space in which to maneuver. He may fake one way and break another, but his most important weapon is a quick start. It is vitally important for the success of the pass pattern that the receivers get downfield quickly, particularly those who are to be decoys. Otherwise they will not be downfield far enough to draw defensive players out of position and the pass pattern will fail.

Once the receiver has succeeded in breaking downfield there are a number of maneuvers that he can use that will be helpful in getting away from the defensive players.

Speed: A fast end is frequently able to break past a defensive halfback before the latter realizes how close he is to his defensive position. A quick line-up or a short cadence sometimes facilitates this maneuver.

Cutting: A good receiver has the ability to fake in one direction and cut sharply in another direction. This is generally accomplished by a step slightly in the direction of the fake, a good head fake, and then cutting sharply away from the foot planted in the direction of the fake. A few receivers in college are able to fake one way, fake another, and then break back in the original direction. Many of the ends in professional football are adept at this and other maneuvers.

A Quick Stop, or "Hook": If the defensive man is covering the receiver loosely the receiver may break sharply for 7, 8, or 10 yards to convince the defense he is trying to run a deep path, stop suddenly, pivot, and receive the ball before the defensive man can recover. The receiver must be careful to watch the ball into his hands, tuck it firmly away and then turn and drive as far as he can. Usually he will be tackled very shortly after receiving the ball.

Running a Pattern: On most pass plays from two to four men will be sent downfield. Frequently two of the receivers will be used as decoys to draw defensive men out of position in order to open up defensive territory for the intended receiver. If the decoys do a good job this is a very effective way to get a man open, and of course the decoys must be ready to receive the ball in case the defensive players do not take the bait.

Choice Passes: Sometimes two receivers will be sent into the territory of a defensive man as, for example, an end running through a defensive halfback with a backfield receiver trailing him. If the halfback covers the end, the shallow man should be open unless the zone is reinforced by another defender. If the halfback takes the shallow man the deep man has a chance of being open. This maneuver has been used effectively by many teams.

Some good examples of various pass patterns and choice passes are illustrated in the diagrams in Chapter 3, The Offensive Plan. Many other team maneuvers are possible. An end or a back may come around behind his own line of scrimmage and receive a short "shovel" pass from the passer. The screen pass is another popular type. In this maneuver the defensive linemen are allowed to come through and a receiver catches the ball over the heads of the oncoming linemen, but behind his own offensive line, who can block for him downfield after he has received the ball. Sometimes the screen of linemen may move out along the line of scrimmage to the right or left and the pass will be completed to the receiver behind them. Of course, in all of these maneuvers the offensive linemen cannot cross the line of scrimmage until the ball is caught.

There are a number of maneuvers, of course, which can be used by an unusually gifted receiver. He can "stop and go" by stopping for a hook pass to draw the defense in, and then breaking past the defensive players. He can go "out and down" by breaking out for a shallow pass to draw the receivers up, and then turning downfield and outrunning the defensive player who has been drawn up. Many successful pass plays tie in very closely with the running attack. Sometimes only one man will be sent downfield on such a play and the running-play action will be so convincing that the receiver, apparently running a path to block downfield, has a good chance to break by the defensive player and get into the open. A quick pass to an end, or a wing back thrown almost immediately to the receiver breaking behind or between linebackers, is another maneuver which has proved highly successful.

Forward passing is a team game. If the linemen and backs assigned to block for the passer do not do their job in holding out the defensive men, even a great passer is in for a tough afternoon. A finely conceived pass pattern which takes 3.2 seconds to develop downfield will go for naught if a defensive lineman breaks through and tackles the passer in 2.5 seconds. However, a fine passer and good receivers will contribute enormously to a team's offensive punch, and by their ability will encourage the rest of the team to work hard to set up the necessary protection.

6. *Protecting the Passer: The "Cup."* The art of protecting the

passer has been developed to a fine degree (see Diagrams 29–33). The basic principle is that of a "cup" protection with the line and backfield protectors guarding the spot from which the quarterback will pass. In general, regardless of the defense, any offensive lineman who has a defensive man playing head on with him will take a well-braced position and let the defensive player show first. As soon as the defensive man indicates on which side he will attempt to charge, the offensive man meets him with a good, solid block. He then attempts to stay with him in close contact, keeping in front of him, and giving ground grudgingly toward the spot he is protecting. Any man who does not have a defensive player on him will step back and act as a clean-up man, ready to meet anyone who has slipped off from a block on the outer wall of the "cup," or any linebacker shooting through. In a normal six-man line, guards will make the defensive guards show and then meet them with a solid block, while the center becomes the clean-up man. The tackles will take a short step back and then meet the defensive tackles with a solid block, and stay in front of them. If the defensive tackle is charging unusually hard, the offensive tackle will place his head across the path of the defensive man, blocking with the inside shoulder, and use the momentum of the defensive player to try to force him on past the cup and deeper than the point from which the quarterback is throwing.

In a five-man line the center will have a man on him and will meet him as the guards did in the six. Guards will step back, each guard acting as a clean-up man for his own side of the line, and then if nothing comes on that side, he will see if he can help on the other side. Particularly in a five, the guards must be alert for shooting linebackers, who may come through with the snap of the ball in an attempt to rush the passer. Guards should know the location of each linebacker and take a good look to make sure that he is not shooting. The clean-up men must be careful not to step back too deep to a point where they will interfere with the action and vision of the passer, but they should be back perhaps 2 yards where they

(1)

(3)

PICTURE 9. *The T-quarterback: (1) stance; (2) step-out action; (3) pivot action* *A.S.U.C., Berkeley).*

PICTURE 10. *The offensive lineman:* (1) *stance;* (2) *pulling out, step-out action, first step;* (3) *pulling out, crossover action, first step* (A.S.U.C., Berkeley).

(2)

(3)

(1)

PICTURE 11. *The offensive right end: (1) shoulder block taking left defensive tackle in; (2) shoulder block, head in front of left tackle, used against penetrating tackle to take him in; (3) shoulder block to take left tackle out (A.S.U.C., Berkeley).*

PICTURE 12. *The left half:* (1) *stance;* (2) *start to right, first movement is complete pivot to right;* (3) *start to right, first step, crossover of right foot;* (4) *receiving ball from quarterback for drive over left tackle* (*A.S.U.C., Berkeley*).

can get a good view of the entire sector they are helping to protect. In case the defense is in a seven-man line, the center and tackles will generally take the men playing on them, while the guards pull out to pick up the defensive tackles. In case any defensive player does not come through, the man assigned to him automatically becomes a clean-up man.

The pass protection blocks are among the most difficult the linemen are called upon to make. A common fault is for the linemen to retreat too rapidly, letting the defensive player penetrate to a point where he interferes with the vision and forward pass of the quarterback. The other extreme is for the linemen to block too soon and too low and go immediately to the ground, missing the man assigned to him. Another common fault is the failure on the part of the lineman to move his feet to keep his body squarely in front of the defensive rusher. Exercises in moving the feet and keeping contact with the defensive man who cuts first to one side and then to the other are helpful in training the linemen on pass protection.

There are variations in the method of protecting the passer. On a running pass, where the ball will be thrown from a point 10 or 15 yards to the right or left of the center of the formation, the type of protection must change. The linemen on the off side, that is, away from the direction taken by the passer, will simply step back and wait for the defensive rush, thus forming a wall. The linemen on the side toward which the passer is moving will be more aggressive. A good block is necessary on the defensive ends on the side toward which the passer is moving, and at least one blocker must be provided as a running clean-up man to pick up any linebacker who comes up to tackle the passer. On other types of plays, where the pass ties in closely with a running play, the block of the linemen on pass protection will be more aggressive, since it is desired to simulate as nearly as possible the action of the running play.

CHAPTER 9 THE OFFENSIVE LINE

THE offensive linemen have always been, and are today, the unknown craftsmen so far as 90 per cent of the spectators are concerned. The natural tendency of most people is to watch the ball and the man carrying it, kicking it, or passing it. The eyes of the crowd take in the territory adjacent to the ball and can appreciate a good block against an end immediately in the path of the ball carrier, or a good downfield block, as well as a well-thrown ball, a great catch, a fine kick, a hard driving run, or a neat side step. A defensive lineman occasionally has the chance to break into the charmed circle when he drives through to tackle the ball carrier for a big loss, but in the congested area up front where the offensive linemen do their job, a great deal of the football game—good and bad—remains unseen and unappreciated. Even the trained scouts in the press box and the players and coaches on the side lines watch the offensive backfield momentarily at the start of a play to obtain a clue as to the point of attack and thus miss the start of the work of the offensive line. The only alternative is to concentrate with field glasses on one particular offensive lineman or at most two, which requires a lot of self-discipline and results in the loss of other parts of the play. In fact, it generally requires a second time over the movies of the game before the coaching staff can see and evaluate all of the action up front.

No one appreciates the work of the offensive linemen to quite the same degree as does a back, for he knows that if the linemen do their job properly he will have a chance to get up a full head of steam and will find a hole to run through.

In our discussion of the offensive line we will be concerned primarily with the T formation, although the principles of offensive line play will not vary a great deal from one formation to another. The discussion in this chapter will be concerned with each position separately and the operations of the line as a unit will be taken up in Chapter 11, Group and Team Drills—Offense.

THE CENTER

The center is a key man in any formation. A single wing back center, if his passes are erratic or inaccurate, can change a smooth operating backfield with a lot of drive into a hesitant, uncertain, and ineffective unit. In any formation the center has a most important function. It is his action in snapping the ball that gets the play under way. He must have an inborn sense of timing and good rhythm to get the ball off exactly on the count. If he is late with the ball, his teammates moving on the count are off side. If he is uncertain—now ahead of the count, now behind—the entire team is hesitant, the get-off is ragged, and the timing is ruined.

In the T formation the center is an especially important player. It is claimed, and with some justification, that a T-formation center can be just as effective a blocker as any other lineman. He makes a blind pass to the quarterback, and unlike the single wing center who must watch his pass to the backs, can keep his head up and direct his charge with his eyes.

1. *Stance.* We have varied the stance of the T-formation center so far as placement of the feet and other details are concerned. At the present time we prefer to have the center take a stance with his feet even, comfortably spread, and a moderate amount of weight on the ball. The center is the only player permitted by the rules to infringe on the neutral zone, but he must not have his head in advance of the front point of the ball. We prefer to have our center place the ball so that a line dropped from the front point of his head guard would hit a spot about 2 or 3 inches behind the front point of the lace of the football. Our center uses both hands on the ball, arms fully extended. Some centers prefer to have just

the right hand on the ball; others make a point of having the laces of the football always up; some like to tilt the front point of the ball slightly. We allow our center latitude in the matter of stance; if he prefers to pass the ball with one hand, we permit him to do so. Nor do we insist that the laces of the ball be in any particular position.

The center's stance is a little higher than that of the other linemen, with the tail approximately even with the shoulders in height, and the head up. The pass from the T-formation center to the quarterback is a quick lift into the quarterback's hand which is placed in the center's crotch. We emphasize the lift with a bend in the elbow of the passing arm. If the elbow remains straight, the center is likely to swing the ball too far back and past the quarterback's hands. It is important that the center's pass be always on the count, always hit the same spot, and with a reasonable degree of force. The natural swing of the center's arm should deliver the ball to the quarterback at a slight angle. That is, in a right-handed center, the rear point of the ball will be turned slightly to the right, which we feel facilitates the handling of the ball by the quarterback. Pictures 8 and 9 show the center's stance and pass, and the quarterback's stance and hands in receiving position.

2. *Punt Formation Pass.* The player passing the ball back to the punter has a lot to do with the success or failure of the kicking game. If the ball comes back hard, fast, and accurately, it gives the punter confidence. If the pass is slow and wobbly, there is danger that the kick will be blocked. If the center is erratic and inaccurate, passing the ball now high, now low, now right, now left, the punter is uncertain and off balance, which is bound to affect his kicking. The pass back to the punter should be thrown as hard as possible and slightly above knee height. The speed of the center's pass is most important. It cannot be made too fast. This is especially true on the center's pass to the punter who is in the spread formation and back 12 to 13 yards. I have found that our centers will vary as much as $\frac{2}{10}$ second in the elapsed time. Those

who are able to get the ball back to the punter in $6/10$ second help speed up the kicking process, while those who take $8/10$ second put the punter under additional pressure.

The player who passes the ball back to the punter need not necessarily be the same one who acts as T-formation center. Under our present liberal substitution rules, a player is frequently put into the line-up to do the punting. The same could be true of the man who is to pass the ball back to him, in case the regular center or some lineman already in the line-up is not equipped to do so.

When passing back to the punter, we prefer to have our center take a stance with one foot back, generally the right foot, in the case of a right-handed passer. The front point of the ball is raised very slightly and firmly gripped by the right hand, with the left hand on the left side of the ball a little toward the rear to guide the pass. This position of the hands produces a spiral. A moderate amount of weight should be on the ball. On the pass to the punter, a slow, floating pass is a distinct handicap to getting the ball away. The center must drive the ball back, aiming at a point just above and slightly inside the punter's right knee. The ball should travel as fast as possible and on as near a straight line as possible. The center's pass to the punter is essentially a forward pass "upside down." It requires not only a good arm, a moderate amount of body movement, but also a strong wrist snap. In training men to pass to the punter, we like to start them forward-passing to each other, with the emphasis on the wrist snap. Next, a forward pass, with two hands on the ball, the right hand doing most of the work, and the left hand guiding the ball, is in order. We have also found it helpful to have the center make a blind pass back between his legs to a man 8 yards back, starting the ball from a position a foot or so above the ground and putting great emphasis on the wrist snap. The center is then encouraged to take his regular stance for passing to the punter and continue his practice with the emphasis still on the wrist snap and the hard drive backward on the right arm. The center must be careful not to lift the ball before passing it back, or make any other preliminary telltale motion which will tip off the defensive players as to his plans.

3. *Center's Blocks.* We work our centers and quarterbacks together as much as possible, since they are the basic unit of the T formation. We like to tell them they are like the pitcher and catcher on a baseball team, and they must work together until the exchange of the ball is automatic and 100 per cent sure. In training a new center, after we have had him work on his stance a bit, we start him working with a quarterback. We ask the new center, after he gets over the ball, to take his left hand and feel the position of the quarterback's hand in his crotch. This gives him confidence that the hand will always be there and that he can drive the ball as hard as he wants into the quarterback's hand. The quarterback starts the cadence and the center joins him in singing it out. The quarterback and center must know each other's assignments on every play. When the center has a tough assignment, the quarterback must be prepared to help him by letting his hand give forward a bit as the ball comes back. This helps the center who is driving ahead as he passes the ball.

As soon as the center and quarterback have begun to show reasonable progress in the exchange of the ball, we like to line a defensive player up opposite our center and begin the blocking process. As stated before, the T-formation center enjoys an advantage over the center in the single wing because the exchange of the ball is blind and the center can watch his opponent as he starts his block. We want our centers to feel that they can be the best blockers in the offensive line. The T-formation center should feel that he has a definite advantage over the defensive player. He not only can watch the defensive man, but he knows where the play is going and when the ball will be passed. The center steps forward as he passes the ball to make use of an advantage which the rules permit him. If he passes the ball and then moves, he is at a definite disadvantage.

If the defensive man is playing on the center, the center must step quickly, to establish contact with the defensive man as he passes the ball. A quick, hard contact is essential. If the center steps to the side to get position first, the defensive man will beat him to the charge. If the play is to the center's right, we want the center to drive hard into the defensive player on him, letting his head slide to his right of the defensive player, driving into him with the full width of the left shoulder, and stepping first with the right foot. The center's action is identical with that described under the Shoulder Block. He must meet the defensive man with a good jolt, and once he has made firm contact he will try to drive him away from the play with short digging steps. If the play is to the center's left, the action is reversed. The center will step with his left foot as he passes the ball, driving his right shoulder into his opponent.

If no defensive player is lined up opposite the center, there will probably be men lined up approximately opposite the guards on either side of the center. Depending on the play, the center will block one or the other of the guards where he has a good blocking angle. Or he may be assigned to go downfield and block a linebacker or a halfback. When blocking a linebacker, the center will drive a couple of steps across the line of scrimmage and then turn to meet his opponent with a solid shoulder block, and drive away from the play and back toward the line of scrimmage, so that the defensive man cannot recover and step back into the path of the play. The center can be a very versatile downfield blocker. We have found him frequently an effective man to use to drive a halfback out on an off-tackle play, or to go through the line and swing out wide in the direction of the play on an end run and act as a clean-up blocker in cutting off defensive players drifting out into the path of the ball. Reasonable size and speed and good coordination are required of the T-formation center because of these many blocking opportunities. Sometimes a boy who has not played center in high school will measure up to these requirements in college. A big, active man at center, who is a hard blocker, is the cornerstone of the T formation.

4. *Center in the Single Wing.* The center in the single wing back formation has a more difficult job than his counterpart in the T. He has a greater variety of passes to make and he must watch the back to whom he is passing the ball; thus he is handicapped momentarily in locating the man he will block. In the single wing the center's stance if right-handed will generally be with the feet well spread, right foot back, tail a little higher than the other linemen but not quite as high as the T-formation center, reasonable weight on the ball, right hand well spread along the right side of the ball, and left hand slightly to the rear of the center acting as a guide hand.

In passing to the tail back who is back approximately 5 yards, he must lead the back on an off-tackle or end-run play so that the back will not have to wait until the ball reaches him before he can start. For this type of play the center will throw a moderately fast ball approximately waist high. If he is passing to the fullback for a play in the spin series, the pass will be slightly softer and aimed at a point just above and slightly to the inside of the inside knee. If the fullback is driving forward into the line on a direct plunge, the center must lay the ball in front of him with a soft pass—a sort of "flip around the corner."

All of these passes must be made accurately to the same spot on each play and with the same speed. An erratic passer will handcuff his backfield by making the backs uncertain and unable to start fast. After the center has made his pass he must raise his head and move into the man he is assigned to block. Sometimes the center finds it desirable, with a man playing over him and charging hard, to drop to one knee and then come up into his block.

GUARD AND TACKLE PLAY

1. *Stance.* The guards and tackles must line up in a position that is comfortable and in good balance. Balance is essential because the player must be able to move straight ahead with power or laterally to the right or left without tipping off the defensive team

as to his intention, and without any unnecessary preliminary motions, such as raising the tail or taking a short, false, or balance step. I have used a variety of stances through the years but the following has proved most satisfactory.

In teaching the stance, we have the lineman stand with his feet 18 to 24 inches apart, toes turned very slightly out, with the toe of the back foot even with the heel of the forward foot. The lineman then squats down like a baseball catcher and we have him roll from side to side and backward and forward until he feels in good balance. He places the hand on the side of the foot that is back lightly on the ground, then rolls forward putting a little weight on his hand, raising the tail to a point where he can charge forward without further change of position. His head is up, looking straight ahead. The opposite forearm rests comfortably across his thigh, and the knees are about as far apart as the hips. He should have just enough weight on his hand so that if he were to raise his hand he would fall slowly forward. Some allowance, of course, must be made for individual variation in build. A long-legged boy, for example, must have the feet a little farther apart than the short-legged boy, and the back foot a bit farther back. The entire stance must be square to the front with the shoulders even in height and parallel to the line of scrimmage. An awkward or unbalanced stance must be corrected as it will handicap the lineman in the execution of his assignments. The lineman should take his position so that he is as close to the line of scrimmage as possible, without infringing on the neutral zone. He is entitled to line up just back of a point passing through the near point of the football. If he lines up 1 foot or 1½ feet back of that point, he is handicapping himself in blocking an opponent, since he has to travel farther.

For nine out of ten boys it is most natural to have the right foot back and the right hand down to the ground. However, we prefer to have our right guard and right tackle assume the natural stance with the right foot back and ask the left guard and left tackle to place the left foot back and the left hand on the ground. This will seem very awkward at first, but most boys in a week or two can adjust to the left stance. The occasional one who cannot adjust to the left stance while playing on the left side of the line we would generally permit to keep his right foot back. In spring practice and early in the season, enough time must be spent in drilling the stance so that it becomes automatic and comfortable. The stance should be checked at least once a week throughout the season, and if the line is becoming careless some time must be spent in restoring a good stance.

2. *Pulling Out.* The tackles occasionally, and the guards frequently, are assigned on a play to move from their positions in the line laterally behind the line to block an end, or to lead a backfield man through the hole in order to block a linebacker or a halfback. If a lineman is to pull out successfully, he must practice it continually until he can move out quickly with confidence, and go at full speed to the point of attack and block with power. There are two generally accepted methods which can be used in pulling out of the line.

The Step-out: In pulling to the right, the lineman will step first with his right foot, gaining about 6 inches toward the sidelines with the toe of the right foot pointed straight in that direction. Simultaneously he will push off with the hand that is on the ground and turn his body sharply to the right. The entire movement must be made instantly with the snap of the ball, and all parts of the body must move simultaneously. This first step is very important. On the second step the left foot will be brought across toward the side lines in a normal running position. The lineman must use his arms to get his body started and to pick up speed. He must not hesitate or "feel his way" as he moves toward the man he is to block, but should get there as quickly as possible. If he is blocking an end out, he should keep as close to the line of scrimmage as possible, so that he will approach the defensive end at a favorable angle. Just before contact he will dip by bending his knees (not ducking his head), keeping his eyes directed at the target, and will jolt the defensive player with a shoulder block. After obtaining solid contact he will continue to drive the defensive player back toward the side lines and also back toward the offensive goal line, keeping his head between his opponent and the path of the ball. This block would be executed with the right shoulder so that the head may remain between the defensive player and the ball carrier.

If the right guard is pulling out to lead a play off tackle to his right, he would follow the same form. As he turns through the hole, the lineman should widen his feet a bit and run in a low, well-braced position, ready to meet instant opposition as he turns the corner. He should keep about a yard distant from the man making the block at the hole, so that he can face squarely downfield. Generally he will expect to meet opposition from the inside, rather than the outside.

If the right guard is pulling to his left behind the center, as he might on executing a trap block or leading a counter play off tackle to his left, his first movement would be with the left foot. Since his left foot is the forward foot he would gain a little more in depth, than he would in stepping to the right. On the first step the left toe will gain about 6 inches toward the side line and be about even with the heel of the back or right foot. The rest of the form is similar to that described in "pulling out to the right." For the left guard the form described above would be exactly reversed. The first step would be made with the left foot in pulling to the left, and the right foot in pulling to the right.

The Cross-over: Another method commonly used in pulling out of the line is the cross-over. In executing the cross-over the right guard, for instance, in pulling to his right would take advantage of the fact that his right foot was already the back foot. He would merely pivot on both feet and step first with the left foot, crossing over to the right in the direction of the pull. He would not attempt the cross-over in pulling to his left, however, since his left foot would be forward. Both the step-out and the cross-over are in common use and both are effective.

3. *Blocking in the Line.* The basic block used in the line will be the shoulder block. When blocking at the point of attack, the offensive lineman should realize that the defensive player must be driven from the ground on which he stands. The general form of the shoulder block has already been described. The blocker will encounter a wide variety of conditions. He may meet a defensive player head on him, or one lined up to his left or to his right and playing on a teammate. The defensive man may be playing high or he may be down on all fours. He may be crowding his side of the neutral zone or he may be lined up back a yard or so. The blocker must get to the man he is assigned to block just as quickly as possible, jolt him hard and then immediately start his legs churning in short steps so that the defensive player has no chance to recover from the initial impact. We tell our offensive linemen that the defensive player determines the level at which the block must be delivered. If the defensive man is on all fours, our blocker must drive his shoulder underneath that of the defensive player, with his (the blocker's) hands on the ground.

Blocking is an art that is not learned overnight. Inexperienced blockers sometimes close their eyes and turn their heads aside and therefore miss the target. They must be taught to keep their eyes open, to drive the head at the target, letting the head slide by at the last minute with the earpiece of the helmet firmly against the defensive man so that the full width of the shoulder is available for the block. Another common tendency of inexperienced blockers is to go to the ground after the initial contact, because the blocker has neglected to bring his feet up under him again after the first impact. It will help the blocker if he will always remember to raise his head as soon as he feels his shoulder in firm contact with his opponent. This will help prevent his going to the ground. If the blocker does fall, he should catch himself instantly with the hand opposite the blocking shoulder, keep his feet churning all the time, and come back up into good blocking position. A lineman must know the path that the ball carrier will take on each play, and must

realize that his duty as blocker is not only to drive his man out of the path of the ball carrier, but also to keep him from recovering into the path. It is not enough to drive a defensive man back 2 or 3 yards if he slides off from the block and tackles the ball carrier after a short gain. The blocker must strive desperately to keep his own body between the path of the ball carrier and the defensive player.

4. *Trap Blocking and Cross Blocking.* Sometimes a hard-charging defensive lineman can be handled best by permitting him to charge across the line against the man opposite him, who steps out of his way and allows the defensive player to be blocked by an offensive man approaching from the side. The player who is executing a trap block will step around the intervening player quickly, head up, to locate the defensive player to be trapped. If the defensive man is charging blindly across the line of scrimmage the trapper's job is an easy one. He can merely ride him on out using the impetus of the uncontrolled charge of the defensive man to help him. A smart defensive player, however, will control his charge. He will only penetrate a short distance before he senses the trap. In that case, the blocker, as he steps around, must be prepared to go up into the hole and "dig him out" wherever the defensive man may be and at whatever level he is charging. The blocker must reach the man to be trapped as quickly as possible, driving him away from the path of the ball, and prevent the defensive player from recovering from the initial impact. The tendency of a green blocker in executing a trap block, is always to step too deep in anticipation of the uncontrolled charge of the defensive man. The blocker should always place himself in a position to block the smart defensive player who is controlling his charge. If the defensive man has penetrated deeper than he has anticipated, he can always adjust his angle. But if he has started too deep, he can never recover a good blocking angle on a man who does not cross the line of scrimmage.

5. *Downfield Blocks.* The most important thing in executing a

downfield block is to get there. Many offensive linemen fail to realize the importance of a block against a halfback or a safety. Such a block, well-timed, may change a 5-yard gain to a 50-yard touchdown run. Safety men tend to play close nowadays, only 10 or 12 yards back, and they play a real part in the defense against the running attack. To block a halfback or safety, a lineman must break sharply from the line of scrimmage the instant the ball is snapped. This quick start is absolutely essential. He must run as hard as he can to the defensive player and then sustain his block. We prefer to have the men blocking downfield use a shoulder block if possible, and keep their feet, rather than use the body block or a roll block and going to the ground. A knowledge of the path of the ball carrier is again very essential here. The lineman blocking downfield must sprint to get in front of his ball carrier and then pick up the defensive player or territory assigned to him.

A good linebacker is hard to block. He will meet the blocker and slide off into the play. Too many linemen raise into an upright position in going through for a linebacker and then have to drop down to a blocking position before making contact. This up and down motion in the short space of 3 or 4 yards takes time. The lineman should shoot through low in order to reach the linebacker as quickly as possible. A block against a linebacker is generally a "moving" block, one that must be sustained with a hard charge. In many respects, especially against a good linebacker, it is the most difficult there is. The blocker must lead him, that is, allow for his movement toward the hole under attack.

6. *Double-team.* Most T-formation blocking is of the one-on-one variety. The offensive blocker is expected to take the defensive man without the aid of a teammate. However, sometimes on plays in which a delay occurs to draw the defense out of position, it is desirable to put two offensive men on one defensive player at the point of attack. There are a number of ways in which these two players can operate. They can each shoulder-block against their opponent and drive him straight back. This has the advantage of

cutting off defensive linebackers, but the defensive player is likely to slip off the block and make the tackle. There is the lead-post principle in which one player maintains his position against the defensive man as a "post" while his teammate, the "lead" man, drives into the defensive man from the side, after which both players join in a wheeling movement. The method we use is slightly different and is an attempt to combine the fine points of each. The offensive player on the side toward which we desire to drive the defensive man, drives into him on all fours with his head in the defensive man's crotch, or with his inside shoulder driving through the knee of the defensive player. We call this offensive player the "low" man. His companion is the "drive" man who executes a shoulder block against the defensive man. The purpose of the "low" man who drives hard and continuously against the defensive player, is to neutralize the latter's charge until the "drive" man can obtain command of the situation. As soon as he has made contact with the defensive man, the "low" man swings his hips toward the "drive" man so that both players present a solid front. It is their intention not to drive the defensive man straight back, but to wheel him and drive him right along the line of scrimmage. We have found an occasional use of the double-team in the T formation to be very effective on trap plays, and occasionally on off-tackle plays as a variation on the basic one-on-one blocking.

END PLAY

The T-formation end has an exceedingly tough job. He is called upon to block the defensive tackle all by himself, and the tackle frequently will outweigh him by 20 or 30 pounds. The problem is further complicated because the end must sustain his block somewhat longer than a guard or tackle, because the ball carrier takes a little longer to reach the off-tackle spot than he does on interior plays. Even more frequently, the end is called upon to block the linebacker or to move quickly downfield to block a halfback or safety. In addition to these duties, which he shares with the other linemen, an end is expected to be a good forward-pass receiver. For this reason, good T-formation ends are not too plentiful. If the end is big enough to stand a good chance of handling the tackle alone on his blocks, he is liable to be a poor pass receiver, and the tall, loose-jointed boy who is an ideal receiver is liable to bounce off a 230-pound tackle. Only by developing quickness and every possible finesse will the end stand a chance to carry out his block. It is always amazing to me that T-formation ends do as well as they do, considering the difficulty of their assignments.

1. *Stance.* The stance of the end is almost identical with that of the other linemen. We ask the right end to have his right foot back and right hand down, and the left end to have his left foot back and his left hand down. Usually the end will line up from 2 to 4 feet from his tackle. Sometimes he will line up 10 or 15 yards outside of his tackle, as a threat to block on wide plays, and especially to be in a good position to go down on passes. Occasionally he will line up in an intermediate position 3 to 5 yards from the tackle. We have generally preferred to keep him in his regular position where he is a constant threat as a blocker in the regular running attack.

2. *Blocks.* Let's consider the right end in our discussion of blocking. His primary assignment will probably be the tackle, who may be lined up in the gap between the end and tackle, on the end's inside shoulder, head on, or even on the outside shoulder. The end's greatest asset in blocking the tackle is his quickness. In blocking the tackle in, we prefer that the end generally step with his back foot; in the case of the right end, the right foot. The end must drive into the tackle as quickly as possible, shooting his head at the tackle's midsection and, in most cases, if the play is to go outside the end, he will shoot his head to the outside of the tackle and make the block with his left shoulder. The general form of the shoulder block is followed, with a particular emphasis on keeping the feet digging and sustaining the block. Sometimes on an off-tackle play, the tackle is lined up inside the end and comes across very fast. If he is permitted to penetrate too far, he will cut off

the interference from the interior of the line, notably a guard coming out to block an end. Against such an alert tackle, the end is permitted to step with either foot, but he shoots his head across in front of the charging tackle and executes a block with the right shoulder rather than the left shoulder. The end must be adept at either of these blocks.

If the end is blocking the tackle out, as for example on a quick opening play, he must shoot the head quickly across inside the tackle and then raise up immediately so that the tackle cannot reach over the end to bring down the ball carrier. On this type of play we do not expect the end to drive the tackle back. If he is able to maintain his position, that is sufficient, because the play hits very quickly.

Frequently the end will be called upon to block a linebacker. This is especially true in a defense in which the tackle plays close enough for the offensive tackle to block him. In this situation the end must drive hard into the linebacker. The ball carrier needs the ground on which the linebacker is standing in which to maneuver. As soon as the end has good, hard contact on the linebacker, he must turn him and keep working him away from the path of the ball.

Sometimes the end will be called upon to block a defensive end. This frequently occurs when the defensive end is crowding in close. If the end can drive his shoulder outside the defensive end and maintain contact on an outside play, this maneuver is frequently successful because it is unexpected. The end also may block the defensive end out, particularly on the quick-hitting fullback off-tackle play. In this case he may go directly for him, or possibly he will step back with his outside foot, and then roll him out of the path of the ball carrier.

The end is generally in a good position to go downfield to block the halfback or safety. Speed in getting to the deep defensive man is again all important.

3. *Pass Receiving.* The end's first duty on going down to re-

ceive a pass is to get away from any tackle or linebacker who will try to hold him up and delay him in getting downfield. Speed is his most important asset, although sometimes if he ducks under the hands of the defensive player attempting to hold him up, and drives on all fours for a yard or two, this maneuver may help him to break loose. The maneuvers of the end and the principles of pass receiving have already been discussed, as have his duties on covering punts. The defensive duties of the line will be discussed in a subsequent chapter.

CHAPTER 10 BACKFIELD
FUNDAMENTALS

A well-trained backfield, operating smoothly as a unit, is one of the most delightful sights in football to spectators and coaches alike. Natural ability counts for a great deal. Speed, agility, courage, and a real desire to play football are all important. A backfield which has played together and has picked up the details of starting, faking, ball handling, and blocking will give spectators many a pleasant Saturday afternoon. A good ball carrier is easy to block for. He gets to the point of attack quickly and the blocks do not need to be held as long. He knows how to take advantage of his interference, when to drive through, how to set up a block, and when to leave his interference and cut for the open spaces. The difference between an ordinary back and a great back is just a little speed, just a little extra drive, which may mean the ability to get by one key defender and turn a short gain into a touchdown run. College football is still a running game and nearly always that team will win whose backs run the hardest.

THE QUARTERBACK

The key man on the T formation, of course, is the quarterback. We are not concerned now with his ability as a passer nor as a field general in selecting the proper plays to use. We are concerned here with his duties—mechanical if you want to call them that—in getting the ball from center and delivering it safely and surely to the other men in the backfield.

In the T formation the quarterback receives the ball from center on every play and is responsible for getting it to the ball carrier at just the right time and at just the right spot, so that the latter can give his best effort.

1. *Hands.* Our quarterback places his right hand against the center's buttocks and well into the crotch, with firm contact. The fingers and thumb are well spread to provide a good target for the center's pass. The left arm is turned, wrist up, the left hand palm up, fingers well spread, with the hand at about a 45-degree angle to the ground. The thumb of the left hand is under the thumb of the right hand, and touching it, with the base of the thumbs separated by an inch or so. The spread of the hands forms a pocket into which the ball can be driven securely and grasped instantly.

2. *Stance.* The quarterback takes a comfortable stance, one foot forward, feet moderately spread, knees bent, body erect, eyes up. The quarterback is neither so close to the center that he is in a cramped position or so far away that his arms must be fully extended. He stands close enough so that the elbows may be slightly bent, and he is relaxed completely. With a short-legged center, the quarterback may have to operate a little bit lower than normally. If this is the case, he doesn't bend the upper part of his body forward, but he bends his knees. On the ball count there is a little extra pressure by the right hand against the center. With the elbows bent, the quarterback can give with the center as he charges forward by keeping the right hand in contact with the center for the inch or two of forward movement which occurs as the ball is being delivered. The natural movement of the center's arm turns the long axis of the ball very slightly to the right and delivers it to the quarterback in a good ball-handling position. The stance and hands of the quarterback, his position in relation to the center and his two basic foot movements are illustrated in Picture 9.

3. *Footwork.* Every effort should be made to keep the footwork of the quarterback as simple as possible. Basically he will use two actions, although the angle at which he will place his foot on the first step may vary somewhat in different plays. The first

action is the step-out, best illustrated in Diagram 4, Play 17, the hand-off to the right halfback. As the quarterback receives the ball he steps laterally, parallel to the line of scrimmage with his right (forward) foot. He continues the lateral action with his left foot preparatory to delivering the ball.

The other basic quarterback action is the pivot, which is illustrated in Diagram 21, Play 38, fullback off tackle to the right. The left foot is forward on this action, and the quarterback pivots sharply on his rear (right) foot, bringing the left foot clear around so that he is in position to deliver the ball to the fullback. The normal pass action is a variation of the pivot. The quarterback will generally have the right foot forward. As he receives the ball he pivots completely on the left foot, turning completely around and pointing the right foot toward the rear. He will generally take three steps plus a hop (or occasionally five steps plus a hop) to reach a position about 6 yards back of the line of scrimmage. He is then in position—left foot forward, pointing in the general direction of the throw—to pick his receiver, and as he throws, step up into the protection of the cup.

4. *Ball Handling and Faking.* As soon as he receives the ball from the center, the quarterback draws it in against his stomach, both for concealment and security. On Play 17, for instance, the quarterback steps quickly to the ball-handling spot carrying the ball in both hands. The right half is driving forward with his eyes on the offensive right tackle. He forms a ball-receiving pocket with his left hand and forearm carried loosely against his body, and right hand in a position to help protect the ball upon receiving it. The quarterback extends the ball into the receiving pocket, hooking it over the left arm and pressing it into the pocket with the fingers. Our backfield operates from a three-point stance, and our ball handling is about a foot lower than most T formations. The quarterback, of course, must be thoroughly familiar with all of his backs. In a tall man the pocket will be a little higher, and some backs will vary a bit as to the manner in which they run

and the exact spot where they like to receive the ball. Some of the Split-T teams like to use a little different method of forming the pocket. On Play 17 the right half would carry his left arm high, forming the upper side of the pocket with his right forearm and hand extended across the body to form the bottom of the pocket. This ball handling method permits a little more deception as the right half can make a much better fake in case he does not receive the ball. However, we have always felt that the method described first is surer and safer. Generally speaking, the same sort of pocket will be formed by the ball receiver in all plays in which the quarterback hands the ball to him directly, and the quarterback's ball-handling action will be similar.

In faking to a back, the quarterback will carry the ball against his body with one arm and make the fake to the back with the open hand. Good faking is essential to the successful T-formation attack. The quarterback must be a sure ball handler and he and the other backs must be good actors to mislead the defense, conceal the ball, and mask the point of attack for the necessary split second to let the blockers get a favorable angle on the defensive men.

In 1951, California was fortunate in having as quarterback Bill Mais, who was unusually adept at concealing the ball. In the first quarter of the Pennsylvania game at Philadelphia we found the going very hard against a rugged and determined Penn line. Just before the quarter ended Bill faked an off-tackle play to the left beautifully and dropped back to pass. Bill's fakes to two of the backs were so good that the Penn defense was drawn in for the vital moment. Bob Beal, our right end, broke downfield and was in the clear when he received the forward pass from Mais. The entire play—pass and run—covered 59 yards and resulted in a touchdown.

The quarterback must work constantly with his center until they become almost like two parts of the same body. The exchange of the ball between the center and the quarterback must be so thoroughly practiced that it becomes automatic. Otherwise in the stress of a tough game, there is likely to be a fumble at the most inconvenient moment. If the quarterback is to work with several different centers, he must become familiar with all of them. It would be ideal to have a quarterback always work with the same center, but sometimes this is not possible. The quarterbacks and centers who are to carry the brunt of the play must be thoroughly familiar with each other. The same holds true for the quarterback and his backfield.

All quarterbacks must be careful to use the same cadence. If they do not, a change in quarterbacks will throw the offensive team completely off. If the new quarterback uses a faster or slower cadence, it is very difficult for the team to adjust to that change. We like to drill our quarterbacks early in the season by having them sing out the cadence in unison to obtain absolute uniformity. Quarterbacks and centers can frequently find some time to practice together while the rest of the team is gathering, or while the punters and place kickers are practicing their specialties.

HALFBACKS AND FULLBACKS

On most T formations the quarterback will do all of the forward passing and ball handling. However, if one of the other backs has unusual passing ability, plays can be devised to take advantage of that situation. Since the halfbacks and fullbacks are relieved of these duties, they can concentrate all the better on running, blocking, and pass receiving. A concentration on details in these departments can help tremendously in the development of a backfield. I consider our backfield coach at California, Wes Fry, to be the very finest there is in the country. I never cease to be amazed at what his concentration on the details of backfield play has been able to produce in the form of a sound, well-rounded backfield, and in the way of fast starting, sustained blocking, and hard running.

1. *Starting.* In the execution of a running play, the first 5

yards are by far the most important. Training in reaction, and the development of the fundamental habits in the elimination of waste motion, can frequently help a back to pick up a yard on a play into the line and 2 or 3 on a wide play. It is always very interesting to me to watch the development of our backs in spring practice and throughout the fall season.

Stance: A sprinter who is only concerned with moving in one direction, forward, would use a stance differing radically from that of a football backfield man who will be starting in directions other than a straight line forward 70 to 80 per cent of the time. Our halfbacks and fullbacks must be prepared to start not only forward but laterally to the right or left, at a 45-degree angle right or left forward, and at slightly less than a 45-degree angle right or left diagonally backward. They must adopt a stance which gives good balance and the opportunity of breaking in any direction. Our stance is wider and deeper than that used by most backfield players. Our backs will generally take a preliminary, upright stance, feet even and well spread, and hands on the knees. From this they will drop into their final three-point stance. On this final stance, the feet will be spread approximately 24 inches apart. The toe of the back foot is 2 to 3 inches behind the heel of the front foot. The hand on the side of the back foot rests lightly on the ground without carrying any weight of the body. The back is fairly straight, the head up, and the leg muscles, especially the muscles of the upper leg, are tense, ready for an instant reaction to the starting signal. We prefer to have our right halfback take a stance with the left foot back and left hand down, and the left halfback with the right foot back and right hand down. The fullback will vary his stance somewhat, although some of our fullbacks have preferred to remain in the right stance at all times. Regardless of which foot is back, the player must be in perfect balance, eyes up, feet firmly set. We like to have the backs operate from the ball of the foot in the belief that the best starting drive comes from the inside of the ball of the foot. For that reason, the toes should point out slightly.

Technique: All backfield starts are made with a cross-over action. That means there is a complete pivot toward the direction that will be taken. If the start is to be a lateral one, the pivot is completely in that direction before a step is taken. If the start is to be at an angle of 45 degrees forward, the pivot is made in that direction. The head and shoulders must snap instantly in the direction of the pivot, aided by the action of the arms. The first step is a fairly long one, with the back foot, or the foot farthest away from the intended direction, pushing off from the inside of the ball of the foot and throwing the weight over on the front, or drive, leg. If a left half, for instance, in a stance with his right foot back, were planning to start to his right, the push would come from the ball of the left foot throwing the weight over onto the right leg with the pivot of the body to the right. On the first step, the body and especially the hips should remain low—noticeably lower than the shoulders. The first two or three steps are all-important. Good drive from the balls of the feet, and vigorous arm action will help accelerate the backs' speed. Teaching a back to start properly is a process that cannot be hurried and one which needs constant review throughout the season. Most backs will have a tendency to pick up the front foot at first, rather than make a complete pivot. It is necessary to drill the starting action until the pivot becomes automatic.

It is important that the back avoid tipping off the defense as to the direction he intends to take. His eyes must be straight ahead, and his body must not lean in any direction. Training in quick reaction to a starting signal is very helpful in correcting any tendency to lean or to sneak into the start. In most starting drills, the backs take the preliminary position with the feet even and the hands on the knees. On the command "set" they drop to the starting position with one hand down and one foot back, as described above. They start on the command of "hike" or a quick hand signal. The starting command may come very quickly after "set" or after a considerable interval. This plan helps a back to develop quick reaction. If the start is made on a regular cadence, the back can anticipate the start. But on a single starting signal which may come early or late, the back must remain tensed and develop an instant reaction to the signal. Once the basic starting techniques have become familiar we find that most backs enjoy the starting drills and the competition of testing themselves against their teammates and against a stop watch.

BALL RECEIVING AND BALL CARRYING

As the ball receiver approaches the spot where he is to receive the ball from the quarterback, the arm on that side is carried loosely against the body, palm up. As the quarterback lays the ball into that pocket, the ball carrier's other hand is ready to help protect it and guide it into the proper carrying position if it is necessary to do so. The fingers of the ball-carrying hand are well spread over the nose of the ball with the forearm protecting the ball. The ball carrier must develop confidence in his ability to protect the ball when he meets opposition. He will generally put the other hand across the top of the ball to help protect it while driving through the line. In training ball carriers we frequently have the ball carrier block a dummy with the shoulder of the ball-carrying arm within 3 or 4 yards after receiving the ball. A back who is careless and has a tendency to fumble can be a great handicap to his team. The man who is entrusted by his teammates with the responsibility of carrying the football owes them the obligation of safeguarding that precious possession. If he fumbles and the opponents recover, his team has not only lost possession of the ball but also the opportunity of kicking it and exchanging 35 or 40 yards of territory for the ball. In a tight game 40 yards might be the difference between victory or defeat. If the fumble occurs on his own 10-yard line, the opponents are presented with an easy opportunity to score. If he fumbles on the opponents' 2- or 3-yard line with a touchdown imminent, it gives them a chance to kick out and neutralizes all of the hard work by his teammates in bringing the ball down the field.

The ability to run hard is the greatest asset a ball carrier can have. A back who dances and spends too much time attempting to elude one opponent forgets that the other ten men on the defensive team are closing in on him and he is not of much value against a strong defense. The back who keeps driving forward on the balls of his feet, has his eyes open to cut when he sees daylight, and who, when he meets opposition with no chance to cut, keeps his forward drive and tries to avoid the shoulder of the tackler and drive through his arms, is the back who can be counted on when the going is tough.

I can recall a number of backfield men who have had this ability to run hard, but perhaps none of them illustrated it any better than Don Heap, a left halfback at Northwestern in 1935, '36, and '37, and captain of the team in 1937. Our statistics showed that in a few of the early season games some of our other backs would have a higher average than Don, but in the rugged games their average would drop decidedly, and Don's would invariably go up. He averaged well over 5 yards per carry in three years against strong opponents.

Another great ball carrier was Jack Jensen, our All-American fullback at California in 1948, who could change direction sharply without tipping off his intentions and with little loss of speed.

We used to teach a number of different dodges to the ball carrier, such as the side step, fadeaway, pivot, as well as use of the stiff arm. We have gotten away from this in the past few years, feeling that emphasis on dodging maneuvers can detract from the drive that a good back should have. If a runner can learn to drive through the line at the point of attack and use his speed, he will gain more yards than by any intricate system of dodges.

BLOCKING

Some T formations require very little blocking from the half-backs, who are used almost entirely for ball carrying and pass receiving, and give most of the backfield blocking duties to the full-back. We have always felt to the contrary, that every back in the T formation, with the possible exception of the quarterback, must learn to block. Even the quarterbacks frequently participate in our blocking drills. A small back, given the initial disadvantage of lightness, can frequently become a good blocker by use of eyes and agility, proper leverage and timing. In our 1948 team at California our best backfield blocker was left halfback Billy Main, who weighed a scant 150 pounds. Billy usually blocked for Jack Jensen at fullback, who weighed 195, and Jack Swaner at right half, who weighed about the same. Billy won the respect of the entire squad by his blocking ability, courage, and determination; and I think all of us got a tremendous kick out of seeing our smallest back block for his big backfield teammates.

A good blocker does not develop overnight. A year or two of hard work and sustained effort is generally required. In 1950 at California we were fortunate in having a backfield all of whom could run well, and were good blockers. Pete Schabarum at right half, Johnny Olszewski at fullback, and Jim Monachino at left half, made an unusual combination. Monachino and Schabarum, our senior halfbacks, were excellent examples of T-formation halfbacks who could block as well as carry the ball and receive passes.

In blocking, as in ball carrying, use of the eyes is all-important. This is even more important in the backfield than it is in the line, because the backfield blocker will generally travel several yards before he applies his block. He must move quickly and yet keep his eyes on the target without tipping off the defensive man as to the direction in which he intends to block. For instance, a right halfback blocking the end on the fullback off-tackle Play 38, Diagram 21, must get a fast start and move directly toward the defensive end. His eyes are open, his head is up, and he drives directly at the belt buckle of the end. Just at the last moment he will slip his head to the inside to drive the end out. If the end insists on closing in, the halfback will slip his head to the outside and take him on in with the fullback cutting out. At the moment of impact the knees are well bent, the tail is well down and driving through to reinforce the shoulder. The halfback's objective is to drive through the end and we are not concerned with which foot happens to be on the ground as the contact is made. As the shoulder hits, the feet keep driving, contact is maintained and the defensive man is driven from the path of the ball carrier. This block does not need to be sustained very long, as the ball carrier is immediately behind the blocker. But the contact must be solid.

A flanker blocking on the fullback end run (Diagram 18) faces an entirely different problem in blocking the defensive end. As the play starts the ball carrier is 10 or 12 yards away from the flanker. If the flanker blocks too soon the end can easily recover and make the tackle. The flanker must realize that he has plenty of time, particularly if the end attempts to drift laterally. If the end cuts in sharply, he can be handled by the lead back and the flanker can turn his attention to another defensive player. Sometimes, however, the flanker will be assigned to cut down an end who is charging in fast. In this case the flanker will drive his body into the end with his head across the path of the end.

A backfield player blocking an end on pass protection will move out part way to meet the end and will make the latter declare himself first as to which side he intends to go. He will then move forward vigorously to meet him.

One of the most difficult blocks for a T formation halfback is on the halfback end run as illustrated in Diagram 11. Frequently the defensive end will attempt to play off the blocker with his hands and float to prevent the play going around him. In that case the halfback blocking the end must sustain his block and keep his feet. If he goes to the ground the end immediately moves in for the tackle. The ability to stay with an end who uses his hands skillfully on a wide play requires good eyes, good balance, and experience, to maintain contact and give the end no chance to recover.

A sound, well-rounded backfield is a necessity for any offense regardless of the formation. Only one man can carry the ball at a time, and he needs the help of ten other men. I can't recall any fine backfields which did not include at least two good blockers.

CHAPTER 11 GROUP AND TEAM DRILLS—OFFENSE

In previous chapters we have tried to discuss the theory of offense and to illustrate some sound plays which have been successful. We have also discussed the fundamentals of the game—those things which an individual or a specialist must master. We are now concerned with the methods of teaching those skills to individual players and finally developing those individuals into team units.

Football coaching is essentially teaching. The theory of the individual fundamentals may be very sound, and the plays may look good on paper; but unless that knowledge is mastered by players it cannot be translated into effective team play. We are concerned in this chapter with group drills for the line, the ends, the backfield, and the entire offensive team.

Planning the day's program is not an easy task. The entire squad, whether it consists of 20 players or 150, must be kept busy—constructively busy—and the instruction must be made as interesting and as varied as possible. Following are some of the drills that we have used and have liked.

DRILLS FOR THE LINE

1. *Teaching Stance.* Early each season and at necessary intervals thereafter the linemen practice taking the proper stance. With a large squad the players would line up in three single lines of perhaps eight or ten men each forming three sides of a square with the men facing in. This "hollow" square arrangement can be used for a number of the line drills. The coach directing the drills is

in a position to observe all of the players and his voice does not have to carry as far as if the players were in a single line. With a large squad we would have probably one coach directing the drill with an assistant working with each line. A small squad, of course, could line up in one line with one man directing the drill.

In teaching the stance the coach illustrates the placing of the feet, the squat, the hand-down, and the roll of the weight forward, and has each man in the entire group go through these maneuvers. He will check each man's stance for the proper position of the feet, square shoulders, and proper balance. Later on the linemen will assume a preliminary stance, with the feet even, back straight, head up, forearms resting on the thighs. On the command "set," the feet will be shifted to the final starting position and the hand will snap down to the ground, all in one fast action.

2. *Pulling Out of the Line.* The same hollow-square formation can be used in teaching the pull, a maneuver we like all linemen to learn, including the center. After getting set, the linemen in unison take the first step only, on the pull to the right and then the pull to the left. The placement of the foot on the all-important first step is checked, as is the push-off with the hand and simultaneous snap of the body in the direction of the pull. The complete movement of the pull-out is then tried by the entire line on "hike," breaking either to the right or left. Sometimes the linemen can be spaced 1 yard apart and each lineman may attempt to catch up with and tag the man ahead of him in the direction of the pull. Another approved pull-out drill is to have ten or twelve linemen all in a straight line one behind the other, and then on the "hike" pull to the right or the left as the case may be, making a 10-yard race of it. With inexperienced linemen, this is sometimes a good idea as there is then no danger of one lineman pulling the wrong way and bumping heads with a teammate.

The next step is to teach the linemen to turn upfield through the hole. A group of linemen are lined up about 1 yard apart facing forward toward the instructor. They count off in threes and pull

on the number, as for example, "Number one, pull right, hike."
Each No. 1 pulls to the right and turns downfield through the hole
left by the No. 1 man on his right. Numbers 2 and 3 remain stationary. Each man must not only turn straight downfield but bend
back at 45 degrees in the direction from which he came. He should
not cut too closely to the man on the inside edge of the hole, or
such action will throw him wide, but should remain at arm's
length from the man forming the inside of the hole. As the lineman turns through the hole, his feet must be well spread ready
to meet opposition, and the inside shoulder should be dipped
slightly. Sometimes it is helpful in teaching the turn through the
hole to have the lineman touch the ground for several steps with
his inside hand. The next step is to have a defensive player hold a
dummy just inside the hole so that the lineman leading through
the hole must be in good blocking position to drive into the dummy
with a hard shoulder block.

3. *Teaching Blocking.* The linemen are paired off, each man
seeking a partner of his approximate size and weight, with each
pair about 3 or 4 yards from the next pair. One player in each
pair representing the defensive man holds a dummy. Sometimes it
is hard to see the block of the individual player if the group of men
composing the drill is fairly large. If there are not too many players,
the coach can go down the line having each man block in turn and
making corrections. A device we like is sequence blocking. The
blocker on the right of the line, for example, is given a "set" and
starts his block on "hike." The "hike" that starts his charge means
the "set" for the next man in line, and so on down the length of the
line. In this way the coach can go rapidly down the line, see each
man block and point out mistakes.

In teaching blocking sometimes various mechanical aids, such
as charging sleds, can be helpful. We have used several different
varieties and have found them useful, although the greater portion
of our blocking is done with player against player.

Another method of dividing the linemen for blocking drills is to have the guards work together, the tackles work together, and the centers together. The guards, for example, might divide into two lines, 5 yards apart, with one line representing the defensive ends. The offensive guards in the other line can practice pulling out of the line and executing the block against the end who is stationed approximately 5 yards away. In teaching this block we like to have the guard pull out sharply, go under good control at about three-quarters speed, and then pick up full speed for the jolt and follow-through. Constant work is necessary in pulling from the line quickly with the ball, getting to the end just as fast as possible at the proper angle, executing the block and turning the end from the path of the ball carrier on the follow-through.

While the guards are working together, the tackles might practice blocking against each other, with one man representing the defensive player, lined up on the outside shoulder of the blocker. Frequently the right tackles will work against the left tackles. In this blocking drill the tackles will practice taking the defensive man out or in. At the same time the centers can practice passing the ball to a teammate representing the quarterback and blocking against a defensive player lined up head on, taking that player either right or left.

Another blocking drill for linemen is what we call the runner-interferer-tackler. The linemen divide into groups of three, a blocker facing the man in charge of the drill, a defensive player lined up head on him with his back to the instructor as if he were a defensive lineman. The third man in the group represents a runner and is stationed approximately 3 to 4 yards back. The instructor signals the blocker which way he wants the defensive player taken. The man representing the runner runs directly at his blocker and then breaks off in the desired direction at the last moment. It is important that the runner not tip off the defensive player which way he intends to cut, or he will make the task of the blocker extremely difficult. In this drill the defensive player obtains practice in meeting a blocker, getting rid of him, and driving through for the tackle. The blocker gets practice in blocking against an active defensive player who is trying to break through, as he would be in a scrimmage play. The three men rotate, taking turns at each position. The blocker can take the defensive man to the right, to the left, or occasionally straight back. He can also block him as he would in pass protection, making the defensive man show first and then driving into him and staying in front of him. On the pass maneuver the man representing the runner takes a step forward, and then drops back as if to pass.

The linemen may also be divided into groups of three for teaching the double-team, or two-on-one. In teaching this maneuver, the defensive player will face the "low" or "setup" blocker. On the "hike" the setup man will drive his head into the crotch of the defensive man, charging forward on all fours. The drive man executes the shoulder block and turns the defensive player straight down the line of scrimmage. The setup man, as soon as he obtains good contact, swings his hip in against the drive man so that they form a solid wall and wheel the defensive player down the line. The three players rotate in being setup man, drive man and defense. The defensive player then plays in the seam between the two offensive men. In this case the setup man drives forward on all fours, driving the shoulder nearest the drive man into the defensive player's knee, and shooting his hand on that side onto the ground between the defensive player's legs. The drive man executes his block as before. With the defensive man in the seam, the setup man must be extremely careful to swing his hips toward the drive man so that there is no split between the two offensive players through which the defensive man might penetrate.

DRILLS FOR THE LINE AS A UNIT

After the group drills in which the line squad is taught the basic fundamentals, it is well to work the entire line as a unit with the men in their regular positions of center, guard and tackle. In this manner, each player becomes accustomed to working with the man who is to play next to him in a game.

1. *Charging*. As a warm-up for the entire line group, a drill that is sometimes used is to have each line come up as a unit and charge off together. Possibly the first time or two they may charge off using a duck waddle from a squatting position, with the body upright, to help stretch the legs. The next time or two they might charge off on all fours for 4 or 5 yards, then raise to a normal charging position. With a "set . . . hike" or with a quarterback calling the cadence, the entire line may practice charging off as a unit straight ahead. A device which is frequently used is to tie a rope between the uprights of the goal posts and have each line charge under that rope to avoid raising immediately with the charge. Another good drill is to have the line charge off with each guard pulling to his side as if to block an end and the center and tackle charging straight ahead. All of these charging and starting drills are useful in helping the line to learn to operate as a unit and to get off together.

2. *Pass Protection*. One of the most important duties of the linemen is to protect the passer from the rush of the defensive players. This duty can best be taught by having the line operate as a full unit. Generally the ends will join the other linemen in practicing pass protection, since on various plays the ends will be called upon to block out the defensive ends. Pass protection is generally taught with three full lines, including the ends, operating together. One line is on defense and may use any defensive line-up they prefer, with a linebacker occasionally shooting through to rush. Another line is on offense, while a third line is waiting its turn and observing the good and bad points in the blocking. The offensive line huddles under the direction of a quarterback, the ball is snapped to the quarterback, and he races back to the passing spot. It is the duty of the offensive line to see how long they can prevent the defensive players from tagging the quarterback. The

addition of an element of competition into the pass protection sometimes helps this drill. Each line in turn protects the passer for three plays in a row, working against a stop watch. The watch is started with the snap of the ball and stopped when the first defensive player touches the quarterback in his passing position about 5 yards back of the line of scrimmage. We like to have each line shoot for a "par" of a total elapsed protection time of 10 seconds in the three pass plays. Protecting the passer under these conditions, where the defense knows the play is to be a pass and can rush without caution, is more difficult than pass protection in a game where the defense is not sure what the play will be. To balance this disadvantage the offensive team is occasionally permitted to run a trap play to keep the defense reasonably "honest."

3. *Line Scrimmage.* A type of drill which is very helpful in developing the linemen on their blocking on all plays inside the defensive end, is the line scrimmage. Essentially it is a full scrimmage of an offensive team against a full defensive team minus the halfbacks and safety. The emphasis, however, is on the line blocking on plays between the defensive ends. Frequently an inexperienced backfield should work behind a strong offensive line, since the experience of having to maintain blocks at the point of attack for backs who hit the hole a little slower than the regular backs, teaches the line to sustain their blocks. In a large squad it is possible to use two offensive teams alternately working against one defensive line and linebacker. If the squad is small and does not include that many men, it is possible to have one side of the line work on offense against the other side of the line who are on defense. In the line scrimmage of a full team against a defensive line and linebackers, it is frequently best to have the defensive ends at first merely meet the blockers coming out against them and not attempt to tackle. The absence of halfbacks and safety reduces the number of men involved in the scrimmage and consequently lessens the danger of injury.

The line scrimmage is an intermediate step between the teaching of basic line blocking to individual linemen and pairs of linemen, and the full team scrimmage. The linemen in the basic blocking drills have blocked against defensive players who have not had the incentive to drive toward the path of the ball carrier. In the line scrimmage, the offensive linemen find that they must work harder to hold the defensive man out of the path of the ball carrier, since the movement of the ball carrier toward the hole brings a defensive reaction toward that spot. After the linemen have learned their basic blocking, the line scrimmage is one of the most useful devices in bringing young linemen along, helping them to appreciate the importance of timing, the location of the ball paths, and the co-ordination of the line acting as a unit. It is a good idea to limit the plays used in line scrimmage to the simple basic plays without too much deception. If the offensive linemen can learn to block the defensive players out of the path of the ball when the latter have a reasonable suspicion as to the point of attack, the offensive line will find their task that much easier when backfield deception is added. As the season progresses and the emphasis is gradually changed from individual blocking techniques to the operation of the line as a unit, the line scrimmage will become an increasingly useful item in the daily practice schedule.

DRILLS FOR THE ENDS

Like the linemen, the ends will be drilled in the offensive stance and in starts. If there is not a separate end coach available, the ends will split their time between the linemen and the backfield men. They will practice the stance, starts, and various types of blocks along with the linemen while they work with the backs on pass receiving, defense against backfield blocking, and in covering punts.

1. *Blocking.* T-formation ends should spend a considerable amount of time in blocking tackles. As mentioned before, this duty is one of the toughest that any T-formation offensive player is called upon to carry out, since the defensive tackle is generally a

much bigger man than the offensive end. Constant drills in quickness and form of the shoulder block are essential if the end is to develop into a good blocker. Blocks against linebackers are extremely important, and downfield blocking must come in for its share of attention, since the ends are generally able to get downfield to block halfbacks and safety more easily than the interior linemen. The ends must also receive instruction in basic pass receiving, as well as in covering punts. They will work with the line on pass protection, on get-off, and in line scrimmage. They will work with the backs on pass drills against men covering them in basic patterns and in skeleton pass setups, as will be noted later.

BACKFIELD DRILLS

The backfield men will need a considerable amount of drilling on the stance, the pivot, and the various types of starts, as indicated in the chapter on Backfield Fundamentals. This can generally be best accomplished by working a group of backs together.

1. *Stance and Starts.* Great care must be taken in setting up the backfield stance properly. A group of backs can be lined up along a chalk line as an aid in taking the stance. As they drop from the "set" position into the starting position, it is helpful to place the front foot in advance of the chalk line and the back foot behind the chalk line. Continued practice in taking the stance will help the backfield men to feel comfortable and at home in what, for many of them, will be a new stance. The next step is to teach the pivot. A group of backs as a unit on the "hike" turn the body, head, and feet, sharply in the new direction without taking a step, all from the starting stance. They next execute the pivot and take one step; then they are ready to attempt some starts. With a large squad, each position may be put together as a unit coming up in turn on the line to take their start, such as left halves, fullbacks, etc. With a small squad the entire backfield group may come up at one time to take their start, straight ahead, right, left, diagonally forward, at 45 degrees right or left, or diagonally

backward. Four or five backs starting together, once they have learned the basic mechanics of the stance and start, can bring the element of competition into the basic drills by making a race out of it for the first 10 yards. In taking starts of this nature, a cadence is not used. The command "set" puts the backs from the upright stance into the starting position, and the command "hike" sets them off together. The "hike" may come early or late and serves to sharpen the reaction of the backs. A sound, well-balanced stance which does not tip off the point of attack, and a fast start, are backfield essentials that take time to develop.

2. *Ball Handling.* Basic ball handling can well be taught by having the quarterback pivot out or step out to the ball-handling spot, and feed a group of backs one after another, starting from their normal stance and normal backfield line-up. The quarterback first lays the ball into the pocket provided by the back who carries the ball in one arm. To gain confidence, the back then proceeds a step or two after receiving the ball and blocks a dummy held by a teammate, using the ball-carrying arm to make the block. The ball carrier, of course, will in a game protect the ball with his other hand at the moment of impact against a tackler, or in going through the line where a defensive player may reach out and attempt to jar the ball loose.

3. *Use of Eyes.* The ball carrier must learn to use his eyes and use his blockers. A simple drill provides a blocker ahead of the ball carrier on the line of scrimmage, working against a defensive player. As the ball carrier receives the ball he must have his eyes open to see which way the blocker is taking the defensive man, and must then cut in the opposite direction to take advantage of the block. A further extension of this drill provides a teammate holding a dummy to represent a linebacker through which the ball carrier must drive. The teammate holding the dummy may retreat with it, advance against the ball carrier, or even throw the dummy at the ball carrier's feet. Any one of these actions assist in helping the ball carrier realize the importance of keeping his

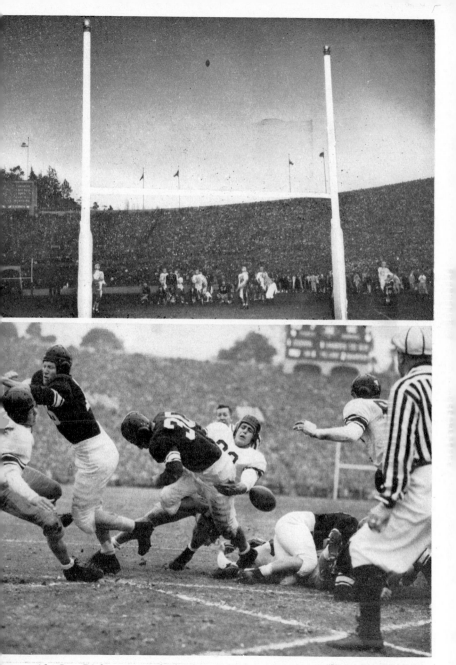

PICTURE 13. *Les Richter (top) kicks first California field goal in years to defeat Washington 30–28 in last three minutes of play, 1951 (A.S.U.C., Berkeley). Murakowski, Northwestern (bottom), scores that much-discussed touchdown against California in the 1949 Rose Bowl. Did he have the ball as he crossed the line? (Wide World Photos).*

PICTURE 14. *Bill Powell* (top) *scores against Minnesota in 1951. Note the l[...]
body angle and hard drive* (*A.S.U.C., Berkeley*). *Jim Monachino* (bottom) *st[...]
arms and cuts away from Ohio State's Vic Janowicz to score in the 1950 Rose Bo[...]
game* (*Wide World Photos*).

eyes open at all times. Sometimes instead of a dummy holder, a teammate or a coach may stand just beyond the hole and indicate with a quick motion of his hand which way the ball carrier should cut.

4. *Blocking*. The backs begin their basic blocking instruction against dummies held by teammates. The form used is essentially that used by the linemen and described under The Shoulder Block. The backs start blocking the dummy from a position 1 yard away, using a moving jolt and trying to block through the dummy. The distance is gradually increased to about 5 yards, and then the same basic blocks are carried through against live men without the presence of the dummy. After the backfield man has learned the form of the shoulder block, he is ready for the basic drill which is shown in Diagram 58. In this drill the back, acting as a lead blocker on a play such as shown in Diagram 21, starts from his normal position in the T and drives at the defensive end who is in his normal defensive position some 6 or 7 yards away. The blocker must start fast and drive his head directly toward the end's belt buckle, giving no indication as to his intentions to take the end in or out. Just at the last moment, if he is taking the end out, he slides his head to the inside and turns him away from the path of the ball carrier. A quarterback feeds the ball to the runner who is in the fullback position, while the coach signals behind the defensive man's back which way the blocker is to take the end— in or out, the ball carrier reacting accordingly. This rather simple basic drill has proved invaluable in developing backfield blocking. Another variation employs a flanker and a lead back working against an end and a linebacker.

5. *Pass Receiving*. A simple drill, which has proved helpful not only to the pass receiver but also to the passers and the men defending against the forward pass, is illustrated in Diagram 59. A passer is lined up in the quarterback spot behind his center, and throws to two lines of receivers who start two at a time from the positions ordinarily occupied by the offensive ends. Two defensive

players are stationed 8 yards in front of the offensive receivers and attempt to knock down or intercept the forward pass. Alternate defenders are stationed 15 or 20 yards back, far enough to be out of the way of the pass, and ready to take their turn on defense. The coach is stationed slightly back of the defensive players where his arm signals can be seen by the passer and the two receivers, but not by the defensive men. A simple signal system can easily be worked out, as one finger meaning a 90-degree cut, two fingers a 45-degree cut, closed fist a hook or stop pass, etc. This drill is good training for the receivers in learning to fake one way and cut in another direction, picking up speed as they take the new direction. It is valuable to the defensive men in teaching them to run backward and not permit the offensive receiver to get

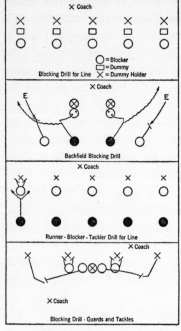

DIAGRAM 58
Group blocking drills

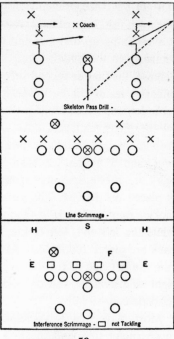

DIAGRAM 59
Team drills—offense

too close to them. It is helpful to the passer in that he has two possible receivers and must instantly pick out the open man. It is a good early season drill and later should be supplemented and succeeded by a skeleton offensive team of center, backs, and ends running pass patterns against a skeleton defensive team of ends, linebackers, halfbacks, and safety. Still later, a full pass scrimmage will be used employing 80 per cent pass plays, and using two offensive teams alternately against one defensive team.

TEAM DRILLS

1. *Learning Plays.* In teaching plays, a common device for a large squad is to use two offensive teams running alternately against one defensive team in dummy scrimmage. Two offensive teams can get off twice as many plays in the same amount of time as one team working against one team, since the second offensive team can be lining up and running its play while the previous team is returning to the huddle after the completion of the first play. On defense, the first or second defensive platoon can be used, or three offensive teams can be used with each team taking its turn on defense for a specified number of plays. If several coaches are watching the offensive players, they will also have an opportunity to make corrections and point out mistakes between plays. If a squad is small and comprises less than two teams, one side of the line can work as an offensive unit against the other side of the line which is placed on defense. For instance, the center, right guard, right tackle, right end, and a complete backfield may be on offense, while the left end, left tackle, left guard, a fullback, and a halfback are placed on defense. After the plays to the right have been run, the left side of the line can take its turn on offense, while the right side assumes the defensive duties so that the plays to the left side can be run.

Most players hate so-called "dummy" scrimmage and would much prefer to spend the time in full scrimmage. However, too much full scrimmage is not advisable because of the danger of injury. It is hard to get the defensive players to come across the line hard enough to provide adequate timing for the offense without the incentive of being able to tackle the ball carrier, but most players are willing to make the effort once they understand the important part the defensive players can play in helping the offense time the block. The defense should make hard contact with the offense on the initial jolt, and then work toward the ball without completing the tackle. The offensive players use full shoulder blocking but do not leave their feet on downfield blocks. As a variation, one or perhaps two of the defensive players at a time may be "active" and allowed to complete the tackle.

In teaching new plays, the assignments may be given on a field blackboard or each man can be told verbally what he is to do. The team walks through the play several times, then goes through at half speed, and finally runs the play full speed. It is important to point out the key blocks, the details of the ball handling, the path of the ball, and the basic purpose of the play, either as a special play against a particular opponent, or a basic part of the week-to-week offense.

Assignments, or the "what to do," are comparatively easy. The details of execution, the "how to do it," take much more time. A play must be lived with for several weeks or even several seasons before all of the important details and proper timing can be mastered.

2. *Types of Team Scrimmage*. Special types of scrimmage, such as the line scrimmage and the pass scrimmage, have been noted above. Another type of scrimmage that is frequently helpful is what may be called an "interference" scrimmage, illustrated in Diagram 59. In this type of scrimmage, an offensive team executes full blocking against a defensive team, all of whom are active in tackling, except the guards and tackles who are stationed in the line. The latter drive hard for the initial contact and then tag, but do not complete the tackle on the ball carrier. The interference scrimmage naturally emphasizes the off-tackle and wide plays and

the forward passes, with just enough plays inside the tackle to keep the linebackers honest and to test the downfield blocking. This scrimmage is frequently used in connection with the line scrimmage. Such a plan really takes a full scrimmage and divides it into two parts, the line scrimmage emphasizing the inside of tackle plays and the blocks against the linebackers, while the interference scrimmage emphasizes the forward-pass plays and the plays outside of tackle. In the interference scrimmage the offense naturally enjoys an advantage, since four of the defensive players are not tackling.

3. *Two-Minute Scrimmage.* A type of intensive scrimmage that can be used late in the week, even as late as the Thursday before a game on Saturday, is the 2-minute scrimmage. In this scrimmage the offensive team is given the ball on the defensive team's 30-yard line and 2 minutes to see if they can score or how many times they can score. The watch is started with the snap of the ball on the first play and the offensive team is not permitted a time out. The only time the clock is stopped is after an incomplete pass, an out-of-bounds play, the enforcement of a penalty, or after a score. The offense soon learns the importance of hustling while the clock is running, and they also learn that 30 yards is too far to go on straight power plays in 2 minutes. The importance of stopping the clock is soon evident, and this type of scrimmage has proved to be a valuable training in making the offense realize the importance of the time element, especially toward the end of a half. Two offensive teams can also generate quite a bit of competition trying to outscore each other in the 2-minute period.

4. *Full Scrimmage.* The best way to learn football is to play it. For all players a reasonable amount of scrimmage in spring practice and in the early fall season is necessary. For the experienced players who will be playing most of the games on Saturdays, little if any full scrimmage should be assigned once the playing season has begun. Dummy scrimmage, occasional partial scrimmages, and contact work of a group nature throughout the

season, will help maintain blocking sharpness, timing, and conditioning. For the less experienced players, once they have had basic instruction in fundamentals (an instruction which will continue as they develop) and have become part of a team organization, scrimmage is very much in order. I am convinced that young men play football because they like the game. The experienced players will have plenty of opportunity to play on Saturday. Those who are developing should have the opportunity to engage in scrimmage at frequent intervals. The scrimmages should be under game conditions. Better yet, if there is an opportunity to provide games with outside teams for the players not yet fully advanced to varsity status, such arrangements greatly benefit the boys. In high school, B-team games, or lightweight games, give many boys opportunity to develop.

At many colleges, unfortunately, that opportunity is not present to the same degree. California for many years has provided a chance for practically all men on the varsity squad to play football in the form of Rambler games. The Ramblers (or junior varsity) play a full schedule of games, and a great majority of varsity players at California have had their first college experience by playing on the Ramblers. These games are generally played as a preliminary to the varsity game, and the opportunity of competition against an outside team, before a crowd, and under full game conditions, has provided experience and the opportunity for development for hundreds of football players through the years. It is only through competition that a player can find and prove himself. Our Ramblers at California are not a separate squad, but an integral part of the varsity, with the same plays and signals. Each year we are proud to see an appreciable number of players advance through the Ramblers into the ranks of the varsity squad.

CHAPTER 12 THE DEFENSIVE LINE

THE defensive line is truly the first line of defense, separated from the offensive blockers by only the neutral zone—the distance of the long axis of the football—particularly at the guard and tackle spots. These players are instantly exposed to the first shock of contact. The success or failure of the defensive plan depends very largely upon how well the defensive linemen are able to maintain their positions. It has been said with considerable justice that the team whose line controls the neutral zone consistently during the game is generally the winner. The defensive line must charge instantly with the snap of the ball, driving in low enough to offset the blockers' charge, then recover from the shock of the block and move quickly to the point of attack.

The defensive line, generally speaking, must drive through blockers rather than step around, and they must penetrate a reasonable distance, stepping forward with the feet, as well as driving the shoulders and upper part of the body across the line of scrimmage, before moving to the point of attack. A defensive line which raises up too quickly, exposing the stomach area to the shoulders of the blockers, or which steps around blockers to avoid contact, can be easily handled by the offensive linemen.

The defensive line must charge hard but under full control. A blind charger is easily cross-blocked or mouse-trapped and spoils the whole defensive pattern by putting additional burdens upon his adjacent teammates. If the defensive player meets no opposition as he drives forward, and senses a trap play, he must instantly drop to all fours and drive to the inside prepared to meet opposition. A sound rule of thumb for the defensive linemen is to fight pressure.

187

That is, if he senses the offensive blocker is trying to take him in a certain direction, he should react against the pressure of the block and battle his way back to the point of attack. If he is slow in recognizing the pressure, or is attacked by two blockers, he may have to momentarily give ground quickly, and pivot or spin backward at a slight angle toward the point of attack.

DEFENSIVE GUARD PLAY

Of all the defensive players, the guards are closest to the ball and their territory can be reached quickest by the offensive backs. The guards have very little time in which to locate the ball and diagnose the play. Their only clue to the point of attack will be the tactical situation facing the opposing quarterback, and the actions of the men on the offensive line within their immediate vision. The guards must charge low and hard enough to neutralize the charge of the blocker opposite them before taking a look to see where the play is going.

The defensive guard should take a well-braced stance, one foot definitely back, in either a three-point position with one hand on the ground, or a four-point stance with both hands on the ground. He should line up head on an offensive blocker, rather than attempting to play the seam between two offensive men where he would be exposed equally to the block of both men. In a six-man line such as illustrated in Diagram 49A, we would prefer to have each guard line up, if possible, with his inside foot back. At the snap of the ball he will step first with the inside foot, which will then be forward as he makes contact, giving him a little better position from which to recover to the outside in case the play goes in that direction. In case the guard feels too awkward in the above stance with the inside foot back we would prefer to have him put the inside foot forward and then step first with the front foot. Above all, the guard must be careful not to raise too quickly and let the offensive blocker get his shoulder underneath; the defensive guard must meet the blocker with his own shoulder at least as low as the blocker's shoulder. The greatest fault of defensive guards is a tendency to raise too quickly and take a look before he has made solid shoulder and forearm contact with the blocker. The defensive guard should be taught first to get off with the ball and then to drive through on all fours. After he has a reasonable working knowledge of these two basic requirements, he may develop other variations in his defensive charge.

The "submarine" is a good basic maneuver against a power attack. In executing this type of charge the guard takes a normal stance a few inches back of the line of scrimmage. At the snap of the ball he shoots both hands forward well into the neutral zone, at the same time dropping his head and shoulders close to the ground, and then driving the upper part of his body forward under his opponent's shoulder and knees, head straight forward, and slightly raised. He then raises the upper part of the body with a push-up maneuver, and starts digging forward with his feet. A well-executed submarine charge is an excellent change of pace and, if unexpected, frequently upsets the offensive blocker and effectively "stacks up" the adjacent area. The submarine charge is sometimes even more effective if aimed at the seam between two blockers. After using the submarine charge a few times the defensive guard may fake a submarine and dive quickly over the top of the offensive blocker. This variation may be successful in getting him quickly into the offensive backfield, but should not be used too often.

1. *Splitting Two Offensive Blockers.* The defensive guard will use his hands against the neck and shoulder of the man opposite him, at the same time driving his own shoulder into the adjacent offensive player. A slight turn of the body and continuous leg drive will frequently enable the defensive guard to drive his body between the two offensive men and break through.

Quick reaction to the pass from center and a low, hard, shoulder charge, however, will always be the defensive guard's real stock in trade. As the guard becomes more experienced he can learn to vary his charge somewhat and try out additional maneuvers, so long as he does not lose the basic charge in so doing. Frequently a guard will develop a special stunt of his own which should be encouraged as a variation. A good defensive guard is an individual who enjoys the hard contact of close line play. He must regard his opponent simply as an obstacle in his path to the point of attack to be neutralized as quickly as possible, and not as a wrestling partner. He must charge, penetrate, neutralize the blocker, free himself and move quickly to the ball, in that order. He must be acutely aware of the tactical situation and know when he must drive low and fight for inches, and when he can play a little higher and be prepared to yield several yards in order to be in a good position to rush the passer or stop a wide play.

When playing over the center in a five-man line against the T formation, the guard is in a position to do a lot of damage to the offense. Rod Franz, our All-American guard at California in 1947, 1948, and 1949, played this position very well, and had the hardest charge I have ever observed in a defensive guard. Certainly the guard playing in the line against any formation is a key man in the five-man line of defense. Footwork is not as important as a hard charge and good defensive range.

DEFENSIVE TACKLE PLAY

The defensive tackles are rightly to be regarded as the cornerstones of the defensive line, if not of the entire defensive team. The tackles are generally stationed so that they can react to plays inside of them, and yet they have enough forewarning to be of value on wide plays. Generally the biggest and strongest men on the defensive team are stationed at the tackle position. The greatest asset that a tackle can have is the ability to recover from a block. One of the finest defensive tackles I have ever observed was Alf Bauman, who played defensive left tackle at Northwestern and was selected as an All-American player in 1940. Alf had an unusual ability to recover from a block and to proceed to the play. I shall never forget his fine defensive play against a great Minnesota team in 1941 at

Minneapolis. Minnesota directed some twenty-five plays at Alf during the game, either inside him, outside him, or right over him. One of the plays made 7 yards, and every other play was stopped for a 1-yard gain, no gain, or a loss.

The ability of a defensive tackle to meet the blocker with hard contact, neutralize his charge, and then recover before the blocker can do so is, in my opinion, far more an inborn thing than even the ability of a punter or a passer. Another player at Northwestern who had that same ability to recover quickly to a marked degree was Bob Voigts, who is now his Alma Mater's head football coach. Bob played right tackle in 1936, 1937 and 1938.

Some tackles have a very quick reaction with the snap of the ball, a fine defensive get-off, and a charge that carries them well into the offensive formation. Occasionally we will find a tackle who has the ability to get off with the ball and to bore in very low, almost on all fours. I think the best man in that respect that I have ever coached was Wilmuth Nemecek, who played defensive right tackle for Oklahoma A.&M. in 1929, 1930 and 1931. Nemecek had unusual ability in boring in very low and he presented very little target to the offensive blockers.

Other tackles are what could be called waiting tackles, rather than charging tackles; their instinct is to allow the blocker to show first and then react to the action of the blocker. This type of tackle play can be just as effective as that of the charging tackle. It is a good plan for the coach to study the tackle candidates and try to decide just what the natural defensive abilities and instincts of each boy may be, and to try to plan the defensive actions of the individual to fit his natural abilities. Our left tackle at Northwestern in 1945 and 1946, Bill Ivy, was a natural "counter puncher." When he lined up at defensive left tackle he did not make the first move, but he had a very quick reaction to any movement made by the blockers opposite him, and his counterplay was very effective.

A weak defensive tackle will put a very heavy burden on the guard playing next to him, on the end on his side of the line, and on the linebackers. But a tackle who can maintain his ground serves as a strong defensive anchor, and makes the play of his three defensive teammates doubly effective. A reckless tackle is wide open for any type of mousetrap play. He is far enough removed from the ball that an uncontrolled charge will bring him into an ideal position to be trapped; a tackle who is vulnerable to a trap can damage his team even more than a guard who lays himself open to the same snare. All sound offensive formations are equipped to put tremendous pressure on the defensive tackle. He must charge hard enough to meet that pressure and yet must keep his charge under control so that he can react to the inside to meet a trap play.

The tackle is in the best position of any defensive lineman to rush the passer. His territory is not quite as congested with offensive blockers as the guard's territory, and he is not required, as is the end, to be concerned with the passer faking a pass and running wide. The ability to pick up his charge, once he recognizes that a pass play is coming, and bore in on the passer is one of the prime requisites of a fine defensive tackle.

Generally speaking, we prefer to have the defensive tackle in a three-point stance, *i.e.,* with one hand down. We prefer to have him place his inside foot back in most cases. The tackle is called upon to play at varying distances from the ball, depending upon the defensive alignment. A tackle on a five-man defensive line, playing against a T formation, will generally play barely on the outside shoulder of the offensive tackle. His inside foot will be back and he must drive through the offensive tackle, and not around him, with a hard shoulder and forearm charge. His play in the five-man defensive line is not unlike a guard. If a defensive alignment calls for a seven-man line, he will be lined up considerably wider and farther away from the ball, being possibly head on the offensive end, or even very slightly to the outside. Sometimes we prefer the defensive tackle on a seven-man line to reverse his feet and have the outside foot forward. He must charge into the offensive end and obtain control of the latter, and then be able to move either in or out to meet the play. In a six-man line the tackle may be a part of a tight six-man defense and his actions will be quite similar to that of the five-man line tackle. Or he may be playing an open six, almost as wide as a seven-man defense.

Regardless of the defensive alignment and the exact position from which the tackle starts his charge and regardless of the distance he is away from the ball, his prime asset will always be his ability to meet the blocker, neutralize the latter's charge, and then move quickly to the play. If he "hangs up" too long on an offensive blocker, and engages in a wrestling match, he is not a top-notch defensive tackle. The tackle, above all defensive linemen, must constantly remember that the blocker whom he first encounters is merely an obstacle in his path and not the final objective. He must break through, strip interference, and, if possible, make the tackle. In situations where the defensive tackle is meeting one blocker, he will use his shoulder and forearm to meet the charge of the blocker, and then use his hands to free himself so that he can move to the point of attack. As he moves toward that point, he must be careful to travel at such an angle that he will meet the ball carrier on or slightly behind the line of scrimmage, and not merely chase him, especially on a play to his outside.

The defensive tackle playing against the strong side of the single wing formation is faced with an even tougher problem than the tackle playing against the T formation. In most ordinary defenses, his position exposes him to the block of two men, the offensive end and the offensive wing back, and an experienced end and wing back can give a defensive tackle a very rough afternoon. This is particularly true if the plan of offense alternates the hard block of the end and the wing back with plays in which the tackle is permitted to come across the line and then be trapped. Unless the defensive alignment is a tight five-man line or a very close six, the tackle will be stationed either head up with the end, in the gap between the end and wing back (who is generally out a yard and back a yard from the end), or head up or slightly on the inside shoulder of the wing back.

His defensive alignment will considerably affect the maneuvers he will use. If he is stationed head up with the end, he must drive in with his shoulder and attempt to obtain control of the end and fight off the wing back as best he can. Generally the tackle will be stationed slightly outside of the end and inside of the wing back. His best defensive plan is a sort of a double coordination movement, in which he will drive his shoulder into the end and neutralize the latter's charge and, at the same time, use his hands to protect his body from the attack of the wing back. In this case the tackle will generally have his inside foot back, stepping forward with the inside foot as he drives into the end, and then moving with his outside foot toward the wing back. Sometimes he can reverse the procedure and have the inside foot forward using his hands on the end and stepping with the outside foot into the wing back, driving against the latter with his shoulder. Some tackles can use a hard charge on all fours, driving right at the gap between the wing back and the end. Another effective variation that some well-coordinated tackles can use is to take a stance with the inside foot forward, and present that leg as a target to the end. As the end drives into the forward foot, the tackle pulls that foot back, shifts his weight to the opposite foot, uses his hands to help get rid of the end, and then drives into the wing back. This "limp leg" maneuver is particularly effective against an end who charges low and hard.

The defensive tackle against the strong side of the single wing must be particularly alert to avoid being trapped. Frequently it will help him to take his key from the actions of the offensive end. If the offensive end moves toward him, the chances are that it will be a play over him or slightly to the outside, or possibly a power play to the inside. However, if the offensive end directs his attention and his block to the inside, the chances are that it will be a trap play, and the tackle must control his charge, turn instantly to the inside, drop to all fours, and be prepared to bore into the blocker who is coming out to trap him and thus close the hole. The tackle playing on the short side of the single wing formation may be lined up either head and head with the defensive end (in which case he will play very similarly to a seven-man tackle playing against a T formation) or he may be lined up on the outside shoulder of the first offensive man inside of the end, playing like a five-man tackle against the T formation. Frequently both men will double-team the defensive tackle on a play in his vicinity, especially if he is playing the inside man and is exposed to the block of the defensive end. Generally the defensive plan will take this matter into consideration and give him some help nearby in the form of a linebacker. But when the tackle is playing close and is blocked by two men, frequently his only recourse, as he feels the block of the end against him, will be to attempt to spin to the outside, reacting to the pressure of the end, and drop back at a slight angle to put himself in position to meet the play.

A careful study of the abilities of each individual tackle is well worth while in order to help him to fit into the defensive pattern. Sometimes it is effective to pair up a hard-charging tackle with a conservative end, and a waiting tackle with a reckless end. The two seem to complement each other. In any event, two good tackles can mean a great deal to the defense and I have always observed that most strong defensive teams are bulwarked by such a pair.

DEFENSIVE END PLAY

Defensive ends are hard to mold into a pattern. I have seen some fine waiting ends, and I have seen some equally good ends who charged with apparent recklessness into the core of the offensive formation. There is a greater variation in end play on defense than in any other spot in the line. We talk about crashing ends, square ends, waiting ends, and I have seen good ones of each of those varieties. I used to think that the answer was to have the end take his stance about 3 yards from the tackle against the normal offensive formation with his inside foot back, and step forward with the inside foot and then the outside foot. On his third step he moved in with the inside foot to meet the off-tackle play, or crossed over with the inside foot to prevent the wide play from turning downfield. I don't think, however, that any particular footwork or any plan of definite steps is the answer. Individual ends vary so widely in the length of step and speed of charge, and offensive plays vary so much in the length of time they take to reach the end's position, that I would much rather instruct the end to take a comfortable position with either foot back, and charge hard, penetrating to protect his position.

Generally speaking, we think the end should charge in at such an angle that he will be able to close the off-tackle hole in case an off-tackle play develops. If, as he charges in, he sees that a wide play is under way, he may then vary the angle of his charge and widen to meet the blockers who are attempting to take him in. In a wide play it is important for the end to make a reasonable penetration of 2 or 3 yards and then fight off blockers, trying to force the ball carrier to proceed laterally in his effort to get around the end. If the end can destroy the angle of the ball carrier on a wide play in this fashion—the ball carrier is not effective until he turns upfield—then the action of the end as indicated above will expose the ball carrier to the linebacker or the halfback.

One of the prime functions of the end against a wide play is to strip the ball carrier of as many interferers as possible. The end will attempt to use his hands in playing off blockers, and keep his feet as long as possible. When he is finally taken by a blocker, if he can reach out and throw an additional blocker off course, he will be of inestimable help to his teammates. On a play inside of him, the end must be prepared to meet force with force. When he sees a play declare itself to the inside, he must bend his knees, lower his shoulder, and meet the blocker trying to take him out with his shoulder and forearm, driving the play to the inside to deprive the ball carrier of room for maneuvering. Perhaps the hardest thing to teach a defensive end is to move and diagnose the play at the same time. Too many ends are hesitant and they want to get a clear picture of the play before they move. It is important that they get under way with the snap of the ball, penetrate and then meet the play with force, whether it is headed inside or outside.

The end's responsibilities will vary considerably with the defensive alignment of his team. If the alignment is that of a five-man line, the end may generally feel free to smash harder because he has some very close support in the form of the linebacker. If it is a seven-man defensive alignment, the linebacker is removed to some distance from the play and the end must play more conservatively. In playing against a wing back the end must be careful to angle his charge in such a manner that he is not exposed to a quick hook block by the wing back. Playing against a flanker presents a number of problems for the end.

If he is a five-man-line end, he may frequently cover the inside and permit the linebacker to cover the outside. This arrangement is illustrated in Diagram 50B. If it is a seven-man alignment, the end must take a greater responsibility to the outside, and if a flanker or man in motion shows against him, he will widen or even drop back off the line a bit in order to help the halfback. This arrangement is illustrated in Diagram 50A. A very wide flanker, say 10 to 15 yards out, seldom presents a problem to the defensive end, since he can get to the "crossroads" and protect himself either against an inside play or an outside play before the flanker can block him. A flanker who is only 3 to 5 yards out presents a much tougher problem. In this case the end cannot charge recklessly across, for the flanker can reach him in time to block him on a wide play. The end can widen, play the flanker first, and be in a good position against the outside play. If the play develops inside, he must be prepared to come right down the line or slightly back of the line of scrimmage to meet the play as soon as possible. Sometimes from his normal position he can fake a charge across and then hold up preparatory to meeting the flanker. Sometimes if he thinks a flanker is wide enough, he may take a chance and shoot the gap to meet the wide play. In any event, playing against a flanker, the end must inform his linebacker and his halfback of his intentions. The three must work together as a unit so that neither the inside nor the outside play is left inadequately covered.

The end can be a very effective rusher against the forward pass. Because of his position on the end of the line and the fact that he can drive in free of immediate blockers, he can develop a considerable head of steam. If the man blocking for the passer is hesitant and doesn't move out sharply to meet him, the end may continue his charge and try to rip right through him with a shoulder block. If the blocker moves out too far the end may on occasion duck inside of him; but he should remember that he is the man who must protect against a fake pass and run, and move to the outside again immediately. Generally speaking, in rushing the passer the end must not leap through the air and leave his feet. He must bore in on the passer with his feet well under him, ready to react in case the passer attempts to run wide. He should try to tackle the passer rather than to jump to block the pass.

A majority of delayed or deceptive plays are designed to take advantage of an overeager end. Any time the play is apparently moving away from an end, he must tell himself that the play is coming back at him in some form. He must follow the play with caution and must be alert for any delayed action back in his direction. Bootleg plays and delayed reverses, as well as fake passes, are favorite plays used against an overeager end. The end on the wide side of the field must be particularly cautious, for if he permits himself to be drawn out of position a long gain or a touchdown may be the result.

Good ends are a great help to the defensive play, and one weak end can do more damage to his own defense than possibly any other player on the line.

LINE DRILLS—DEFENSE

The first thing the defensive lineman must learn to do is to react to the ball with a good defensive get-off. At frequent intervals during the season we like to line up several defensive lines, one after the other, facing a center, and concentrating on reaction to the ball. As soon as the center moves the ball (and the pass may come early or late), the defense must react immediately. Sometimes it is a good idea to have the center shout or make a false motion in an effort to draw the defense off side. They must remain rock steady until the ball itself moves, and then they must react instantly. The next thing the defensive line must learn, especially from tackle to tackle, is to drive forward low on the defensive get-off. As was mentioned earlier, linemen can be drilled in the low charge by making them charge under a rope held at the proper height.

A drill we have used a lot for defensive charge and reaction to the ball is illustrated in Diagram 60A. An offensive center is lined up with the ball, and offensive players hold dummies, indicated by the square figures, in the approximate position that would be occupied by offensive blockers in the line. Two other offensive players hold dummies at the spot where the ends would meet opposition normally on a play inside of them. The ball is snapped to an offensive player representing a ball carrier, stationed 5 yards back. The purpose of the drill is twofold. First, the defensive linemen must drive hard into the dummy representing the offensive blocker. Then they must find the ball and move toward it as indicated by the various lines. The man representing the ball carrier may drive forward at an angle, or move laterally right or left upon receiving the ball, or he may take a step forward and then drop back to pass. The defensive linemen from end to end must drive into the dummies representing offensive blockers, and then must free themselves from the dummies and move to the ball. We have found this to be a good basic drill for the linemen's defensive charge and rally.

The reaction of the defensive player to an individual blocker is best taught in a drill similar to that in Diagram 58, The Runner-Interferer-Drill, in which the defensive player must meet a blocker, get rid of him, and then make the tackle. A variation of the same drill can be used, in which the defensive man may be blocked by the man opposite him, or the man opposite him may pull in either direction and an adjacent offensive player may execute a trap block. The latter drill is good training in meeting a trap. The defensive linemen, of course, will receive further training on rushing the passer in pass scrimmages and in all-round defense with the full defensive team.

LINEBACKERS

The very foundation stones of a good defense are the linebackers. It is an old adage among football coaches that good linebackers can make an ordinary line great, and poor linebackers can make a good line look like a sieve. Modern football puts more strain on the defensive linebackers than any other position. The linebacker is expected to move quickly to support his line, and plug any holes that develop. He must rally to meet wide plays, and he must take a very important part in the pass defense, by dropping back quickly to cover men in the flats or in the area in front of the halfbacks and safety.

No other defensive position requires quite the versatility of the linebacker, and no other position is exposed to more types of pressure. If he plays too close, he may get tangled up with his own line on a wide play, especially if a defensive lineman is driven back.

If he plays too far back, he is a sitting duck for good offensive blockers who have a chance to get an angle on him. He must be prepared to be blocked from any angle. The free linemen opposite him may move forward instantly to contact him, or he may be taken from the side by a blocker he does not see.

All coaches are on a constant search for good linebackers, and I know of no position that is harder to coach. One of the basic purposes in using different defensive formations is to vary the position of the linebackers so that they will not always be in the same spot. Good linebackers have always been very important from the early days of football to the present, but under the platoon system they are the true specialists of the defensive unit. Most spectators watch the ball, but of late years I think the linebackers have begun to come into their own so far as spectatorial appreciation is concerned. Good linebackers have been appreciated for a long time by players. Ask any lineman who has been caught slightly out of position and then been saved by a timely tackle by his linebacker. Ask any halfback who has seen a linebacker hold up an end on a pass play, or knife through and strip the interference on an end run. So much is expected of linebackers that it amazes me that as many successful ones turn up each year, as is the case.

In 1947 California played Stanford, a team which had not been too strong defensively during the season. Stanford used a seven-man line against us in the big game and it was only by a fortunate pass in the last 2½ minutes that California was able to win. Stanford's linemen played fine football, but George Quist, the Stanford linebacker, was a tremendous bulwark of strength all afternoon. I have seldom seen one man make more tackles or mean more to the defensive plan than Quist did on that occasion.

With a six-man line, of course, there will be two linebackers, and we met some fine linebackers in the 1950 and 1951 Rose Bowl games. Both Ohio State and Michigan used a six-man line as a basic defense, and Lininger of Ohio and Momsen of Michigan gave us a fine display of linebacking. In the ordinary five, there will be three linebackers. At California we have used that defense as one of our basic plans for the past five years, and we have had some excellent linebackers. One of the first things we always look for in the spring of the year and in the early fall are men who have the ability to play this difficult position. A good linebacker must be stout enough to meet and neutralize a blocker coming through for him. He must be able to delay ends and occasional wing backs who are going down as pass receivers. He must have the speed to move laterally and reinforce the flanks, and he must have the alertness to drop back and help in the pass defense.

In the five-man defense we like to have our corner linebackers, who are generally the defensive center and fullback, stationed about 1 to 2 yards back, and slightly outside of the offensive ends in a normal T formation. We like to have them well-braced, knees slightly bent, and the inside foot forward, where they are in a position to watch the blockers, especially the ends who are in position to make immediate blocks, and also watch what is happening in the offensive backfield. As the blocking end or potential pass receiver moves toward the linebacker, the latter must meet the blocker with vigor, driving his shoulder and forearm into him, and then, like the defensive linemen, he must get rid of the blocker and move to the play. The linebacker must work very closely with his end and tackle and there will be occasions when we like to have the linebackers "shoot" by driving through the line with the snap of the ball. This maneuver can be very effective if used with discretion and at the right time.

On a pass play the linebacker must hold up any eligible receiver within his area, and then drop back to help in the pass defense. Frequently a linebacker is assigned to the flat area on his side. We like to have him angle back to the outside, ready to cover the flat if the ball goes out there, but also ready to react to the inside in case the ball is thrown downfield or over the middle of the line. If the ball moves in the opposite direction, the corner linebacker on the side away from the point of attack must be particularly cautious, and must be alert for any delayed pass play or delayed running play coming into his territory. In the 5-3-2-1 defense, the middle linebacker, who frequently is a guard but might well be a center or a player from any other offensive position, is a very important man. He has greater freedom than the corner linebackers. He may play at times almost in the line and may work a "stunt" with the guard who is playing in the line. In passing situations he can be back 5 yards or more to help protect the vital area over the middle. We like to have the middle linebacker play a roving sort of a game; he can afford to be a little more reckless than the corner linebackers. Les Richter, California's All-American guard in 1950 and 1951, was an exceptional middle linebacker who covered a great deal of territory.

To be a good linebacker, whether in a seven, six, five or four-

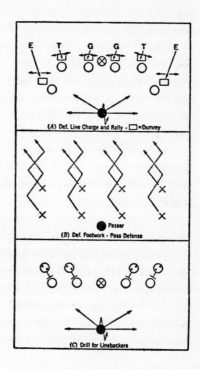

(A) Def. Line Charge and Rally - ☐=Dummy

(B) Def. Footwork - Pass Defense

Passer

(C) Drill for Linebackers

DIAGRAM 60
Drills

man defensive setup, requires alertness, and ability to get rid of blockers, and speed in moving to the point of attack. Diagram 60C illustrates a drill that is used for linebackers. Each is stationed about a yard back of the line of scrimmage, and slightly to the outside of the man who may block him. His inside foot is forward. The ball is snapped to a man representing the ball carrier, and he may move in any direction or step back to pass. The blockers will attempt to take the linebackers in or out according to signal, or may go down to receive a pass. The linebacker must meet the blocker, then move to the play if it is a running play, or if he senses that the blocker is trying to get away from him to go down to receive a pass, he must hold him up and then drop quickly back to cover. The linebacker will soon learn that if he attempts to step around the blocker, or meet him too high, he will not be in any position to stop the play. He must neutralize the blocker first before he moves to the play. One of the worst mistakes that a linebacker can make is to play too high and be driven back by an aggressive blocker, giving the ball carrier plenty of room to maneuver. Generally one of the linebackers will be the defensive quarterback and give defensive signals for his team but all linebackers must be acutely conscious of the tactical situation, and must play their game right along with the offensive quarterback.

The first thing to look for in a linebacker is the ability to meet a blocker and get rid of him. Any player with reasonable size and coordination, regardless of the position he may play on offense, might be a man to work into the linebacking spot.

DEFENSIVE HALFBACK AND SAFETY

The defensive halfbacks and safety must work together as a unit, both against the running attack and against forward passes. In Chapter 4 we have discussed some of the requirements of these players in meeting the pass attack. There is no easier way to lose a ball game than to allow a pass receiver to get behind a halfback or safety for a long and costly completion. Similarly, on a running play, a missed tackle by a halfback or safety can do more potential damage than a similar misplay on the line of scrimmage or on the part of a linebacker. The halfbacks and safety are frequently the last defenders between a ball carrier who has broken loose and the goal line. We have discussed in Chapter 4 the manner in which the defensive backs will rotate to meet a running play. We are now concerned with a more detailed discussion of the requirements on the part of the men to play these positions, and the methods of teaching them to meet the various situations that they may encounter in a ball game.

Speed and a fast defensive reaction, either to the ball carrier or pass receiver, are very essential on the part of defensive halfbacks and safety. A halfback or safety who is slow or hesitant about coming up to meet a running play may cause his team just as much damage as if he lets a pass receiver get open behind him. The halfbacks and safety must play as a unit, not only on passes, but against a running attack. They must talk to each other constantly, and move up rapidly to support each other in meeting the particular play at hand.

It goes without saying that all three must be excellent tacklers. They will receive training in bringing down a man in the open field, in approaching in good balance, and in otherwise carrying out the form of a good tackle. They must appreciate the importance of a side line. The offensive ball carrier cannot gain any ground going out of bounds, and if they can maneuver him into a position where he is forced out of bounds, they are executing in effect the surest tackle in the game. The halfbacks and safety will do a lot of running in the course of a ball game. They must take nothing for granted; even if it appears that a lineman or a linebacker is in a perfect position to make the tackle, they must assume that he is going to miss the ball carrier and must place themselves in a position where they can instantly execute the tackle. They will not, of course, pile onto a player who is down, but as long as a runner is on his feet, they will keep coming in to make the tackle.

The defensive halfbacks and safety must always be aware of the down and the distance to gain, the time remaining to play, and all other factors that will enter into the tactical situation. They must be alert for long passes and prepared to counter odd offensive formations. On each down they must check to make sure that there isn't a flanker or an end stationed out wide. If one man is stationed wide, say 10 to 20 yards out from the normal offensive tackle spot, the halfback must widen to meet him. If two men go out wide, the halfback must give warning and call for help on the part of an end or a linebacker in covering the two wide men. At all times, the halfback must observe very closely the actions of the end and any wing back or flanker on his side. Frequently the actions of these men will tip off a projected pass play. If they move immediately downfield, the chances are good that it will be a pass. If they block, the chances are that it will be a running play coming to that side of the field. The halfbacks and safety are generally the ones who anticipate a pass first, and they must warn the linebackers, so that the latter can drop back to help out in the pass defense.

The defensive halfbacks and safety, in covering passes, must be trained to run either straight or diagonally backward, and while so doing to change direction without getting their feet tangled up. Several drills are used in teaching footwork for pass defense.

1. A group of backs are lined up in a single line and on the "hike" they sprint backward, facing a man representing the passer. In order to keep them in proper balance, sometimes they will be signaled to run forward, sometimes they will be signaled to run backward.

2. A group of backs will be lined up facing the passer, as in Diagram 60B. They will start out running diagonally backward to the right at an angle of 45 degrees. When the passer calls "cut" they will reverse and run at 45 degrees to the left. They must learn to change direction in this manner smoothly, without tripping up and, most important of all, without losing sight of the passer. This drill can be used for a small number or a large number of backs, and

can be combined with the passer actually throwing and having the backs play the ball.

3. *Ball reaction.* This is one of the first and most basic drills for pass defense. An entire backfield, including linebackers, is lined up facing the passer, who is back behind his line of scrimmage in approximately the position that a forward passer would occupy in a game. The defense is in good balance ready to react instantly to the ball, since no receivers are going down. The passer will fake several different directions and then will try to throw the ball in such a manner that it will strike the ground downfield, anywhere from 5 to 30 yards, before a defensive man can get it.

The defensive players must learn to react instantly to the ball and they must talk to each other as the play develops. When one is about to intercept it, he must call, "I've got it," and his teammates must then form interference for him. After the defensive backs have had some work on reaction to the ball and in running straight and diagonally backward, they are assigned to covering a receiver. They must learn not to let the receiver get too close to them. They must remain in good balance so that the receiver's fake will not throw them off stride. Then, as the ball is thrown to the receiver, they must learn to go for the ball. Pass defense drills will later be extended to cover a full pass scrimmage.

As training for a specific opponent advances further, the defensive backs will receive practice in defending against the favorite pass patterns of the opponent. The positions and favorite paths of the best receivers will be pointed out to them. Above all, the safety and halfbacks must learn to give instant warning of a pass. Also, they must warn each other of men cutting across from one side of the formation to the other by calling "Man across." They must learn to go for the ball once it is in the air, and must be made to realize that they have just as much right to the football, once it is in the air, as the offensive player. Sometimes it is a good idea to throw a ball midway between an offensive and a defensive player, 15 to 20 yards downfield, and have each of them go for it aggressively.

Aggressiveness in playing the ball is a very important part in pass defense.

TEAM DEFENSIVE DRILLS

After the linemen have received instruction in the proper stance, in getting off with the ball, and in the various maneuvers to overcome blockers; after the linebackers have received their specific training; after the backs have received instruction in pass defense, in footwork, and in the method of rotating to meet a play; then it is time to put the entire defensive plan together by working with team units. A start can be made by having a full defensive team working in dummy scrimmage against an offensive team using almost any normal offensive formation. The offensive team will run wide, right and left, they will slant off tackle, they will hit straight up the middle, and they will drop back to pass. The defensive team must learn to react to all of these maneuvers. In early season or spring practice scrimmages, men with good defensive reaction will be noted, and gradually a defensive unit will be formed.

In preparing for a specific opponent, it is a good plan if possible to have a team run the opponent's plays and pass patterns against the defensive unit. An entirely new system of offense, of course, cannot be learned by a reserve team, but their four or five favorite plays could be selected and thoroughly illustrated for the benefit of the defense. The same is true of their most frequent pass patterns. One of the great problems with such practices is getting enough plays run off fast enough. Because of unfamiliarity with the opponent's system, it takes quite a bit of time to run off the plays on the practice field. Sometimes it helps the situation to have a full offensive team running the opponent's plays but concentrating mostly on running plays, and alternating with them a skeleton team of center, ends, and backfield, which will throw passes only. The offensive team will receive their play, possibly diagramed on cardboard if the opponents are using a formation or style of play different from ours; then they will line up and run that particular play. Meanwhile the skeleton pass team is receiving a pass pattern, and as soon as the full team has completed their play, the skeleton team goes up and runs a pass pattern. Meantime the full team is receiving the next play. In that manner we have found it possible to run off about twice as many plays as would be possible with just one offensive team. While the skeleton team is running off the pass pattern, the defensive coach in charge of the line can be discussing with his linemen mistakes made on the previous play and, while the full offensive team is running off their play, the coach in charge of the defensive backs can be discussing with them any mistakes made in covering the previous pass pattern. This team defensive drill is illustrated in Diagram 61 on practice organization.

After the season once starts most of the hard contact work in practice during the week will be confined to group work in which the linemen, the ends, and the backs, working in separate units, will receive fundamental instruction. Some full defensive team scrimmage is necessary early, but once the playing season has started, this full team scrimmage will be kept to a minimum. In becoming familiar with an opponent's plays, the defensive line can hit hard for the first contact, and then go to the point of attack without tackling. Contact can also be minimized by having only the line tackle, or only the linebackers, or only the safety man and halfbacks. Team defensive coordination is just as important as team offensive coordination, and team defensive drills should be carried out at a speed comparable to game conditions, even though very little tackling may be done. Thus the various defensive players may have a realistic picture of the opponent's offense.

CHAPTER 14 THE ORGANIZATION OF PRACTICE

FOOTBALL is a race against time. The game itself, with the ball in play for approximately 12 minutes of the elapsed 60 minutes, is a battle against the timer's clock. To an even greater degree, football coaching and the preparation for the various games is a true race against time. The amount of time available for practice will vary at different schools, but the total amount will always be limited.

At California last fall from the first day of practice until the last game we spent 126½ hours on the practice field and 18½ hours in meetings and blackboard talks, a total of 145 hours. Sixty-one hours of field practice and meetings, or 42 per cent of the season's total hours, were spent in the first three weeks before classes started. In that 145 hours the basic fundamentals of the game must be taught to a squad of 80 or 90 players, the specialists must become proficient in the ball fundamentals, an adequate kicking game must be developed, a basic offense and a basic defensive plan must be taught, the players must be properly conditioned, and specific preparations must be made to meet ten separate opponents. Unless the utmost value is obtained from every single minute during the season, some phase of the game will be neglected and team development will suffer accordingly. Football is a highly competitive game and the team which can make best use of practice time available will enjoy a considerable, and perhaps decisive advantage against its opponent.

There are a great many factors which limit the time available for football in an educational institution. Most conferences have rules which state the date upon which football practice for member institutions can start in the fall. Once classes start, laboratories and late afternoon sections rigidly limit the amount of time available for practice on any given day. Many high schools which serve a large community and whose students are transported to school from outlying districts by school busses, find that the hour when the school bus departs in the afternoon to take the students home is another very definitely limiting factor. Even if there were no rules and no afternoon classes it would be unwise to practice much over two hours. The law of diminishing returns goes into effect very shortly after the end of that period; players become tired, lose their sharpness and timing, and practice becomes ineffective.

Not only the time available, but the size of the squad and the number of men available to help with the coaching, will vitally affect the plan of organization. A large university squad of eighty or ninety men composing a varsity and a junior varsity group, with eight or nine coaches available, may present a more complex problem in organization than a squad of thirty players coached by two men. Regardless of the size of the squad, careful planning of the practice is extremely important. Each player on the squad should be given an opportunity to develop progressively as an individual and as a team member in learning the game. A player can learn a great deal by watching what goes on at practice and by listening to what is said, but he will learn infinitely more and develop himself much faster if he has an opportunity to participate fully in the drills. Practices must be planned so that the entire squad and all of the coaches available can participate actively. There should be a minimum of activity in which only a few members of the squad participate while the rest watch. Every practice must be thoroughly set up beforehand in a staff meeting, so that each member of the coaching staff knows the program thoroughly and understands what his part in it will be. He must know exactly what he is going to do, how he is going to do it, and how long he will have to achieve his objective. Football practice must operate on a careful time schedule, realistically planned, and yet flexible enough to adjust to those unexpected difficulties which one always encounters.

SELECTION AND ORGANIZATION OF THE COACHING STAFF

Football coaching today is no longer a "one-man-band" proposition. The modern game demands a well-knit staff of several men of highly developed ability who can teach effectively the infinite details of the game. A minimum number of men to handle a small university squad of forty-five players would probably be four in number—a head coach, a coach of the line, a backfield coach and an end coach. With a larger squad of sixty to ninety men who may be playing a varsity and a junior-varsity schedule, six to eight coaches will be more effective. A small squad can be managed by two men, one of whom will generally handle the line and the other the backfield, and either of whom may be the head coach. Adequate coaching help is particularly important in high school because of the desirability of separating the players into various age and weight groups to avoid injury. A good coaching distribution for a fair-sized high school might be two men handling a varsity squad of thirty-five or forty, one man handling a j.v. squad and one or two men coaching a lightweight or frosh-soph squad. The importance of adequate teaching and supervision of high-school players cannot be overemphasized. Possibly not many high schools can work up an organization such as that developed by Paul Brown when he was coaching at Massillon, Ohio. Coach Brown carefully coordinated the junior-high-school and the high-school teams and provided well-trained coaches and fine supervision which turned out strong outfits year after year.

A well-balanced coaching staff will be made up of men who vary in temperament. Their different personalities will give the staff stability, like a folding screen, each section of which stands at a slight angle to the other sections. Reasonable age and background differences among members of the coaching staff frequently add strength to the entire unit. The staff should be composed of men who

FIGURE 15. *Two fine catches: Jim Monachino's against Southern California in 1950 (top) (Wide World Photos), and Morley's (Stanford's left end) against California in 1951 (A.S.U.C., Berkeley).*

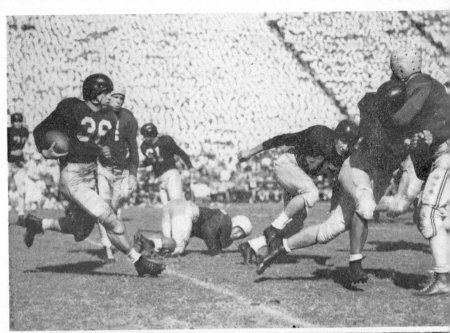

PICTURE 16. *California back Oszewski (top) goes 13 yards against Santa Clara 1951 behind good blocking (A.S.U.C., Berkeley). California's Don Robison (bottom) (45) swings around Stanford end behind fine blocking of Richter (67) a Powell (A.S.U.C., Berkeley).*

love the game of football, enjoy dealing with young men, and are willing to work hard and teach with genuine enthusiasm.

Whatever success California has enjoyed in the past five years has been due in large measure to the contributions made by my staff: Wes Fry, backfield coach; Bob Tessier, and, after Bob's untimely death in 1950, Herm Meister, line coaches; Eggs Manske, end coach; Nibs Price, backfield coach and scout; Zeb Chaney, general assistant and rambler coach; and Harold Grant, freshman coach. A university team playing a strong schedule needs the concentrated effort of a strong staff and I feel that I have been most fortunate in having the help of an ideal group.

On a large staff, each man must be an expert in his own department and yet have full knowledge of, and the ability to coach, the team offensive and defensive plans. In addition, the various specialties, such as scouting, the coaching of punters, passers, place kickers, and kickoff men, must be assumed by the various members of the staff. The head coach on a large staff must assume responsibility for the proper organization of the squad and the staff itself. He should delegate responsibility freely, but his is the final responsibility to see that all parts of the organization work together smoothly. All staff members will contribute ideas toward the general offensive and defensive plans to be used, but the head coach has the responsibility of final decisions. He should be able to coach any of the specialties that other members of the staff are not equipped to take care of. He will, of course, have many off-field duties in addition. These are discussed in Chapter 15.

SPRING PRACTICE

The foundation of most college football teams is laid in the spring. This off-season practice is most important for individual and team development, but the practice period should be held to reasonable limits. Until 1952 the various conferences throughout the country varied somewhat in the amount of spring practice permitted by conference regulation. In the Pacific Coast Conference, spring practice was limited to thirty practice sessions. In some other sections of the country there was no time limit placed on spring drills. At the National Collegiate Athletic Association meeting in January of 1952, a regulation was passed limiting all schools to not more than twenty spring practice sessions within a period of thirty days. In February of 1952, the eight colleges in the Ivy League—Brown, Columbia, Cornell, Dartmouth, Harvard, Pennsylvania, Princeton, and Yale—announced that they would drop spring football practice altogether.

Fall practice is a race against time and is much too short a period for squad development without the opportunity of spring practice. The spring period will enable the coaches to accomplish to a greater or less degree the following objectives:

1. To get acquainted with the new men and get an estimate of their strong and weak points as individual players in order to help them develop. We like to encourage everyone who is interested in football to come out in the spring, and each spring we find a number of new men, some of them without high-school experience, who show promise as potential varsity players. The screening process is most essential, for the practice must move fast in the fall and the squad must be reduced to workable numbers.

2. To teach the basic system of play. This will include the fundamentals of the game, the basic plays of the offense and the basic defensive plan. In addition, men will be developed in the ball specialties, such as passing, punting, and place kicking.

3. To experiment with new additions to the basic plan and try out players at new positions where they might be more effective. Each football team is custom-made. Special abilities may permit the use of plays that were not feasible the year before. Better blocking assignments on certain plays may develop through experiment in spring practice. A variation in the basic defensive alignment may be indicated by a change in personnel from the year before. Sometimes the graduation of a number of men at one position makes it necessary to move players from other positions

to fill that weakness. Sometimes a player who has not been particularly successful at a certain position, may find that he fits in much better at a new spot. Men who have been used primarily on the defensive the year before may show marked offensive ability, and vice versa.

Spring practice is a very essential preparatory period for the fall campaign. It provides each individual an opportunity for further experience with the game, and a chance for sound development. The practice periods should not be too long and should be made as interesting as possible. Scrimmages and practice games conducted in a manner similar to the games to be played in the fall will add to interest and provide opportunities for individual and team development under competition.

Men who are proficient in other sports and desire to participate in such sports during the spring should be given the opportunity to do so. The sport in season should take precedence. Freshmen who are not yet eligible for a varsity spring sport and who have a possibility of fitting into the varsity football plan should be encouraged to give precedence to football if they care to do so. The emphasis in the spring should be on new and less experienced players.

FALL PRACTICE

Most schools set the date for the opening practice in the fall, generally by conference rule, so that there is an opportunity for approximately three weeks of practice before the first game. This is about the right time to condition and develop a team for the first test. Generally the date of the opening practice will be early enough so that the greater portion of this three-week period comes before classes start.

Early fall practice is exceedingly important. Last fall at California we had the opportunity to get in 61 hours of practice in the first three weeks before classes started. This amounted to some 42 per cent of the entire practice time for the season. We had the opportunity to practice twice a day for a portion of this period, and to hold evening meetings which are most important in rapid team development. It is often said that if a football team does not develop into an effective unit within the first month after practice has started, that it probably never will develop, and there is considerable truth in this thought. Hence the importance of a fast start in the practice season.

A detailed chart of the first week of practice is outlined in Chart 2. During the first week we like to practice five mornings and hold five 45-minute meetings either before the afternoon practice or in the evening immediately after dinner. On the morning practices we spend about 1 hour and 45 minutes on the field, a period given largely to the learning of plays, the development of the kicking game, and the practice of various ball fundamentals by the specialists. Pass offense and defense are also stressed in the morning workout. The afternoon workouts are somewhat heavier and stress is placed upon group work and the development of individual fundamentals. More contact is used both in individual and team drills in the afternoon workout.

During the second week of intensive early-season practice, we will generally have three morning practices. I have always felt that eight double practice days are about the maximum that can be assimilated by a squad in the first two weeks of practice. The number of squad meetings will also be cut from five to four. During the second week the tempo of the practices should pick up a bit, with greater emphasis on the pass game and upon the development of team offense. Conditioning work such as sprints and covering punts will continue, as will group work and individual development. During the second week team scrimmages of various kinds will take place, culminating in a game scrimmage on Saturday.

The third week of practice will consist of single practice sessions only, although they will continue to be about 2 hours and 15 minutes in duration—a little longer than during the regular season. A final scrimmage will be held on Wednesday and then practices

CHART 1: FIRST WEEK OF FALL PRACTICE—MORNING PRACTICE

Time	Monday	Tuesday	Wednesday	Thursday	Friday	Saturday
9:45 Early group	Punters Passers	Ends and backs and two centers		Punters Pass group	Punters Pass group	Punters Pass game
10:15	Pass receiving Entire squad Group work—Stance and starts	*Group work* Line—Block vs. dummies Ends—Stance, pass receiving Backs—Stance Start Ball handling	11 A.M.—Lecture: The Kicking Game No practice on field	*Group work* Line—Block 1 on 1 dummies Ends—Block vs. dummies Defensive charge Backs—Starts Ball handling	*Group work* Line—Block 1 on 1 Ends—Block vs. tackle and linebacker Backs—Starts Block vs. dummies	*Group work* Line—Block Pass protection Backs and ends— Pass patterns Pass defense
11:00	*Form teams* Set up the offense formation Learn 2 plays	*Form teams* Add 2 running plays and 2 passes		*Form teams* Add 2 plays 2 passes Set up punt formation	*Form teams* Add 2 plays 2 passes Punt—Cover and return	*Form teams* Add 2 plays Punt—Cover and return
11:45	End morning practice	End morning practice		End morning practice	End morning practice	End morning practice
Lecture 1:45 or 7:00 P.M. (45 min.)	The formation 4 basic plays (on blackboard)	Adjustment to defense 2 running plays 2 passes	5 running plays 2 passes	2 running plays 4 passes	The defensive plan	(No lecture)

CHART 2: FIRST WEEK OF FALL PRACTICE—AFTERNOON PRACTICE

Time	Monday	Tuesday	Wednesday	Thursday	Friday	Saturday
2:45 Early group	Centers and quarterbacks	C. and q.b.	C. and q.b.	Punters Place kickers Kickoff men	C. and q.b. Pass group	1:30—C. and q.b. Pass group
3:15	*Group work* Line—Stance, Start Pull Ends—Bl. vs. dummies Backs—Starts Ball handling	*Group work* Line—Live blocking Ends—Block vs. tackles Backs—Starts, block vs. dummies	*Group work* Line—Pull, live blocking Ends—Pass receiving Block vs. line-backers Backs—Ball handling Live blocking	*Group work* Line—Block 1 on 1 Runner, Interferer Tackler Ends—Defense vs. backs Block vs. tackle Backs—Starts Block vs. ends	Cover punts Pass scrimmage	2:00— *Form teams* Step plays Review offense Interference scrimmage
4:00	*Cover punts*	Sprints by position	Cover punts	Line scrimmage Interference scrimmage	Punt—Protection Cover Return	Line scrimmage Pass scrimmage
4:25	*Form teams* Add 2 plays Wind sprints In at 5:30	*Form teams* Review all plays Signal drill In at 5:30	*Form teams* Add 1 play—2 passes Review offense Wind sprints In at 5:30	5:00 Form teams Signal drill Team starts In at 5:30	2-min. scrimmage In at 5:30	In at 5 P.M.

will be shortened considerably on Thursday and Friday in preparation for the opening game on Saturday.

Once the playing season has started and classes have begun, less practice time will be available. During the regular season we spend approximately 8½ hours on the field Monday through Friday in preparation for the game on Saturday. Monday practices are considerably shortened, especially for the men who have played the major portion of the game on the previous Saturday. Generally such players will work in sweat suits, running new plays for use against next Saturday's opponent, and reviewing mistakes made in the previous Saturday's game. Other players who did not see much action in the game will very likely scrimmage. The heavy work of the week is done Tuesday and Wednesday, with Thursday devoted to a final review of the offense, the passing game, and the kicking game. Friday will be a light workout in sweat suits of about 45 minutes' duration. A typical midseason schedule is illustrated in Chart 3 below.

SEASONAL PLANNING AND STAFF MEETINGS

A football team should operate under three practice plans—a seasonal plan, a weekly plan, and a daily plan. The seasonal plan will naturally be a rather general one. Each football team usually has two or three rivals for whom they like to be at a peak. This fact should enter into the seasonal plan and every effort should be made to see that the team is thoroughly prepared for those two or three key games. The defensive and offensive plans must be well developed for each game, and some variation is probably desirable in those plans for peak games. The weekly plan will be worked out in considerable detail. It should take into account mistakes made in the previous game, and allow practice time to correct them. The daily plan will be a thoroughly detailed outline, carefully timed. The weather, or a lag in team development may cause a modification of the weekly plan which can be corrected in considering the workout for the next day. The full coaching staff should thoroughly

CHART 3: VARSITY—BASIC WEEKLY PRACTICE SCHEDULE

October, 19–

	Monday	Tuesday	Wednesday	Thursday	Friday
3:45–4:10 Early groups	Place kickers— Kickoff Pass group (informal)	Tackles Pass group Punters	Guards Pass group C and q.b.	Place kickers— Kickoff Punters	Organize at 4:20
Practice organized at 4:10	Set up offensive plan for Saturday Sweat suit group run plays (30 min.)	Group work (40 min.) Line Ends Backs	Group work (30 min.) Line Ends Backs	Form teams at 4:10	Line ⎫ Backs ⎬ starts (10 min.)
	Remainder of squad—Group work (30 min.), emphasis on individual development	Set up defensive plan for Saturday Team B—Defense vs. opponent Teams A and C—offense	Continue defensive work A and C—offense B—defense	Review punt game— Protection Cover Return	Review place kick and Kickoff return
	Scrimmage	B and A—switch	B and C—switch	Pass game— Review protection and patterns for Saturday	Run plays (15 min.)
		Short pickup period to cover special situations or team weaknesses	Open period to be filled as needed	Goal-line offense and defense	
		Team starts In at 6:10	In at 6:10	In at 5:55	

CHART 4: DAILY PRACTICE SCHEDULE

TUESDAY (Week of third game on the schedule)

3:45—*Early group*

Guards—Block vs. ends   Punters and centers—Warm up
        Lead through hole   Kick for
                                            out-of-
                                            bounds

4:10—Call squad together—announcements, etc. Calisthenics

4:20—*Group work* (35 Min.)

Line —Runner-interferer-tackler drills (Diagram 58)
        (15 min.)
        Pass protection

Ends —Block vs. tackles (15 min.)
        Join line in pass-protection drill

Backs—Starts
        Block vs. defensive ends (Diagram 58)

4:55—Call squad together

Explanation of defensive plan for Saturday

Show opponent's formations—identify key players—mention favorite plays and pass patterns

Defensive team line-up in various defenses planned for Saturday

5:05—Defensive team work against opponent's plays and passes as run by scout team and skeleton pass group (Diagram 61)

Two offensive teams dummy scrimmage against team using defense which opponent might use (Diagram 61)

During last 12 min., defensive team switch with either offensive team; the latter will then work on defense

5:45—Two teams alternate on offense vs. one defensive team—all three teams rotate

Pass Protection—full blocking (8 min.)

Punt Protection—full blocking; no tackling of receiver (12 min.)

6:05—All teams three good starts—each team on in to the showers after completing three satisfactory starts.

discuss the daily plan so that each man understands when he goes on the field what he is to teach, how he is to teach it, how long he will have, and the staff members and players with whom he will be working.

A football staff will spend a surprising amount of time in preparation for each individual practice. During the so-called off-season, frequent meetings will be held to discuss any change in plans for the forthcoming season. A considerable amount of time will be spent in reviewing movies of the past season. Just before the start of each season, spring and fall, an intensive series of meetings will be held to review and discuss the teaching of all fundamentals of the game. During the regular playing season in the fall, a minimum of 2½ hours will be spent in staff meetings for each hour that is spent in coaching on the field. Practice plans will be discussed very thoroughly, movies will be studied, scout reports will be heard and discussed, and the defensive and offensive plans to be used against each opponent will be considered very carefully by the entire staff.

Each staff will vary widely in the number of meetings and time spent in meetings, but the following schedule of staff meetings, which is a rough approximation of a midseason week at California last fall, might be illustrative.

SUNDAY

5:30 P.M. *to 12:00.* Three to four hours are spent in a careful study of movies of the game of the previous day. After a discussion of the movies and a discussion of team personnel, the coach, who has been scouting the next week's opponent, makes his report. The offensive plan for use against the opponent is discussed and then set up in its final form.

MONDAY

2:30 P.M. *to 3:30.* Discussion and assignment of duties to staff for Monday workout.

8:00 P.M. *to 12:00.* Further discussion of scout report after which the defensive plan for the week is set up.

TUESDAY

1:30 P.M. *to 3:30.* Thorough discussion of practice plan, and assignment of duties for the practice. In case the defensive plan does not work out well on the practice field, a further staff meeting is held at 8:00 P.M. Tuesday night.

WEDNESDAY AND THURSDAY

2:00 P.M. *to 3:30.* Discussion of the kicking game, and any modification of pass patterns, general offensive plan, or general defensive plan which may be made necessary by developments during the week. Discussion of the daily practice plan and the assignment of duties for the practice field.

FRIDAY

3:00 P.M. A very short discussion of the afternoon's practice plan.

The time spent in staff meetings each week during the season is largely unappreciated by the general public. For a staff to go on the practice field with only a vague idea of what is to be accomplished would waste a great portion of the time and effort of the players and coaches alike, and also would result in some important point of preparation for Saturday's game being overlooked. All members of the staff must be given a free opportunity to express opinions and make suggestions regarding the team offensive and defensive plans, as well as the practice schedule. In a strong staff, differences of opinion will inevitably result. These differences should be talked through thoroughly, a decision arrived at, and all loose ends tied together in the staff meeting. When the coaching staff steps onto the field, they must be entirely in accord; then each man can effectively teach his part of the general plan.

The planning sessions of a staff of two or three men, handling a small squad, are equally important. Even if one man is coaching a squad entirely by himself, it is very important that he set aside a few minutes before practice to organize his thoughts and plan how he can most effectively use the time of his players and himself in the practice period available to him.

STAFF PROCEDURE—DAY OF GAME

The function of a coaching staff on game day is to give all possible help, support, and encouragement to the men who are playing the game. The coaches cannot play the game for the players. An attempt to over-control the game from the bench is undesirable. If all decisions, even minor ones, are made from the bench, such procedure tends to atrophy the initiative of the players and to remove some of the zest from the game. The experience and judgment of the coaching staff should be a reservoir upon which the players may draw as needed during the game.

Perhaps the best way to discuss staff procedure on game day would be to follow in sequence a typical game day from the time the players report to the dressing room at the stadium until they leave after the game.

The squad that is to suit up for the game will report to the dressing room about 1½ hours before game time (twelve-thirty if it is to be a two o'clock game). Most of the routine taping of ankles, etc., will have been done by the training staff shortly after breakfast, but there will still be thigh guards to tape on, as well as other special taping and adjustment of pads for specific individuals.

12:40—The defensive signal callers and linebackers will meet with the defensive coach and head coach in front of the blackboard. A final review of the defensive plan will be gone over carefully, including defense against the punt formation and the kicking game.

12:50—The offensive plan will be covered with the quarterbacks with emphasis placed on the running plays and passes to be stressed in the early part of the game. The defensive personnel of the opponents will be discussed very briefly, as well as defensive patterns that they have used in previous games and might use today. However, the quarterbacks must be warned that all information available is good only until 2 o'clock when the game starts. The opponents might come up with an entirely different defense.

1:05—The entire squad is assembled and the head coach first reviews the defensive plan with particular reminders regarding favorite plays and pass patterns of the opponents, and certain of the opponents' players who must be watched carefully on specific plays. The punt game is covered briefly as it pertains to the particular opponent. The offensive plan is then covered, with a reminder as to the plays to be stressed early, and a warning to be alert for any change in the opponents' defensive plan.

1:20—The starting line-ups will be announced for both the offensive and defensive units, and the team will start toward the field for a warm-up period. During this period each coach will be assigned to one group of men to make sure that they are thoroughly warmed up in preparation for the game. One coach might watch the centers and punters and punt receivers, another might watch the place kickers and kickoff men, another might watch the passers and the receivers, another might watch the linemen as they take starts and practice pulling out. Each player knows the warm-up procedure thoroughly, and if there are only one or two coaches available a senior player might take charge of a group for the warm-up. After all players, including the specialty men, have had a chance for a brief workout, the squad will return to the dressing room. The entire warm-up procedure will take about 15 minutes.

Before returning to the field for the game, the head coach will call the squad together and talk briefly with them, reminding them of their opportunities and responsibilities in the game that afternoon, and giving them all possible encouragement and support for the contest ahead. The day of the inspired locker room oration has long since passed. If a team is not ready for the game at 1:45, nothing that happens between then and the opening kickoff can prepare them. Good preparation comes from long hours of hard work on the practice field, and a thorough knowledge of the game plan. The squad will leave the dressing room in plenty of time to reach the field at least 3 minutes before the opening kickoff. If necessary the captain or co-captains who will meet with the officials for the flip of the coin, will leave a minute or two earlier.

2:00—The game begins.

With the present liberal substitution rules it is very important to have the bench well organized so that a minimum of confusion will occur during the game. Each player should have a definite place to sit on the bench, so that he can be located quickly to enter the game. One way of accomplishing this would be to have the offensive signal callers seated immediately to the left of the coach. Just beyond them should be either the offensive or defensive team, whichever was not in the ball game at the moment. And still further beyond them to the left, should be the additional backfield men. To the coach's right might be the defensive signal callers and centers and beyond them the linemen who are not at the moment in the game with either the offensive or defensive unit. Sometimes it is a good idea to have the ends seated together.

The coach in charge of the bench will have a busy afternoon, and needs all the help he can get. In making substitutions, it will avoid confusion if, when the offensive team comes off the field, any changes that are to be made in the make-up of the offensive unit for the next sequence are made immediately or as soon as possible after they come off the field. The same would be true of changes made in the defensive unit. In that way a sudden change of the ball would not cause confusion and delay on the bench, and the new men to go in with their respective unit will have a chance to sit with the members of the offensive or defensive team and find out how things were going in the ball game.

The coach in charge of substitutions should have his order of substitution for each position, offense and defense, carefully planned out and written down. Thus, in the heat of the game, he will neither forget a player or be delayed in making the substitution. Any players who are to go in automatically in special situations, such as a punter or a center on a kicking situation, or a center, holder, place kicker, or blocker on a point after touchdown, should be so informed, and must take the responsibility of being ready to go in instantly when the occasion arises, without delaying the game.

The bench is probably the worst spot in the stadium from which to see a football game. The players and coaches on the bench are generally seated at least 15 or 20 feet from the side line in a low position with very little perspective. Their angle of vision is such that the bodies of the players nearest them cut off the action which is happening on the other side of the line. The coach on the bench, therefore, needs all possible help. He may ask players not in the game to concentrate on one man each, and he will check with the offensive and defensive units when they come out each time. But he will rely far more on the telephone connecting him with an observer in the press box. In our games at California we always have Wes Fry, our backfield coach, in the press box as an observer to give us information as to opponents' defenses and other pertinent facts upon which any modification in the plan of attack must be based. The observer in the press box with field glasses has a good perspective since he is looking down upon the field of play, and he is in an ideal position to see exactly what goes on. Generally, we will have two or possibly three men in the press box, with perhaps one man watching our defense very carefully, and, if possible, a third man to help either the offensive or defensive spotters and to keep statistics. Sometimes it is not feasible to have three observers in the press box, but at least one observer is essential to get the proper information to the bench. If enough coaches or observers are available, it is sometimes helpful to have one stationed in one end zone with a telephone to either the press box or the bench to give information on line spacing, or to pick up any angle charging on the part of the defense.

One of our toughest games in 1950 was with Joe Kuharich's

strong University of San Francisco team. The game was played in a pouring rain and the middle of the field was a quagmire, with water standing in big puddles. Late in the third quarter, with the score tied 7–7 and neither team able to gain consistently, we intercepted a pass on S.F.'s side of the 50-yard line. After several plays and our one completed pass of the day, we had the ball on S.F.'s 7-yard line near the right-hand side line in one of the few fairly firm spots remaining on the field.

Wes Fry in the press box had noticed that when California stationed a flanker to the wide side of the field, the S.F. defense moved out toward the middle of the field, leaving the short side toward the side line rather thinly guarded. He suggested that we put a flanker to our left and then run a play wide toward the side line with our right end blocking the S.F. left end. These instructions were sent in and everything worked out perfectly. Our right end was able to block the S.F. end, and Jim Monachino, behind the blocking of Johnny Olszewski, swung around S.F.'s left end and drove into the end zone for the winning touchdown.

The use of the phone between the press box and the bench must be carefully planned. If possible, an assistant coach on the bench should handle the phone so that he can accumulate pertinent information and then pass it on to the head coach or whoever is making substitutions. In the absence of an assistant coach available to handle the phone, sometimes a player, preferably a quarterback, or a manager may be able to perform this duty. The head coach will be frequently talking to the observer in the press box in order to ask questions as to the opponent's defense, where the opponent is gaining if they have the ball, and other significant information. Facts and data should be carefully screened by the man handling the phone. Background material should be allowed to accumulate, but emergency information, such as a defensive deficiency if the opponents have the ball, should be passed on immediately.

The platoon system provides unusual opportunities for adjustment of the game plan, either offensively or defensively, as the game proceeds. If, for example, the opponents are presenting an unusual defense which might call for one or two changes in blocking assignments, those changes can be given to the entire offensive unit while they are on the bench during the period in which the team is on defense. The quarterback can also be given information about the opponent's defense which he may not be aware of on the field. Similarly the defensive unit, when they are on the bench while the team is on offense, may be given information regarding a change in defensive emphasis to meet something new or unexpected that the opponents are showing in their attack. In general the offensive quarterback will be given suggestions as to the particular type of play and particular area of the opponents that seems to be open. In almost every game, in addition, there will occur once or twice a situation which calls for a specific play immediately before the opponents can change their defense. Two or three times in the afternoon, a "must" situation will arise in which the quarterback is bound to follow immediately the explicit instructions from the bench. Most of the time, however, a well-trained quarterback who understands the defensive tactics of the opponents will do better if the responsibility of calling the individual play rests upon him.

At half time, the players must be urged to rest and relax completely for the first 5 minutes after they reach the dressing room. During this period the coaches will consult and evaluate very rapidly the happenings of the first half. It may be that the opponent's defense has begun to settle into a pattern and a change in the general offensive plan may be indicated. Perhaps certain defenses used by our team may have been rather ineffective. Other defensive patterns will have to be emphasized during the second half. Toward the end of the rest period, the head coach and offensive coach will consult briefly with the quarterbacks with suggestions as to any change in the plan of attack. The head coach and the defensive coach will then check with the defensive signal callers on any changes. Then the entire squad will be alerted to any offensive or defensive changes in the general game plan and also to any developments which need attention in the kicking game. The half time period is far too short for extensive indulgence in verbal pyrotechnics. The dressing-room activities must be very well organized, for a great deal must be accomplished in all too short a time. Someone should be assigned to warn the coaches 5 minutes before the start of the second half so that the team can return to the field in plenty of time.

When the team returns to the dressing room after a hard-fought game, they are still very much in the spirit of the contest. It is generally a good idea to keep everyone out of the dressing room for a few minutes after the game. This gives the coaches a chance to have a word with each boy, and perhaps a few brief announcements or observations for the entire squad. If the game has been won, an expression of appreciation is very much in order, together with a warning that the season is not over and another tough game looms next Saturday. If a hard-fought game has been lost, a word of encouragement tempered with regret will be helpful. Any technical evaluation of the game is very much out of place at this time. It is always well to remind the squad to check very carefully with the doctor and trainers on any possible injury, no matter how slight, which might have been overlooked in the heat of the contest. It is human nature to enjoy winning and to hate to lose, and no player ever need be ashamed of these very natural emotions. If he can rejoice in winning without crowing about it or running down his opponent, and if he can feel badly about losing without attempting to alibi or blame someone else, then he is achieving an emotional stability and maturity which will be a lifelong asset.

PLANNING FOR A LARGE SQUAD

The practice plan for a large squad of seventy to ninety men with five to eight coaches will be a complex one. Naturally some players will be more experienced and farther along in the process of development than others. The experienced players must not be held down to the pace of those less developed, but must be brought along as rapidly as possible. Neither must the younger players be neglected. To accomplish both objectives will require considerable ingenuity. In group work the younger players can work with advantage under a separate coach and yet be a part of the same general setup, say a line drill, where they can watch the more advanced players and yet be going through the same drills themselves. As the younger men develop they can be tested against the more experienced players and an accurate measurement of their progress be thus obtained. In team development the younger players can work against the more experienced men. Diagram 61, for example, illustrates a possible practice field setup for a squad of seventy or eighty men. In Diagram 61*A,* two experienced teams are working offense against a team that is learning to play defense. The defensive team might well employ the defensive pattern of the opponents for the following Saturday. In Diagram 61*B* the defensive team is working against a full team of younger players who are learning to play offense. Alternating with the full offensive team will be a skeleton pass group which will specialize in putting on the pass patterns of the opponent to be met next Saturday. Extra men can be used to alternate in either setup; for example, an extra offensive backfield or two or three extra offensive linemen might alternate in 61*A* and several extra defensive backs or linemen might take their turn on the defense in 61*B*.

One of the great problems in dealing with a large squad is to coordinate the various groups and drills so that each group will finish its work at about the same time. Thus, no group is being hurried or cut short on a vital point, and no group is being forced to prolong its workout to accommodate a slower group.

THE SMALL SQUAD

A squad of thirty to forty men with two coaches can follow most of these basic principles. In group work, one coach can take the linemen, while the other coach can take the backfield men. The ends might work one time with the line on blocking and another time with the backs on defense against backfield blocking, or as part of the pass pattern. With two teams available, plus alternates, the team development might come a little slower than with a large squad, since in all probability a number of the players will have to play on both offense and defense.

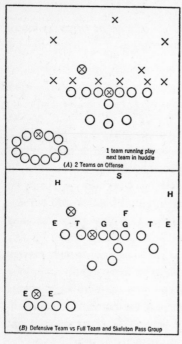

DIAGRAM 61
Team drills

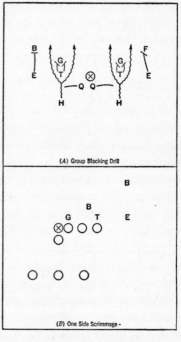

DIAGRAM 62
Practice drill for small squad

A small squad of barely two teams or less, coached by one man, will present some problems. Basic blocking and tackling drills might be executed by the entire group as a unit, or drills could be devised such as 62A. In this drill the backs practice receiving the ball from the quarterbacks and driving into the line behind the block of the tackles. The defensive guards can work against the tackles and extra backs can work as linebackers on defense against the block of the ends. Diagram 62B illustrates a "one-side" scrimmage that could be used both for offensive and defensive development. The right side of the line might work on offense against the left side on defense, and then the left side take the offense and run the plays in their area while the right side of the line took over the defensive duties.

Each squad will present its own problems in the organization of practice, but careful thought by the coaching staff in laying out each day's work can pay great dividends.

SCOUTING

It is not our purpose to investigate in great detail the subject of scouting nor to present a complicated scouting form. Scouting is very much a part of the game of football, and is used almost universally by all teams, college, high school, and professional. If a member of the coaching staff has had the opportunity of seeing an opponent play, a much more intelligent plan of attack and defense can be worked out to meet that opponent. With a large coaching staff, three or four of the staff may have scouting duties on any given Saturday, and additional scouts in the form of former players or alumni may also be active. Scouting is occasionally overdone and many conferences have rules which limit the number of scouts that can see a prospective opponent and the number of games in which a prospective opponent may be scouted. Scouting an opponent in several games instead of just one is distinctly helpful.

An alert, experienced scout can be a tremendous asset to his team. An inexperienced scout may not be too helpful. I recall Ike Armstrong (now athletic director at Minnesota) telling me that when he first went to Utah he was very shorthanded and he sent his football manager to scout the opponent for the following Saturday. The football manager was very inexperienced and did his best, but when he came back, the only information he could give to Ike was that the right guard was cross-eyed. Incidentally, the manager turned his talents in other directions after graduation, and is now the president of one of the country's leading universities.

A scout can bring back too much detail. I like to tell our scouts at California that they have a very easy task. They have to answer only three questions: 1. "How can we win?" 2. "Where can we gain?" 3. "What and whom must we stop?" We ask our scout to make a very brief summary answering these three questions on page one of the scout report.

We also ask our scout to prepare a form in which he will attempt to give specific information on the following:

Opponent's personnel: Offense and defense lineups, jersey numbers, approximate weights, and whatever information about each man he feels may be helpful.

Opponent's punt game: Formation, coverage, return.

Accurate diagrams of all offensive formations, giving the exact spacing and jersey numbers of players.

Offense: Favorite running plays based on effectiveness and use. Other dangerous running plays, favorite pass patterns with notes on receivers, and ability of passers. Other dangerous pass patterns.

Defenses used by opponent, listed in order of frequency of use and effectiveness.

There will be many other items and additional details that the scout will bring back. We naturally want to know as much as we can about the type of play an opponent likes to use in various situations, such as in scoring territory, near the side line, or when he must go for big yardage. We are also interested in knowing how other teams have gained against our prospective opponent and what defensive plans have bothered them in the past. Sometimes a statistical study will help make clear a pattern in their offense or defense that might otherwise be missed. The scout should be a man who is familiar with the personnel and the offensive and defensive plans of his own team, so that he can make practical and specific suggestions. The considered judgment of an experienced scout will be of more value than a mass of unrelated details, and a

good scout may easily be the difference between his team's winning
and losing the ball game.

L. W. "Litz" Rusness turned in many fine scouting perform-
ances for Northwestern during my twelve years there. Litz seemed
to do a particularly good job on the University of Minnesota, and
his report invariably was very helpful in planning our offense and
defense for the great series of games between those two schools.

At California, "Nibs" Price and "Eggs" Manske do a very fine
job of scouting for us. In 1947 Eggs brought back a very careful
analysis of the Wisconsin team. He told us that the Wisconsin halfbacks, and particularly the right halfback, were fine tacklers against
running plays but came up too rapidly on pass plays. We planned
several pass maneuvers against the Wisconsin right halfback which
worked out very successfully indeed. Although Wisconsin made
more first downs than California, we completed three passes for
touchdowns behind the Wisconsin right halfback, which contributed materially to the California's 48–7 victory.

QUARTERBACK TRAINING AND STRATEGY

The player who is called upon to select the plays for his team
and direct the offense on the field inevitably must accept a heavy
burden of responsibility. He must be a real leader with a sound
general knowledge of football, and a very thorough and specialized
knowledge of the offense of his own team. However, it has always
seemed to me that the quarterback must accept an unfair burden
placed upon him by most spectators. The team makes the quarterback far more than the quarterback makes the team. If the team is
blocking sharply and timing their plays well, almost any sound
play will work; if the team is not doing a good job on the fundamentals of the game, like blocking and timing, the best quarterback in
the country will look bad because nothing that he will call will have
a fair chance of succeeding. The quarterback, however, can be
helped, both by the coaching staff in giving suggestions during a
game, and in receiving training during the season in evaluating

various situations that he will meet on the field. The quarterback must not be too mechanical nor too rigidly confined by a great many hard and fast rules. He must use his eyes and think in terms of living men rather than words or diagrams on a sheet of paper.

Playing experience is a great asset to any quarterback. All quarterbacks will make mistakes of judgment at times. It is a part of the learning process and the quarterback should have the responsibility of directing a team under game conditions as often as possible.

Our California quarterback in 1950, Jim Marinos, was a senior without one minute of varsity playing experience. He had, however, played a great deal with the Rambler squad in the two previous seasons and had had the opportunity of getting some of the inevitable mistakes of the young quarterback out of his system and developing a reasonably good football background. Jim was a good ball handler and enjoyed the confidence of his teammates. That confidence was manifested when his teammates selected him as game captain in our fourth game of the season—a crucial contest against U.S.C.—and he justified that confidence by his steady play throughout the remainder of the season.

We do not use a hard and fast set of rules for the guidance of the quarterback, but the following are a few basic suggestions that a young quarterback might find helpful:

1. *A Good Field General Is a Real Leader*. You must command the respect and confidence of your teammates. If the other ten men believe in you, they will block and run that much harder and make your task easier. You must know your offense thoroughly—not every assignment, but the essential blocks and the type and purpose of each running play and pass. Think football off the field as well as during practice and games.

2. *Use Your Eyes on the Field and on the Bench*. Know how the defense is lined up; don't guess. Know where each linebacker and halfback is stationed and how he moves up. See how the defense reacts to motion or a flanker. Get information from your team-

mates at time out or between plays (never in the huddle). Find out how the defensive guards, tackles, and ends are charging.

3. *Keep the Pressure on the Defense Constantly.* Fifty-eight minutes is not enough. Don't get anxious if the score, the wind, or the breaks are against you. Force your opponent to make the mistakes.

4. *Mechanics.* Look over defense and plan your next play until the huddle has formed. Step into the corner of the huddle next to the left halfback and talk just loud enough for the right end to hear. Give your play number, then pause, starting cadence, pause again, "Hike," and everyone moves to the line.

Deliver your starting cadence in a loud staccato voice. Remember you have only 25 seconds to put the ball in play from the time the referee walks away from it at the end of the previous down. Save time by making the huddle form quickly. Move briskly and with decision, but make sure everyone has the play and starting number before you break the huddle.

You must practice your center pass, ball handling, and footwork until all are automatic and do not require thought in a game.

5. *Kicking.* Nothing keeps the pressure on your opponents like a sound kicking game.

You will average about five to nine kicks in a tough ball game.

Inside your 10-yard line, get the ball out as soon as possible (very few exceptions).

From mid-field on, place your kicks. Instruct your punter to shoot for the coffin corner.

Don't lose the ball on downs outside of your opponent's 30.

On fourth down outside your opponent's 30, kick unless behind with less than 5 minutes to play.

6. *Choice of Plays.* In a normal game, you have about sixty-five chances to advance the ball through running plays or passes. You will come into possession of the ball about thirteen times during the game, one or two of which are liable to be so deep in your territory that you will have to kick out immediately. Therefore,

you must not waste time and energy attacking the strong spots in the defense. Find where the defense is weak as to personnel, spacing, or faulty adjustment to man-in-motion. Use running plays and passes which hit those spots. When defense adjusts to meet your attack, hit the new weaknesses. Attack the blind side of the lineman who commits himself, and pass in the territory of a back who rushes up to stop running plays. Choice of play is important, but execution is even more so. A poor play choice that you and the team have confidence in will gain more than the ideal play.

Never forget the score, never lose track of the time.

Don't use short-yardage plays or short passes when you need long yardage for first down.

Don't use long-yardage plays or delayed plays when you have short yardage to go (3 yards or less).

Shoot for a touchdown on the first two plays of a series. Use a play that should get 5 yards and has a good chance to go all the way. Drive for first down on the third-down play. You must make good yardage on that first play or you are in the hole.

Study the situation in front of you, then choose a play that is designed for that situation or that defense. Then call the play number. Don't think in numbers.

Know who made the tackle on the last play. You may find a "guesser" on the other team. Such a man makes costly mistakes of which you must take advantage.

When you find a weakness, take full advantage of it. Keep repeating plays that are gaining this Saturday, not last Saturday or two weeks ago, but vary them. Don't let your opponents anticipate correctly.

7. *Pass Game. Don't* throw passes in territory of the best pass defender.

Don't let a pass be intercepted. If opponents intercept one out of six or seven of your passes, they will probably beat you on that factor alone. If the receiver is covered, take your loss or overthrow so that no interception is possible. Each interception is worth at least 40 yards to your opponents.

Don't use short passes when you are ahead or have the game under control.

Pass to a tall end covered by a short back. Pass to a fast receiver covered by a slow defender. Second down and one or two to go is a fine spot for a pass or play which may go all the way.

In a pinch, pass to your most reliable receiver.

Pass when the defense is not expecting it. Don't get in a rut and wait until third down and 8 yards to go.

Use trap plays occasionally in a passing situation. You will find the line rushing and the backs playing deeper. Your sweeps are also good in this situation if the ends are rushing hard.

8. *Scoring Territory.* Inside your opponent's 20-yard line urge your team on. Caution the team against off-side. In close, use quick hitting plays—not delayed plays. Don't hesitate to go wide if the defense is playing close.

A quarterback is just an ordinary fellow who knows the mechanics of his position and can use common sense.

CHAPTER 15 THE FUNCTION OF
THE COACH

THE coach has come to occupy a unique and peculiar position in our American educational system. Because of great public interest in sports, most colleges, universities, and high schools find themselves willingly or unwillingly in the entertainment business. This applies to a varying extent to several different sports, but on a countrywide basis it has particular application to football. Because of intense public interest in football, a coach is no longer a seasonal instructor on the athletic field, if indeed he ever was. More and more is expected of the coach in the way of off-field and out-of-season activities. He must be not only an athletic instructor, a counsellor of students, a practical public relations man, an acceptable public speaker, but in many cases a proselyter (in the widest and best sense of the term) and, on occasion, an employment manager.

First and foremost, a coach is expected to win slightly more than his share of the contests in which his team engages. The American public enjoys watching a good contest, and it is human nature to want your team to win. The fact that on any given Saturday afternoon only 50 per cent of the teams can win while the other 50 per cent must lose puts considerable pressure on the coach, and has presented problems of rapidly increasing complexity to educational institutions. The pressure to win is a hard, realistic fact which must be faced and accepted by anyone who chooses his livelihood in the field of sports.

Even in the field of high-school coaching, where in theory the coach is a teacher and hired on the same basis as any other teacher, that pressure is not absent. No educational institution which supports a football team is entirely free of the compulsion to win, although the pressure is much greater at some institutions than at others. It is even more true today than when Bob Zupke first said it —"A coach is responsible to an irresponsible public." Competition, of course, is an accepted fact of our American way of life. The lawyer is expected to win his case. The salesman is expected to outsell his competitors. But in very few fields is there as much public interest in the outcome of the contest; nor does it take place in the presence of so many thousands of interested and partisan spectators.

It has always seemed to me that one of the most important, but unlisted, functions of a coach is to act as a buffer between the educational process and the entertainment demands of the public. The game of football has many intrinsic values; that is why football and other games are sponsored by educational institutions. Football must be taught as a game and played as a game, and the coach must absorb whatever outside pressures there are, so that the game may be played for the enjoyment of the players and their fellow students.

A coach must be prepared to take criticism—even at times uninformed and unfair criticism. He may not like it or feel that he deserves it, but he must accept criticism as an integral part of coaching and must not waver in his determination to see that football is maintained as a game primarily for the benefit of the participants. After the Michigan-California Rose Bowl game on New Year's Day, 1951, I recall one newspaper headline which stated, "Ortmann wins—Waldorf loses." Ortmann was the Michigan left halfback who played a very fine game that afternoon. When the player receives the credit and the coach the blame, such procedure is in line with the latter's natural responsibilities. The reverse would be unthinkable.

In recent years, many fine, well-trained young men have gone into coaching as a profession. It is to be hoped that some measures can be taken to give a greater stability to coaching. Some sincere, though thus far ineffectual, efforts have been made by the various athletic conferences and the National Collegiate Athletic Association in that direction. At the end of four years at the University of California, I was the oldest coach in the Pacific Coast Conference in point of service. Of the ten head football coaches at member institutions when I came to California in 1947, not a single one is now in the conference. Two of the 1947 head coaches are coaching outside of the conference, and the rest have turned to other and in most cases more profitable activities. The rapid turnover in football coaches is by no means confined to the Pacific Coast Conference. But the situation illustrates rather concretely the present lack of stability in the coaching profession. Whatever steps have been made toward tenure and reasonable security have been made by only a few individual institutions.

Football coaches are individualists who work in a highly competitive field. For the coaches of my generation who have been at it for twenty-five years or more and who have developed a sort of protective scar-tissue, security is not too important. For the young coaches, who have been coaching three or four years and are not yet sure about their lifetime plans, security is not yet an issue. But for the many fine young men between the ages of thirty and forty, who have been coaching long enough to want to go into it on a permanent basis, and who have had a chance to demonstrate ability in the coaching field, it is to be hoped that some greater stability may be achieved.

A COACH IS BASICALLY A TEACHER

Most men start coaching football because they have played and enjoyed the game, and because they enjoy working with boys and young men. In spite of whatever pressures there may be connected with it, coaching brings many rich rewards, one of which is the association with young men and the pleasure of watching them develop. A coach is fundamentally a teacher. It was H. L. Mencken who said of the teaching process:

> It consists of a deep belief in the interest and importance of the thing taught; a concern about it, amounting to a kind of passion. A man who knows a subject thoroughly, a man so soaked in it that he eats it, sleeps it and dreams it, this man can almost always teach it with success. That is because there is enthusiasm in him, and because enthusiasm is as contagious as fear or the barber's itch. An enthusiast is willing to go to any trouble to impart the glad news bubbling within. He thinks that it is important and valuable for everyone to know. Given the slightest glow of interest and a pupil to start with, he will fan that glow to a flame. He drags his best pupils along as fast as they can go, and he is so full of the thing that he never tires of expounding its elements to the dullest.

Most coaches feel that kind of enthusiasm. They are full of football; they eat it, sleep it, talk it—and love to teach it.

A football coach should be an ideal teacher of his subject because of natural enthusiasm and because of the fact that he is full of the subject. Not only that, but the subject he is teaching coincides with the natural interest of most young men. Plato once said that the natural interest of boys up to the age of twenty-five was in sports and games. A coach on the football field has, therefore, some advantages over the teacher in the classroom or the laboratory, because his pupils have a natural and active interest in the game being taught.

But the coach must realize that enthusiasm on both the part of the teacher and the player is not enough. He must strive constantly to improve his teaching methods. He must plan his work carefully. He must keep the instruction simple. He should pick out the important points and stress them, and he must not try to teach too much at one time. After all, both the team and himself are judged not by what he knows, but by what he is able to impart to his teams.

He must be thorough, but must be careful not to overcoach. He must let the team know that he expects a high level of performance, but not an unreasonable one, and he must constantly encourage them to reach that level. He must vary his practice plan to avoid monotony and maintain interest. Otherwise, he will find that the players have not absorbed as much of the instruction as he had wished. Finally, he must constantly strive to improve the effectiveness of his teaching methods.

RELATIONSHIP WITH SQUAD

No one should enter coaching who does not enjoy working with young men. Each squad is slightly different than the one before, and yet basically the same. The atmosphere of the practice field should be relaxed, but never to the point of carelessness nor pointless horseplay. There may be times and places when something approaching military discipline might be necessary, but I have always preferred an easy, informal spirit on the field. I enjoy an occasional wisecrack, and feel that a team practices best in a businesslike but relaxed atmosphere.

The relationship of coach and player by its very nature should be a very close one, both on and off the field. Most coaches are sincerely interested in their players, not only as athletes on the field, but as students off the field. It is a most natural thing for a player to feel free to bring any of his problems, athletic or personal, to some member of the coaching staff whenever he feels the need of help or advice, and the coach must be ready to help on any problem that comes up. The opportunity of getting to know, and occasionally to help, a fine group of young men year after year is one of the great rewards of coaching. To watch players graduate and then make names for themselves in their business or profession, is one of the coach's genuine pleasures.

The coach expects loyalty from his players and his associates, and in turn he owes an even greater loyalty to them. Football is an unpredictable game, and a football can take a lot of funny bounces.

A team that looks good in the spring may not pan out at all well in the fall on games won and lost. The coach owes a particular loyalty to a team which is having a bad season. They are trying just as hard as he is, and their combined efforts just are not productive of winning games. Such a team needs to be encouraged, and the coaching staff must call on all of their resources to help the players over a tough time. Sometimes losing seasons or losing games are the means of drawing a squad and a staff closer together. Some of the finest friends I have are men with whom I have shared a tough and disappointing season. Friendships made in adversity are even more lasting than those made in the flood-tide of success. Experience and maturity in a coach can perform no finer service than to help a team enjoy victory without becoming cocky, and to meet defeat without loss of faith.

PUBLIC RELATIONS

The coach's activities in the field of public relations have multiplied geometrically in the past few years. The growth of public organizations interested in sports such as quarterback clubs and touchdown clubs, as well as the various luncheon clubs and especially alumni groups, together with the increase in award dinners for high-school athletic teams, indicate a great broadening of interest in athletics. Every coach is called upon to attend and speak at occasions of this kind. Every coach that I know faces a very busy schedule at the end of the season, which keeps him traveling throughout most of December and well into the spring of the year. A strenuous speaking schedule is disruptive of family life, and takes the coach away from the campus more than he would really like to be. However, most coaches gladly accept the role of traveling salesman and ambassador for they feel that they are representing not only themselves but far more so the school with which they are associated. Such outside duties have come to be an accepted and growing part of a coach's job. Most colleges and universities recognize that, properly handled, the traveling and speaking activities of members of the coaching staff can be a legitimate and effective part of the public relations program of the institution.

One of the most important parts of a coach's job and frequently one of the most pleasant, is his contact with newspaper and radio men. Most colleges and universities employ the services of an athletic publicity man and he can be of great assistance to both the coach and the newspapers. However, there will be many occasions on which the newspaper men will seek information directly from the coach, and the latter should always be available either for a personal visit, or by telephone, and should be free and frank in providing information. The attempted use by the coach of exaggerated stories of injuries in the futile hope of making the opponent overconfident has been almost entirely discontinued. I was cured of that some twenty years ago on the only time I attempted to use the device. I stated that one of my Oklahoma A.&M. players was more severely injured than was the case, and might not see action in the next game. The story was printed and I received a phone call the next day from a very anxious mother. That cured me.

Most newspaper men have a genuine interest in the game, and feel very keenly their responsibility to the public to write accurate and interesting stories. Journalists and coaches have jobs that have many things in common. With the newspaper man the story and his obligation to the public must come first. The coach owes an allegiance to the public, but it is secondary to the development and the welfare of his team, and each should respect the other's primary interest. The growing practice of weekly meetings between all of the newspaper men and all of the coaches in a given area has done a great deal toward enabling each to do a better job and provide the basis for better understanding.

It goes without saying that the coach owes an unswerving loyalty to the organization that he serves, and to the faculty and administrative officers with whom he is associated. If he is unable to give loyalty for any reason, he should seek other opportunities, for coach and player alike need to believe in their institution. Above all, a coach must conduct football in such a way that it may rightfully be called a part of the educational process.

Most coaches would probably obtain greater financial rewards if they put the same energy and effort and enthusiasm that they put into the game of football into a business or a profession. But in spite of the pressures and the insecurity that are a part of coaching, I do not know any football coach who doesn't thoroughly enjoy his work. Association with young men keeps one young in spirit, and there is the never-ending joy of watching fine boys gradually change from a collection of unrelated individuals into a smooth-working organization playing with spirit a game they truly enjoy. Even the men who have left coaching for more remunerative fields, look back with nostalgia on the joys and sorrows and solid satisfactions of their coaching experience. I guess old coaches never die. They just fade away, reluctantly.

CHAPTER 16 AMERICAN FOOTBALL —AN APPRAISAL

FOOTBALL is a game of high emotional content. It has a great fascination for player and spectator alike. When a game attracts annually some 600,000 high-school players, some 50,000 college players, as well as unnumbered thousands of boys who play the game in impromptu games on street corners and sand lots, such a game certainly has its influence on high schools and colleges throughout the country. When a game attracts millions of spectators, many of them in crowds of 50,000 to 100,000 people, and occupies large sections of the sports pages and commands the interest of a considerable portion of our population during the fall season, that game can be said to have assumed some importance. The methods of conducting the game of football in high schools and colleges have been criticized severely at times, in many cases with justification. As a game of hard physical contact, football has been criticized as dangerous and prone to cause injury. There can be no doubt that accidents do occur. Safety measures are extremely important, and it is up to all those who play, supervise, and even watch the game, to see that every possible precaution is taken for the welfare of those playing. Such is the popularity of this fall sport, however, that the game would undoubtedly continue to be played on an impromptu basis even if abolished by high schools and colleges.

One type of criticism expresses the feeling that it is not the proper function of an educational institution to sponsor a football team and go into the entertainment business by building stadia and charging admission to sporting contests. Others question the educational

248

benefits of football to players and student-spectators alike. Still others express the thought that the emphasis upon winning football teams has led to extensive proselyting and subsidization of outstanding high-school players, thus placing too heavy an emphasis on what is supposed to be only a game.

On January 1, 1952, I was one of some 100,000 spectators who paid approximately $500,000 to watch a Rose Bowl game between the University of Illinois and Stanford University. The television and radio rights were sold for nearly the same amount. It is estimated that some 30 million people saw and heard the game while sitting in their living rooms all over the United States.

In direct contrast was a statement by President James B. Conant of Harvard University some three weeks after the Rose Bowl game. "We have arranged for the coming football seasons without regard to gate receipts and provided for lighter schedules." He reported the Crimson's 1950–1951 intercollegiate and intramural athletic programs resulted in a net expense exceeding $350,000. "This sum is not to be regarded as an athletic deficit," Dr. Conant said. "It is as much a proper charge against the resources of the faculty as the maintenance of a library or a laboratory."

There is undoubtedly some justification for charging admission to football games, in that such gate receipts do pay the expenses of a wide variety of sports in which hundreds of students participate. At the University of California, football receipts pay the cost of supporting twenty-four different sports in which hundreds of students participate. The students competing in the twenty-four sports last year took part in some 375 intercollegiate contests. Most years the football receipts pay for the entire sports program, with little help, if any, from the student ticket, the receipts of which can thus be channeled into nonathletic activities. The same situation is true to a greater or lesser degree at nearly all institutions which support an athletic program.

Football as a game has many fine intrinsic values. Football as a business, which carries the financial load of the entire sports pro-

gram, has presented many problems and many temptations. At the
N.C.A.A. meeting in Cincinnati in January, 1952, a committee of
college presidents headed by President John A. Hannah of Michigan
State, presented a report which was critical of certain phases of
college sports, and football in particular. The report pointed out
that in some cases the proselyting and subsidization of high-school
players by colleges and universities had been carried beyond proper
limits. The report was critical of Bowl games and suggested their
abolition. It also called for the discontinuance of out-of-season
practice, particularly in football and basketball.

I do not pretend to be wise enough to answer all of the criticisms
of American college football, nor to be able to present any easy
solutions to all of the problems surrounding the administration of
the game. Certainly one of the most hopeful signs of progress toward
the elimination of abuses and excesses is the interest of college
presidents and administrators in the problem. Many athletic conferences throughout the country had already taken steps in the
direction suggested by the Presidents' Committee.

The Committee might have gone a step further and pointed out
that the abuses surrounding the game of football stem directly from
the pressure to win. On any given Saturday in the fall, only 50 per
cent of the teams playing can possibly win—the remaining 50 per
cent, with the exception of the possibility of a few ties, are mathematically sure of defeat. It is a natural and healthy thing to want
your team to win, but if the demand for a winning team on the part
of the public, students, and alumni becomes excessive, there develops the temptation to take short cuts to insure a winning team.

To what extent colleges and universities practice proselyting and
subsidization in their sports program, and particularly in football,
would be difficult to say. It might depend largely on a definition
of the term. Nearly every student attending any college or university has probably been proselyted in the broadest sense of the
term, in that some alumnus or friend has attempted to point out
strong points of the school and the advantages of attending it. All

colleges are interested in young people who are good students and indicate leadership possibilities, including those with athletic ability. All colleges attempt to provide financial opportunity for promising students who need such help, whether they are athletes or not, and whether such help be in the form of a scholarship, a grant-in-aid, or a job. Just where legitimate and reasonable proselyting ends and excessive subsidization begins is a line of demarcation difficult to set. A boy who is dependent entirely on his own resources to attend college, and who desires at the same time to compete in athletics, faces a difficult problem. The time necessary to do justice to his studies, to support himself, and to compete in athletics will require a tremendous expenditure of energy and time.

The N.C.A.A. is making a sincere effort to regulate college athletics, particularly in the fields of subsidization and scholastic standards. Whether such regulation on a national scale is feasible and enforceable remains to be seen. The efforts of the N.C.A.A. to enlist the support of all colleges and universities toward a solution of the perplexing problem of television of athletic events gives hope that other problems may be solved by the same kind of concerted effort.

The various athletic conferences throughout the country have accomplished a great deal in the past thirty years. Such conferences are made up of colleges and universities which, for the most part, are of the same general size and standing, and from the same geographic area. They are governed by faculty members—a representative from each institution. This in itself is a long step toward making certain that the athletic tail will not wag the academic dog. These faculty men have made long strides toward the proper regulation of athletics. The tramp athlete is a thing of the past, and the various conferences are making consistent efforts to insure that the student athlete makes proper progress toward graduation. There are many complex and continuing problems surrounding the administration of college athletics, but the accomplishments of the various athletic conferences in the past thirty years show promise that solutions may be gradually found.

In the final analysis, proper control of the athletic program must inevitably depend on the integrity of the individual institution. I probably oversimplify the problems involved, but it seems to me that if an educational institution insisted that its football team must be composed of students certified as acceptable to that institution, playing a game against a team of students from a university of comparable academic standing and scholastic requirements, then that institution would be justified in supporting a football team.

I have always felt that if three conditions hold true, an athletic program is a constructive part of the curriculum of an institution whose aim is education.

1. The athletes who participate in the sports program must enter by exactly the same process as any other student. They must be required to maintain the same scholastic standard, including progress toward graduation. They should, with very few exceptions, come from the same general geographic areas as other students.

2. The students participating should derive some fun from the sport. Football and other sports should be enjoyed as a game and not worked at as a business.

3. If four years after an athlete has graduated, he is emotionally well adjusted to life and making reasonable progress in his business or profession, then the university has performed its proper function in giving him his start on a lifelong education. And the chances are that he has benefited from his participation in sports at least as much as from any academic course.

Before you dismiss the above conditions as hopelessly naïve and not susceptible of administration, I will readily admit that no set of rules could be drawn to insure proper enforcement. Such application would depend entirely on the spirit and integrity of the institution and the men administering its educational and athletic program. If that spirit is there, very few rules are necessary. If it is absent, a code in a volume weighing 10 pounds would prove inadequate.

FOOTBALL AS A SYMBOL

The football team at any given institution tends to become, in the minds of many people, a symbol of that institution. This tendency is responsible for a great deal of the interest surrounding the game, but also it has engendered many of the problems. A football team can be a true and healthy symbol of a student body provided that the members of the squad are truly representative. If they are from the same geographical area, if they are required to enter by the same process as other students and maintain comparable scholastic standards, the football team may be not only a healthy extracurricular activity for the participants, but may also serve as an equally vicarious interest and outlet for the entire student body. Such an athletic team may well serve as a rallying point and a unifying force for the student body. As such, the team might well have considerable value, especially in a large university with its many departments, diverse interests, and increasing complexity of organization. If, on the other hand, a football team is a paid group of gladiators from a different section of the country, then it is not representative of the students and has very little in common with them. Such situations are unfortunate and justly open to criticism.

One of the most valuable but generally unrecognized functions of spring practice is to give any student the opportunity to try out for the team representing his institution. In the fall, the period before the first game is so short that there is little opportunity for the untried student to have a fair chance to make the team. In the spring, without the pressure of an immediate game, there is an opportunity to learn skills and demonstrate abilities. I have always been particularly happy that at California we have had a large spring turnout which has included many boys who have not played football in high school. Each spring a number of such boys have had a chance to learn the game. In the past three years there has always been at least one boy on our starting offensive or defensive teams who never played in high school.

By the very nature of the game, football is not merely a bundle of techniques, but far more a thing of the spirit. It is inconceivable in our American sports tradition that a man trying out for a school or college football team should ever give less than his best effort. Football teams are never selected on the basis of weight or because the team members take a nice-looking photograph. The things which can be measured, such as weight and speed tested against a stop watch, are important, but the imponderables, the elements and values which cannot be measured by any device known to man, are far more important. The qualities of courage, and the ability to rise to meet a tough situation, can be recognized only in the heat of competition.

This fact I learned on my first coaching job, at Oklahoma City University in 1925. My teacher was a boy by the name of Merrill Bartlett who weighed 152 pounds and had never played high-school football. Bartlett was slow and not too well-coordinated on offense, but he was an exceedingly stubborn defensive player. I recall that at the end of the first season, in making plans for the next year, I felt that right guard, the position played by Bartlett, was an outstanding weakness in our team. The next fall I found a 185-pound guard who had a fine record in high school, and thought that my problems at that position were solved. Early in the season, such appeared to be the case. The new guard could beat Bartlett by about 10 yards in a 50-yard sprint, and by every measurement I could devise, he appeared to be far superior. However, about the second game of the season, we met a very tough opponent, and things were not going well at all. I sent Bartlett into the game and everything seemed to pick up for our team; somehow Bartlett became a fixture once again at the right guard spot. In preparing for the third season, I still felt that right guard was the weak spot. We had several big guards, all much faster than Bartlett, and I thought that surely they would solve my problem. But the same process as the previous year was repeated once again. I kept trying the physically superior men, but somehow it was only when Bartlett came into the game that our team began to move on offense and to tighten up on defense. Merrill Bartlett enjoyed football, liked physical contact, and just naturally hated to lose. I have always tried to remember what he and the other Oklahoma City University boys taught me in my first coaching job.

In 1934, when I was coaching at Kansas State, we had a football team that was the despair of photographers. Our starting team varied about as widely as to size, height, weight, and general build as the average subway crowd. It looked as if someone had gone over the campus and had picked blindly any eleven men. They ranged in the line from a little guard, Gene Sundgren at 166, to big George Mattox at 220, and in the backfield from Leo Ayers at 140 or less, to our blocking back, Leland Shaefer, at 200. They didn't take a very impressive team picture, but what they lacked in size, they more than made up in spirit and stamina. In seven out of ten games we were tied or behind at the half, but we scored 75 points in the fourth quarter of all games while holding our opponents scoreless. In the final game of the season, we scored three times in the last half to defeat a favored Nebraska team and give Kansas State the only football championship it ever won.

At California in the past several years we have had many boys who have demonstrated repeatedly that in football those intangibles which cannot be measured except in the heat of competition are the truly important things after all. In 1948 we had an end by the name of Frank Humpert who was just a little bit slow, and didn't get to play very much that year. In spring practice in 1949, Frank worked as a center on offense and a linebacker on defense, both positions entirely new to him. That fall in our early season practice Frank was about our sixth center, as I recall it. In an early-season blocking drill he drove hard at the man opposite him, fell, and broke a bone in his right hand. A T-formation center with a broken right hand is about as valuable as a hunting dog without a sense of smell. But

Frank kept in good condition by running, and a little later when the
hand had begun to heal and the doctors consented to allow him to
practice with a protective pad, we worked Frank quite a bit as a
linebacker. About the third or fourth game, we sent him in for a
kickoff. In watching the movies of that game, our staff noticed that
on the kickoff one player was down fast and made a beautiful tackle.
We couldn't catch the jersey number, but we did notice the pad on
the right hand and knew it was Humpert. A little later our opponents
were kicking and way back near the safety man as he received the
ball we noticed in one corner of the screen a beautiful block. Again
we couldn't catch the jersey number, but noticed the padding on the
right hand. We felt that even though Humpert was not fast he loved
to play football, and somehow could cover the ground in spite of his
lack of speed. From then on, he became our regular linebacker on
defense and did a fine job all season.

Our safety man at California for the 1949 and 1950 seasons was
Carl Van Heuit. Carl is short, 5 feet 7, not too heavy—about 163—
and definitely too slow to figure much in the offensive picture as a
halfback. It was only when we were desperately trying to find a
safety man in the early 1949 season that Carl had a chance to play.
His courage under fire and his ability to analyze and anticipate opponents' moves and to direct our defense, far outweighed any lack
of speed or height. He was a fine safety and never once fumbled a
punt. Football will cease to be football on the day it has no place for
a boy like Carl Van Heuit, who is by any measurable standard too
short, too slow, and too light to make a college football player.

Every boy or young man who has ever played football retains a
most pleasant memory of the team of which he was a member. Not
only are the incidents at games and practices remembered, but also
friendships made on an athletic field are likely to be lasting ones.
A boy takes pride in his team. Possibly no organization to which
a man will belong in later life will receive quite the unselfish devo-
tion or have the all-around *esprit de corps* as a high-school or college football team. High moments and low, tragic events and

humorous ones, shared together at a stage in life when interest in athletics is by nature high, weld a group of individuals into a single unit. From a coaching standpoint, there is no greater thrill or finer sense of achievement than that moment when a group of individuals suddenly become a team, a working organization, in which the sum total of the group adds up to so much more than the individuals which constitute it.

Football, perhaps more than any other game, is a hard, contact, team sport. It emphasizes competition of a direct and personal kind. I don't know any coach or educator who has been able to express adequately the innate desire of a young man for competition—a desire to pit his best against the best of an opponent. Perhaps that desire for competition was best expressed by Theodore Roosevelt when he wrote:

> It is not the critic who counts, not the man who points out where the strong man stumbled, nor where the doer of deeds could have done them better. The credit belongs to the man who is actually in the arena, whose face is marred by dust and sweat and blood; who tries and comes short again and again; who knows the great enthusiasms, the great devotions, and spends himself in a worthy cause; who in the end, at best, knows the triumph of high achievement and at the worst, if he fails, at least fails while daring greatly, so that his place shall never be with those cold and timid souls who know neither victory nor defeat.

Competition on the athletic field can be an important part of the educational process. I trust that we will never "de-emphasize" the sports program in our colleges and high schools. Instead we should "re-emphasize" our sports program, eliminating any undesirable features but emphasizing the many fine things which can contribute so much to individual development.

O